D0214316

Railroad Mergers and the Language of Unification

Railroad Mergers and the Language of Unification

James B. Burns

QUORUM BOOKS
Westport, Connecticut • London

Library of Congress Cataloging-in-Publication Data

Burns, James B., 1969–
    Railroad mergers and the language of unification / James B. Burns.
        p.   cm.
    Includes bibliographical references (p.   ) and index.
    ISBN 1–56720–166–0 (alk. paper)
    1. Railroads—Mergers—United States—History.   2. Railroad law—
United States—History.   3. Railroads—United States—Finance.
I. Title.
HE2751.B88   1998
385′.1—dc21   97–21854

British Library Cataloguing in Publication Data is available.

Library of Congress Catalog Card Number: 97–21854
ISBN: 1–56720–166–0

First published in 1998

Quorum Books, 88 Post Road West, Westport, CT 06881
An imprint of Greenwood Publishing Group, Inc.

Printed in the United States of America

The paper used in this book complies with the
Permanent Paper Standard issued by the National
Information Standards Organization (Z39.48–1984).

10 9 8 7 6 5 4 3 2 1

To my Lord,
who taught me that to increase
in wisdom and knowledge is to increase
in grief and sorrow

Contents

Acknowledgments

My sincere appreciation goes to Roy V. Scott for opening my eyes to the wonderful worlds of railroad and economic history. Besides his providing me with invaluable guidance during the research and writing of my manuscript, his honesty and candor taught me to approach issues directly and without reservation.

I am also grateful for encouragement and assistance provided by Charles D. Lowery, Lorenzo M. Crowell, John F. Marszalek, Johnpeter H. Grill, Lynn K. Barker, and William E. Parrish. I am particularly grateful to Lorenzo M. Crowell and Charles D. Lowery for their detailed review of my work. Their suggestions were important in helping me to enhance the quality of this study.

Very special thanks go to my family, whose encouragement and understanding throughout my life made this endeavor possible. Particular appreciation is extended to my mother, whose hours of computer assistance on this project were critical in the production of such fine quality maps and charts.

1

Introduction

And the Lord came down to see the city and the tower, which the children of men builded. And the Lord said, Behold, the people is one, and they have all one language; and this they begin to do: and now nothing will be restrained from them, which they have imagined to do.

Genesis 11:5–6

As the nation's earliest big business, the railroad industry was the first to understand the power of unity so vividly related in the Book of Genesis. In the early 1860s, for example, railroads employed Samuel F. B. Morse's telegraph to coordinate intercarrier exchanges and thereby promote service beyond the rights-of-way of individual systems. The Union Pacific and the Central Pacific joined lines in 1869 at Promontory Point, Utah Territory, thereby permitting the first transcontinental flow of traffic. A collective agreement to standardize time zones in 1883 allowed rail carriers to schedule interstate service, and the adoption of the standard gauge by southern railroads in 1886 facilitated a fuller interchange of cars and speedier operations nationwide.

While these joint efforts generated enormous benefits for railroads and the public alike, rail officials learned that the corporate merger was the most powerful tool for intercarrier cooperation. Mergers could integrate the operations of multiple lines under a single management. They could facilitate new and more direct routes to markets, attract new traffic with single-system service, and permanently eliminate internecine competition. Indirect benefits included a decline in fuel expenditures, the elimination of superfluous line segments, a reduction in labor costs, and better utilization of rolling stock and other equipment.

Railroad companies could also benefit from combinations with corporations outside the business of railroading. They could diversify their investment bases, secure new avenues of capital, and acquire competing modes of transportation. Diversified investment bases might allow rail carriers to withstand more effectively declines in rail traffic while obtaining needed capital from nonrail holding companies or nonrail subsidiaries. The acquisition of water and motor carriers could open door-to-door markets served exclusively by trucking companies and facilitate access to international markets dominated by shipping lines.

From the time the first fledgling systems were operational in the 1830s through the late twentieth century, railroad leaders sought to exploit the benefits of unifications. Combinations were so numerous in the 1880s and 1890s that by the turn of the century, more than 15 percent of the nation's carriers had been involved in mergers.

A century later, by the 1980s and 1990s, every major railroad could be tied to a combination with another system, and most either owned or were affiliated with other modes of transportation.

Almost as soon as rail companies started combining with each other, the federal government began regulating intercarrier relationships. For example, the Interstate Commerce Act of 1887, which first undertook to regulate interstate railroads, included stipulations outlawing railroad pooling arrangements. By the turn of the century, the Supreme Court ruled on the legality of certain combinations, ordering the dissolution of the Northern Securities Company and other attempted unions that were "in restraint of trade." The Panama Canal Act of 1912 and the Motor Carrier Act of 1935 empowered the Interstate Commerce Commission (ICC) to ensure the independent development of the motor and water-carrier industries by restricting railroad acquisitions of these modes.

During the early years of regulation, the ICC was critical of mergers. Commissioners believed that combinations could be a threat to competition, and the agency sought to prevent violations of the Sherman Antitrust Act (1890) and the Clayton Antitrust Act (1914) before the Justice Department brought cases to the Supreme Court. Meanwhile, Congress was so preoccupied with granting the Commission powers to regulate railroad rates that it did not consider fully the benefits that corporate mergers might afford.

Legislators, however, were prepared by 1920 to give greater attention to the issue of rail mergers. Nationalization of the railroad industry during World War I gave government officials special insight into the realities of railroading and the advantages that mergers could provide. With the Transportation Act of 1920, Congress urged the combination of the nation's rail carriers under the direction of the ICC. Federal officials hoped that such a move would preserve the benefits realized during nationalization after they returned railroads to the private sector.

Twenty years later, officials in Washington continued to believe in the benefits of combinations, but they then realized that the arranging of mergers should be left to the private sector. Congress legislated its modified viewpoint in the Transportation Act of 1940. For the next three decades, railroad executives decided for themselves when and with which systems their companies would merge, while it was the Commission's task to ensure that the unifications were "in the public interest."

One of the main reasons the Commission supported so enthusiastically the unification of the nation's railroads after 1920 was the realization that operating a railroad profitably was difficult. Federal operators could not do it during nationalization, and in the half century following privatization, only a few railroad companies prospered.

By 1970, the nation's railroads were under enormous financial strain. Returns on net investment and returns on equity were at dangerously low levels, the railroad market share of freight shipped and the numbers of passengers transported were spiraling downward, and railroad trackage and equipment were deteriorating. The industry was facing a crisis as numerous railroads filed for bankruptcy; and corporate mergers, which became commonplace in the 1950s and 1960s, seemed unable to ameliorate the situation.

The blame for the industry's troubles lay in antiquated and burdensome regulation, poor railroad management, and competition from other modes of transportation. Regulations governing rates prevented railroads from generating adequate income, while other laws limited the ability of the carriers to abandon unprofitable lines. These constraints contributed to a growing pool of incompetent managers who, mesmerized by Commission restrictions, failed to develop new approaches to operations as did the leaders of other industries in the decades after the World War II. Finally, railroads faced enormous competition from motor carriers which increasingly absorbed a greater percentage of freight transportation markets. This challenge to railroad viability limited railroad market expansion that often had helped carriers overcome financial burdens in the past.

This latter problem was augmented by the federal government's funding of other modes of transportation. Between 1946 and 1975, for example, the trucking industry received over 69 percent of all federal aid to transportation. Twenty-nine percent was allocated to the automobile, airline, and barge industries, and a mere 1 percent was set aside for railroads. This disproportionate allocation of federal transportation funds to the trucking industry was important in providing motor carriers rights-of-way into traditionally rail-dominated markets.

By the 1970s, federal officials realized that they had to act if they wanted to preserve the railroad industry. Between 1970 and 1980, Congress passed legislation that heavily funded ailing systems, gave carriers greater corporate and operational flexibility, and promoted combinations. The Rail Passenger Service Act in 1970 relieved carriers of unprofitable passenger operations and consolidated that service under a National Rail Passenger Service Corporation (Amtrak). The Regional Rail Reorganization Act of 1973 provided funding for a pseudo-public company, Consolidated Rail Corporation (Conrail), to unify the operations of numerous failing freight systems in the Northeast. Finally, the Railroad Revitalizaiton and Regulatory Reform Act (1976) and the Staggers Rail Act (1980) freed railroads from regulations that prevented operational flexibility and continued to inhibit unifications in the private sector.

As legislators transformed the regulatory structure, railroads continued to combine with other carriers. Rail officials, like many federal regulators, still believed that mergers could be a panacea for many of the difficulties inherent to railroading. In a freer regulatory environment, officials assumed that they might realize the benefits of mergers that combining systems of the 1950s and 1960s had not achieved. Consequently, dozens of merger applications were filed with the Commission during the 1970s and 1980s, and the ICC was predisposed to approve them.

As railroads unified with other rail systems, they began to acquire other modes of transportation as well. While carriers avoided direct violation of the Panama Canal Act and the Motor Carrier Act by the establishment of holding companies, the Commission sanctioned intermodal unifications in a liberal interpretation of the law. As a result, railroads joined with trucking and shipping firms to form global multimodal transportation enterprises.

By the 1990s, the industry had changed significantly. Reduced regulation, mergers with other transportation companies, and affiliation with huge diversified conglomerates helped railroads stem the decline in their share of intercity freight. Rail carriers had access to new domestic and international markets through a booming intermodal industry, and a resurgence of the shortline industry permitted the larger carriers regularly to abandon service over superflous or marginally profitable line segments. As a result, railroads reported returns on investment at levels not seen in decades, and they boasted of highly advanced equipment and rights-of-way in first-class condition.

The consolidation that transformed the nation's rail carriers between 1970 and 1995 was important not only in changing the prospects of the railroad industry but was also significant in that it represented a phenomenon sweeping corporate America at about the same time. During the 1980s and 1990s corporations in numerous industries engaged in mergers that awed Americans in both their frequency and value. This merger mania was most significantly felt in the chemical, petroleum, drug, food, defense, banking, telecommunications, media, healthcare, and retail industies.

As in the railroad industry, the stimulus for large-scale combinations was economic pressure. The stagflation that characterized the late 1970s, and that culminated in a recessionary economy by the end of the decade, influenced congressional support for legislation that liberated industry from federal regulation. This support for deregulation measures, which continued in the 1980s, stimulated corporate reorganization in much the same way that regulatory relief in the railroad industry encouraged corporate adjustment. As in the railroad industry, moreover, this adjustment manifested itself in a merger craze that set records in both the number of combinations that transpired and the value of those unifications. Also, as was the case with railroads, other businesses found that corporate combinations afforded numerous operational and financial benefits which they had not been able to realize in the past.

This study will show that corporate combinations with other companies between 1970 and the mid-1990s were a panacea for many of the financial and operational problems of the nation's major rail carriers. This thesis rests on the idea that the successful operation and financial performance of rail carriers depends on a single variable—access. As rail executives and industry regulators know, all railroad operational and financial ills can be traced to either a lack of access to capital or a lack of access to markets. Assuming that rail managers strive to achieve peak efficiency in daily operations in order to generate the greatest profits possible and that federal regulations do not interfere with that method of operation, a given railroad's performance will directly relate to its access to both capital and markets. Intensive capital investment is critical for the purchase and maintenance of expensive equipment and right-of-way; and huge markets, capable of providing adequate levels of traffic, must be exploited if railroads are to be profitable.

Corporate mergers that transpired in the railroad industry between 1970 and 1995 ensured railroad access to both markets and capital. Through combinations with other systems, railroads formed the most efficient network yet realized for delivering freight to existing rail markets throughout the United States. Unifications with motor and water carriers generated comprehensive transportation networks for delivering freight door-to-door domestically and to markets around the world, and combinations with companies outside the business of transportation ensured railroad access to capital.

This access contributed to the improved health of the railroad industry by the mid-1990s as evidenced by operational and financial performance data. Increasing ton-miles of freight hauled reflected increased operating efficiency in rail markets, while growing numbers of trailers and containers hauled suggested increased penetration of motor carrier and water carrier markets. Rising returns on both investment and equity indicated an increase in the worth of railroads, and declining debt-to-equity ratios suggested greater access to equity capitalization.

At first glance, this thesis appears to challenge directly that in Richard Saunders' *Railroad Mergers and the Coming of Conrail* (1978). In his study, Saunders argued that mergers were not a panacea for the ills of financially ailing railroads in the period between 1954 and the collapse of Penn Central, the juggernaut of the Northeast, in 1970. He contended that although rail officials were able to treat the symptoms of financial illness through combinations, unifications failed to provided a cure. As far as Saunders was concerned, a decade had been wasted on the wrong medicine, on a panacea that proved to be a placebo.

The present study, however, does not challenge the assesment made by Saunders for the period that he addressed. Clearly, the railroad industry was in dire straits by the early 1970s, and many scholars judged railroad mergers unsuccessful up to that time. Mergers did not stem the degeneration of the industry as a whole nor did they appear to provide short-term solutions to the problems of individual systems involved in them.

How then does one reconcile the two sharply different perspectives about mergers during two contiguous periods? If mergers were deemed a failure for the period from 1954 to 1970, how can they be singled out as a panacea for railroad problems between 1970 and the mid-1990s?

The answer lies in the changed times. This study demonstrates that railroad officials, industry observers, and federal regulators were correct in their belief that corporate mergers could remedy many of the difficulties intrinsic to railroading. The pre-1970 environment in which the industry operated, however, did not permit rail carriers to exploit fully the advantages that mergers afforded. Transportation regulation, which discriminated against railroading, prevented it.

By the 1980s and 1990s, however, the entire regulatory structure of the industry had been reorganized; and railroads were permitted to conduct operations like any other business. Once railroads obtained a level playing field with other industries and other modes of transportation, they showed how effective combinations could be.

This study focuses strictly on the nation's Class I rail systems. For purposes of organization, the ICC arranged carriers into three classes based on gross annual operating revenue. Class I carriers were those systems with the largest operating revenues and usually the longest lines. Although the threshold dividing class rose with the growth of the industry, Class I operations accounted for more than 90 percent of all railroad traffic in the nation for every year between 1970 and 1997. Class II and Class III carriers, that is, regionals and shortlines, made up the remainder. They participated in mergers of their own.

When 1970 opened, there were seventy-three Class I carriers in the nation. Thirty-two crisscrossed the Northeast, fourteen dominated the South, and twenty-seven covered the West. The railroads in the Northeast participated primarily in the movement of manufactured products, coal, and other ores. Western carriers dominated movements of agricultural goods from the plains states and connected the major industrial regions of the Northeast to western ports. Southern carriers connected the growing lumber, paper, and pulp industries to manufacturing centers outside their region, while they interchanged agricultural products, manufactured goods, and ores with northern and western lines.

By 1997, only ten Class I carriers remained. As a result of bankruptcy, merger, or a changing classification threshold, some sixty-three systems had disappeared from the Class I category. Because of the economic malaise surrounding the industry in the 1970s, several carriers, including the Chicago, Rock Island & Pacific (Rock Island) were either divided, sold, or left to rust. As a result of numerous combinations, many Class I carriers fused into a single system. For example, the Great Northern's merger with the Northern Pacific and the Chicago, Burlington & Quincy, among others, reduced by two the number of carriers on the Class I list. Finally, the Class I threshold changed three times between 1970 and 1997. In 1970, a carrier was a Class I if it had annual operating revenues in excess of $5 million. That number was raised to $10 million in 1977, $50 million in 1978, and $250 million in 1992. As a result, a few carriers were downgraded to Class II status.

While railroad growth required changes in revenue classifications, the sheer size of the newer systems necessitated a change in geographic classification. No longer could regulators, rail officials, or industry observers speak of railroads as belonging to one of three districts. Combinations among carriers in the Northeast, South, and West rendered that categorization meaningless. In 1986, carriers were considered to be either eastern or western sytems. By 1997, as a consequence of further combination, even that classification was being challenged.

The research for this study was based on three major kinds of primary sources—finance dockets of the Interstate Commerce Commission, reports by federal agencies and congressional committees, and trade journal articles. ICC dockets provided the bulk of the information relating to specific combinations of two rail carriers or of a railroad and another mode of transportation. Reports by federal agencies and congressional committees contained the majority of the material used for assessing both the financial and operational health of the industry and the advantages and disadvantages of corporate combinations. Finally, trade journal articles were immensely important in helping to tie together developments over the period as a whole.

The ICC's finance dockets include a plethora of information. Each docket consists of the application filed by merging parties with explanations of forecasted benefits and possible detriments, the objections and/or compensatory claims of competing transportation systems, the views of numerous third parties that expect to be affected by a given merger, the comments of federal agencies, and the analysis and decision of the Commission. Some merger cases fill more than three dozen volumes consisting of from five hundred to one thousand pages per volume, so sifting through such material can be daunting. Fortunately, however, the ICC published a neatly organized version of the more important dockets in a series of regulatory volumes found in most federal depository libraries. With the sunset of the ICC in December 1995 and the transfer of its functions to the Surface Transportation Board of the Department of Transportation, these kinds of sources became that much more of a convenience.

The reports produced by federal agencies, associations, and congressional committees were the most helpful in assessing the industry and mergers as a whole. Studies and annual reports of the Interstate Commerce Commission, the Department of Transportation, the Association of American Railroads, and the Senate Committee on Science, Commerce and Transportation were among the most useful. They provided detailed analyses for regulators and federal legislators on nearly every issue concerning rail operations.

A variety of journal studies and articles supplemented the government documents and offered their own analyses and perspectives. Considering the dearth of books on the issue of recent railroad mergers, one must depend on these sources to provide a broad perspective of the period. Articles assessing individual combinations helped relate the federal data to the socio-political environment of the period while comparing or contrasting proposed unifications with those of the recent past.

2

Legacy of Merger

The merger movement in the railroad industry originated in 1838, when the Wilmington & Susquehana merged with the Baltimore & Port Deposit to create the Philadelphia, Wilmington & Baltimore. This was only eleven years after the nation's first regularly operating railroad, the Baltimore & Ohio, was chartered.[1] That first merger in the railroad industry was an insignificant transaction at the time, but combinations of various kinds would become a widespread and integral element in the evolution of the nation's burgeoning rail network that has continued to the 1990s.

MERGERS TAKE ROOT

The importance of unifications was not evident, however, until the latter half of the nineteenth century. Prior to the Civil War, general "antigovernment sentiment in the political culture of the United States" precluded federal coordination of railroad growth. This gave rise to "a [private] patchwork of roads each developing according to local needs at first, and then coming together due to changes in markets, technology, personnel, politics and vision."[2]

Nevertheless, federal activity during and after the Civil War generated many later changes. The government contributed to the expansion of the railroad system which grew from 23 miles of track in 1830 to 166,703 miles by 1890. Federal land grants of nearly 131 million acres between 1850 and 1871 and federal and state financial assistance of some $350 million up to 1873 were important in that expansion.[3] Still, there was not a true national railroad network. The industry required continuing reorganization and integration.

The idea of integrating the nation's railroads was a radical one. Rail systems had developed independently for half a century, and individual railroad companies were hesitant to share operational control with other carriers. There had to be clear and powerful incentives for them to do so.

Depressed economic conditions combined with the challenges of operating a railroad profitably in the three decades after the Civil War provided the necessary incentives. Owners of small railroads stubborn enough to continue independent operations often found themselves in trouble. In 1893 alone, the courts assumed control of more than 27,000 miles of track, and investors lost nearly $2 billion in railroads which could not meet their financial obligations.[4]

While numerous financially weak carriers fell into bankruptcy, the acquisition of a large number of small lines by stronger firms accelerated the growth of the more secure systems. Railroad barons like James J. Hill, Edward H. Harriman, and Jay Gould began acquiring these smaller systems on a massive scale. Between 1884 and

1888, for example, there were 425 consolidations, and by the turn of the century about one-sixth of the railroads in the United States had been involved in mergers.[5] This large-scale consolidation led to the emergence of railroad empires that dominated entire geographic regions of the country. Using horizontal integration strategies, railroad executives coordinated railroads at every level to create increasingly larger systems. Railroads serving enclaves were joined to form county systems. Those operations grew into state, then district, and then regional systems. Subsequently, interregional connections created what resembled a national transportation network.

The emergence and continued development of the nation's railway network, however, was not as simple as it appeared at the macroscopic level. Railroad owners often battled over important connections or links to new markets. They used rate wars to drive competitors out of targeted markets and established agreements with shippers to monopolize the transport of specific products. Such economic strife was unhealthy for rail carriers which required stable revenues and consistent traffic levels to remain profitable.

In order to eliminate this internecine competition the more experienced rail executives often turned to informal agreements known as pools. Pools provided territorial standardization of rates and maintained existing market conditions as determined by the pool members. Theoretically, such agreements provided an ideal remedy to the destructive aspects of intercarrier competition. The first genuine pool was formed in Iowa in 1870 among the Rock Island, Chicago & North Western, Michigan Central, and the Chicago, Burlington & Quincy. After the depression of 1873, William Vanderbilt of the New York Central pooled operations with his two great competitors, the Erie and the Pennsylvania; and in 1875, Albert Fink of the Louisville & Nashville arranged pools with thirty-two different lines.

Although rail executives put a great deal of hope in pools, these popular mechanisms failed to ameliorate intercarrier relationships. Rail leaders rarely remained faithful to such arrangements. As Joseph Nimmo, Jr., leader of the federal government's first rail statistics department, realized, "Pooling agreements would never work unless made legally enforceable."[6]

To many groups in the nation, railroads that unified or coordinated operations through pools were able to offer beneficial services. Bankers, merchants, timber interests, and coal and iron interests, among others, were generally satisfied with rail service designed to meet the needs of heavily populated industrial cities.[7] Rail competition at these centers produced reasonable railroad rates and, at times, substantial discounts.

To other groups, however, railroads that unified or coordinated operations through pools were little more than corporate predators. The first voices espousing this idea in the late nineteenth century were the nation's farmers. Agriculturists were often the railroads' most unhappy customers. The farmers offered railroads only relatively light traffic, and there were fewer industrial or manufacturing products inbound to those rural areas to supplement the outbound agricultural shipments. So carriers charged higher rates in an attempt to meet fixed costs or compensate for losses incurred in competitive urban centers. In addition, the fact that farmers were small shippers ensured that they would not receive railroad rebates offered to customers who filled large numbers of rail cars. With usually little access to more than a single railroad, many farmers were wholly dependent on one system for the shipment of their agricultural products. They were consequently subject to the rate practices of the railroad monopoly serving their respective markets. Agriculturists believed they were being exploited, and in many cases they were.[8]

Organizing into local farm groups known as granges, disgruntled farmers called on local and state officials in the 1870s for railroad regulation. These "grangers" obtained enough power to gain control of state governments in Illinois, Iowa, Wisconsin, and Minnesota; and by the mid-1870s, these four states had initiated regulation of the nation's railroads. Besides establishing rate ceilings, states prohibited rebates, mergers, and similar mechanisms employed by carriers. For every complaint made by the farmer, there was an attempt at remedial regulation.

The judicial system soon tested the constitutionality of state regulation. In the Granger cases of 1877, the Supreme Court upheld the right of states to regulate the rates public utilities charged. One of the six cases, Munn v. Illinois, for example, focused on an Illinois law that established maximum rates that warehouses and grain elevators could charge customers. The case established an uneasy relationship between federal and state governments, for state regulations would not necessarily be deemed in violation of the due process provisions of the Fourteenth Amendment or contrary to the interstate commerce powers set aside for Congress if applied to interstate businesses. Supreme Court Justice Morrison R. Waite emphasized the importance of protecting the public against the practices of large enterprises vested with such significant public interest.

Unfortunately, state legislatures and state commissions charged with overseeing such regulation were often uninformed and uninterested in the financial and logistical difficulties their laws presented to rail carriers. Both institutions frequently enacted regulatory measures at the local level without consideration of the possible debilitating effects that such measures would have on individual carriers. In many cases, these laws threatened the healthy operation of rail systems. In response, carrier executives objected vociferously and complained to the federal government, but there was little rail owners could do in the absence of a centralized form of regulatory oversight.

Change came rapidly, however, when the federal government intervened in the business of state regulation in 1886. In Wabash v. Illinois, the Supreme Court, still under the leadership of Chief Justice Morrison R. Waite, pointed to the need for federal intervention when it concluded that state regulation of interstate railroads hindered the fair and equitable operation of the services that such carriers supplied.[9] Railroad owners had made the same argument. As early as 1884, many leading rail executives, disgusted with the random nature of state oversight, requested that federal regulation replace state governance. Moreover, in addition to seeking alternatives to haphazard state policies, rail leaders also hoped federal involvement might eliminate the problems of rate cutting, over-expanded facilities, and profitless rebates.

In 1887, Congress passed the Interstate Commerce Act. The new law established the Interstate Commerce Commission (ICC) and authorized that agency to assume regulatory jurisdiction over the nation's interstate railroads. As the first federal regulatory agency, the Commission monitored rate levels, outlawed rebates for preferred customers, ended higher rates for short hauls, and served as a watchdog for unfair or unequitable practices employed by carriers.

However, the new law was vague and of limited effect. Rulings and cease-and-desist orders involved the Commission's interpretation of nonspecific features of the Act. Since the job of interpretting the law belonged to the judicial branch of government, railroads appealed unfavorable rulings to the courts. Judicial review took many years to complete. Moreover, if the court of jurisdiction ruled in favor of the ICC (and many times it did not), railroads would appeal. While a given case was under review or appeal, the railroads in question were not required to comply with the Commission's order.

Meanwhile, the new law strengthened internecine competition. The Commission prohibited pooling, so rail carriers lost the only available means to protect themselves against the damaging effects that accompanied loosely regulated rate practices. Subsequently, vigorous rate wars combined with a national economic malaise to drive numerous carriers into bankruptcy in the 1890s. Not for another two decades would the federal government awaken to the problem.

By the time federal officials realized the need to strengthen the ICC, state legislatures, under the auspices of progressive leaders, had enacted hundreds of laws regulating the intrastate operation of railroads. In 1909, for example, 41 states enacted some 664 railroad laws. At the same time, local leaders sent numerous proposal to their representatives in Congress. Between 1912 and 1915, more than 4,000 bills affecting railroads rolled through Congress and state legislatures.[10]

At the federal level, Congress passed four pieces of legislation granting the ICC greater authority over railroad rates. Congress enacted the Elkins Act (1903), the Hepburn Act (1906), the Mann-Elkins Act (1910), and the Valuation Act (1913) in a continued effort to transform the Commission from a de facto investigative body into a regulatory agency with the power to actively protect the public against the perceived wrongs of railroad officials.

The Elkins Act outlawed the railroad practice of granting rebates to large shippers who demanded kickbacks in return for their business. Published rates would be maintained as legal rates, and violators of the law would be subject to stiff penalties.[11] The legislation was popular among small companies, rail executives, and members of both political parties, as the federal government placed railroad rates beyond the control of other large industries.

Three years later, however, Congress passed the Hepburn Act restricting the power that even railroads had over their rate practices. The new law gave the ICC the power to replace existing rates with "just" and "reasonable" maximum rates. The Commission also outlawed free passes, established a minimum period for adjusting published rates, and established a uniform system of railroad accounts and reports.[12]

In 1910, the Mann-Elkins Act augmented the ICC's power over railroad rates. The law gave the Commission the power to suspend rates for up to ten months pending investigation and without a prior complaint by a shipper. In addition, railroads had to prove that established rates or rate increases were "just" and "reasonable."

Although the Commission was making regular determinations on the "justness" and "reasonableness" of railroad rates after 1906, it was not until 1913 that the ICC considered a formula to properly determine what constituted a "just" and "reasonable" rate. In accordance with the Valuation Act, the ICC began the tedious process of evaluating railroad property values in order to establish an asset base on which to determine the "reasonableness" of rates. The study, which cost millions of dollars to research, took twenty years to complete. In the meantime, the Commission determined rates based on the value of service. Value-of-service pricing was defined as establishing a price based on what the service was worth to the customer rather than what the service cost to provide.[13]

Unfortunately for the industry, the ICC followed a regulatory policy that capped railroad income but prevented carriers from cutting costs. By restricting rates to a maximum level based on value-of-service pricing, the ICC was essentially limiting the railroads' ability to increase revenues on the shipment of freight. Meanwhile, restrictions on combinations prevented carriers from achieving cost efficiencies that become critical in markets of limited revenue potential. Consequently, most railroads remained financially weak throughout the Progressive era.

In the first decade of the twentieth century, the federal government completely reversed its policies. Instead of applying adequate regulation to an undisciplined industry, federal officials strangled the industry with overregulation. Not only were unhealthy competitive practices eliminated, but so too was the ability to compete. Reacting to this enigmatic regulatory storm, Henry Cabot Lodge, a Republican senator from Massachusetts, noted, "The ICC has undertaken as its mission not the protection of the public, but the destruction and prosecution of the railroads."[14] Rail owners throughout the industry shared Lodge's cynicism.

As Progressives constrained the industry with rate regulations, federal officials cracked down on consolidation practices. Progressive leaders resolved to teach owners that "railroads ceased to be private possessions when they became public utilities."[15] Federal officials began to enforce the long-neglected antitrust law.

The most famous case brought before the Supreme Court under this policy involved the Northern Securities Company, the famous railroad holding company of James J. Hill. During President Theodore Roosevelt's administration, the Justice Department charged the company, which received financial backing from J. Pierpont Morgan, with violating the Shermann Antitrust Act of 1890. The Act outlawed contracts and combinations or conspiracies in restraint of trade, and Northern Securities had consolidated the three major carriers serving the northwestern United States: the Northern Pacific, the Great Northern, and the Chicago, Burlington & Quincy. In 1904 by a narrow margin, the Court ruled in favor of the Justice Department and ordered Northern Securities to disband.

James J. Hill, however, was not the only baron singled out by reformers. Edward H. Harriman, who controlled the Union Pacific, Southern Pacific, and Illinois Central, also became a target.[16] Elsewhere, federal officials blamed underhanded machinations of Pere Marquette executives for the financial collapse of the Cincinnati, Hamilton & Dayton, and they damned J. Pierpont Morgan for his unsuccessful attempt to monopolize New England rail transportation and for inadvertently leaving the New Haven in financial ruin.

Unfortunately, in its prosecution of the railroad industry, the federal government failed to realize that the systems at the turn of the century were not those of the Gilded Age. The economic depression of the 1890s had eliminated much unhealthy competition that infested the industry and harmed the public. The "new" railroads were no longer "poorly integrated corporate entities ridden by rate wars which reduced the profits of the best situated roads drastically and drove the weaker ones to the wall of bankruptcy."[17] The new roads favored stability through intercarrier operating agreements, they sought rate levels that guaranteed reasonable returns, and they eschewed internecine competition.

But by the turn of the century, when the federal government awakened to the problems of the Gilded Age, it acted as though the railroads were still operating in that era. Too often, outdated policies were applied to a modernizing industry—a phenomenon that would continue for decades.

Not until the onset of the World War I and the weakening of progressivism did the federal government fully realize the weaknesses in the nation's rail network. The enormous demands of war revealed an inadequate system of national transportation. That insufficiency stemmed from action taken by legislators of the Progressive era who utilized macroscopic legislative measures to combat complex issues. As a result, the industry as a whole suffered, leaving a transportation system too unreliable and decentralized to serve large-scale national demands.

The severe weather of the winter of 1917–1918 exaggerated the industry's frailties. Rail cars moving munitions to terminal points on the Atlantic Coast clogged rail arteries, creating nationwide car shortages. The problem climaxed when hopper car shortages threatened the supply of coal in the nation's urban centers. Antipooling regulations together with rail paranoia of voluntary agreements with competitors precluded a resolution.[18]

In December 1917, President Woodrow Wilson ordered the nationalization of rail operations and named William McAdoo head of a newly formed United States Railroad Administration. The public generally supported the president's action, while special interests expected personal gains. Labor groups sought hour reductions and wage increases under federal control. Shippers sought reduced rates, rail administrators expected expedited traffic movements, and railroad executives hoped for the security of guaranteed income. Nationalization fulfilled the aspirations of many of these groups, and there were other benefits. The designs of cars and locomotives were standardized, circuitous routes were eliminated, and traffic movement was coordinated. Nationalization had all the characteristics of a panacea for industry ills.[19]

FEDERAL ENLIGHTENMENT

At the end of the war, federal officials investigated ways to return the industry to private management. Nationalization was designed as a temporary measure, and the peace settlement at Versailles eliminated the immediate need for federal coordination. Nevertheless, the experience of running the entire industry taught rail regulators some important lessons. The largest was that running a system profitably was a difficult challenge. In the two years of nationalization, the federal government lost over $1.2

billion in rail operations despite raising passenger fares by 18 percent and freight rates by 28 percent.[20]

In order to preserve the stability of the market that federal control engendered, federal officials devised compensatory plans to return railroads to the private sector. Federal administrators now better understood the difficulties of railroading, and they wanted to assist in the railroads' continued development. So Congress considered a variety of strategies to meet the needs of an industry on the brink of denationalization.

Republican Senator Albert Cummins of Iowa offered one strategy. Cummins understood the need for consolidation, and he promoted it. He also recognized that railroads required stable revenues in order to maintain their financial health. Therefore, Cummins proposed a two-part plan. First, railroads would be given the opportunity to consolidate voluntarily for a specified period. Then unification would be compulsory. Cummins believed consolidation was a key to long-term stability, and he thought that the number of the nation's railroads should be no more than two or three dozen.[21] Second, to provide the stability required for unifications, Cummins proposed a "recapture plan." Under the plan, railroads would be guaranteed a 6 percent rate of return. Those systems unable to attain this level on their own would receive loans from a fund supported by those roads which surpassed the 6 percent level.

Unfortunately for the Cummins plan, conservatives in the House of Representatives gutted the "fair return" provision. In addition, they refused to make consolidation mandatory. Legislators believed that a strengthened ICC would ensure returns by mandating fair and reasonable rates. There was nothing of significance left in the bill.

While federal officials were still debating the Cummins plan, a lawyer from Chicago offered an alternative strategy. Glenn Plumb, who recently had been named general counsel for the railway brotherhoods, submitted a plan that labor favored. Plumb believed that labor and the public had enough vested interest in railroads to be included with management in their operation. Plumb proposed that the federal government purchase all railroad property and then lease it to federally chartered corporations the stock of which would be divided between managers and wage earners.[22]

Unfortunately for the Plumb Plan, anti-Bolshevik hysteria swept the nation in 1919. The Plumb Plan smacked too much of socialism. Moreover, on the labor side, the proposal lacked the support of labor leaders like Samuel Gompers who believed that labor and management had to bargain independently for their own best interests. The plan faded away completely by 1922.

After the Plumb and Cummins plans were studied, ideas from each were included in the Transportation Act of 1920. Under the Act, the railroads were returned to private control.[23] Rate controls were readjusted, and carriers were permitted to pool operations and use terminals jointly in certain circumstances. In addition, the Commission was given the power to regulate railroad mergers and line abandonments. Finally, the ICC was charged with drawing up a plan to consolidate the nation's railways. This last goal was never achieved. By 1921 "its legislative mandate [was] ignored with the tacit consent of all concerned."[24] The Commission could not devise a comprehensive plan that did not alienate a particular group.

Despite the incapability of the ICC to consolidate the nation's railroads, the Transportation Act of 1920 represented a change in policy by the Commission. The ICC's task of "keeping rates down and competition up [before the war] was replaced by the broader, and more positive, challenge of planning a railroad system that would meet the needs of shippers and the country as a whole."[25] This was to be an era of positive regulation.

Meanwhile, the Commission adopted Albert Cummins's ideas on rate adjustment. The ICC was responsible for ensuring that railroads were able to earn a 6 percent rate of return on investment. This level was determined to be the "base for a fair return and was the point below which the railroads were allowed to keep all revenues."[26] In order to ensure that this policy had a chance, the Commission agreed to a variety of individual rate increases until the industry stabilized itself after denationalization. Thereafter, the Commission permitted few rate adjustments.

After the Transportation Act of 1920 returned carriers to private management, the Commission continued the study of rail unifications. The Commission hired Harvard Professor William Ripley, author of various works on rates and regulation, to formulate a policy. The plan Ripley devised called for a two step overhaul of the industry. Ripley wanted to begin by creating rail monopolies by subregion throughout the nation. Then, the rail lines in these subregions would be geographically balanced to facilitate smooth connections from region to region. Ripley expected to bring together all railroads in the United States in twenty-four systems.

As the Commission studied possibilities of general unification in the 1920s, railroad executives expressed their support for consolidation. W. W. Atterbury, president of the Pennsylvania Railroad, expressed the general feeling. He noted, "The public can have cheaper railroad transportation and better service at the same time if it is willing to forgo the excessive competition between railroads heretofore insisted upon, and permit nationwide consolidations of a character to produce more effective results."[27] On the other hand, rail executives did not favor compulsory consolidation by the federal government. They believed such interference would be a violation of their rights and would be harmful to the country. Rail officials argued that "Governmental operation, even in the hands of trained men, inevitably means political domination and waste."[28]

Ultimately, however, worries over compulsory consolidation proved unnecessary. Throughout the 1920s and 1930s, the Commission remained divided on the details of such a plan. Members found the task of coordinating district systems almost impossible. For example, in 1929, after six years of study, two ICC plans for the consolidation of eastern carriers remained unresolved.[29] One plan called for the consolidation of eastern carriers into four basic systems—the Pennsylvania, New York Central, Baltimore & Ohio, and Chesapeake & Ohio. A five-system plan included the same four railroads with each contributing to the creation of a fifth carrier. The sanction of any detailed plan alienated one or more rail officials.

Such was the case with a consolidation plan formulated by Frederick H. Prince, former president of the Pere Marquette Railroad and president of the Association of Railroad Securities Owners. The plan called for a national network composed of seven railroads. There would be two roads in the East, two in the South, and three in the West. While the plan never materialized, it generated further ICC discussion and helped drive new transportation legislation through Congress.

Congress passed the Emergency Railroad Transportation Act in 1933. This legislation established the Coordinator of Transportation and directed that official to reduce duplication in the industry by promoting pooling arrangements of track and rolling stock. Railroads were exempted from a variety of antitrust regulations, and rail debts owed to the federal government were forgiven. The law also established new fair rates of return to compensate for inflation. Finally, the legislation expanded the ICC's power to regulate all forms of rail combinations, including those transacted through holding companies, thereby eliminating any questions as to ICC jurisdiction.[30]

In some ways, unfortunately, the legislation was a failure. Joseph B. Eastman, the Transportation Coordinator, did not force railroads into compliance, so railroads disregarded many of his suggestions concerning line rationalization. Moreover, the law did little to help carriers achieve a fair rate of return. On the other hand, rail officials took advice from the newly established Association of American Railroads, a nonprofit organization formed in 1934 specifically designed to help railroads coordinate operations.

Meanwhile, the Roosevelt administration continued to promote coordinated consolidation. The president appointed a Committee of Three, known as the Splawn Committee and composed of the ICC's most progressive commissioners, to formulate a plan. This committee ultimately proposed the union of all railroads into a single system under private ownership. In May 1938, FDR expressed his delight with the idea, and railroad labor scrambled for compensation agreements with management pending a presidential decree of compulsory consolidation. The president, however, avoided premature action.

To alleviate the tension within management and labor circles over the idea of compulsory consolidation, the president appointed a Committee of Six composed of management and labor representatives. This Committee offered its own recommendations which proposed little more than voluntary consolidation of rail systems. Its members were inclined to accept the notions that rail executives had held since the Transportation Act of 1920; they believed that a compulsory consolidation strategy would not remedy industry ills. So the Committee of Six rejected compulsory consolidation and instead supported new legislation allowing rail officials greater latitude in formulating their own strategies of unification.[31]

AN ALTERNATE APPROACH

The Transportation Act of 1940 required that rail mergers be approved by the ICC if the agency found them to be consistent with the "public interest."[32] This meant that unifications would be evaluated not simply on the basis of their effect on competition, but would also include consideration of improved service, transportation facilities, and operations. The stipulation simply legislated what the ICC had been doing in the few mergers that had taken place in the previous twenty years. Merger of the Gulf & Ohio with the Mobile & Ohio was one example. In its approval one year earlier, the Commission pointed to the maintenance of through routes and existing gateways of a bankrupt Mobile & Ohio as being in the public interest.[33]

The law also amended the Interstate Commerce Act and thereby established the first statuatory criteria for evaluating mergers. According to Section 5(2)(c) of the Act, the ICC would use four factors to determine whether such combinations were in the "public interest." They included the effects of unifications on adequate public transportation service, on other carriers, on the total fixed charges of the carriers involved, and on the employees of the carriers involved.

In addition, the new legislation eliminated the provision in the 1920 act requiring the Commission to devise a comprehensive merger plan. Combinations would henceforth be judged on their own merits.[34] Discussion of compulsory consolidation was at an end.

Before the effects of the Transportation Act of 1940 could be felt, the country was again engrossed in a world war. Rail officials would have to wait a few years to test adequately the provisions of the new law. Only then could they decide whether or not unifications were "a panacea for a weak railroad problem."[35] Meanwhile, the nation's railways enjoyed the temporary prosperity that a wartime economy evoked. Revenue and ton-mile statistics literally skyrocketed. Net income doubled for Class I railroads during the war years, and in 1944 carriers handled 300 percent more ton-miles than in 1932.[36]

Unfortunately for railroads, the wartime prosperity was short-lived. The prosperity carriers experienced during the war, ironically, sped the financial decline of rail systems following the conflict. Railroad infrastructures became exhausted as a result of wartime traffic increases, and maintenance costs soared. In 1940, Class I rail systems spent $819 million on maintenance of equipment and $497 million for maintenance of way. By 1945, those figures were up to $2.15 billion and $1.41 billion, respectively.[37]

To help ensure the viability of companies financially threatened by deterioration and expensive maintenance costs, the Commission used its broadened "public interest" power to sanction several major combinations. The Gulf, Mobile & Ohio was permitted to purchase the struggling Chicago & Alton in 1945; and two years later the Pere Marquette, already controlled by the Chesapeake & Ohio, was allowed to merge its operations with those of the C&O.

Between 1947 and 1953, four other control agreements were expected to promote efficiency and rationalization in the industry. Control of the Wheeling & Lake Erie was intended to augment the Nickle Plate's competitive position; control of the Detroit, Toledo & Ironton by the Pennsylvania removed the DT&I from the shadow of Pennroad Corporation, a noncarrier holding company with interests other than railroading; and the Central of Georgia's control of the Savannah & Atlanta in 1951 and of the South Western in 1953 provided access to real estate investment companies and expansion of rail access.[38] The Commission hoped that by permitting such transactions, it might preclude further financial and operational decline of the industry.

Beginning in the mid-1950s and extending into the 1960s, however, the government lost interest in the railroad business. The federal response to the industry's problems was "either to ignore the problems of the railroads or to dole out regulatory relief in a piecemeal and insufficient fashion."[39]

This disinterest was particularly evident following the Korean War. Railroads prospered again during that conflict, but after the crisis was over the recession of 1954 set in. The capital intensive railroads were extremely sensitive to national economic downswings, and the recession meant a serious financial blow for many ailing systems. As in the past, rail officials looked to Washington for financial assistance to meet the high fixed costs associated with rail operations, but the federal government offered no financial help. By themselves, railroads had to face the facts that war demand was over and that the benefit from dieselization, exploited since the late 1920s, had reached its peak.

In the absence of federal aid, railroads looked to efficiency gains through corporate combinations as a way to obtain some operational and financial relief. Between 1956 and 1960 so many carriers were involved in negotiations about unifications that the period has been recognized as the beginning of the modern merger movement. Major carriers in the West involved in these discussions were the Union Pacific, St. Louis-San Francisco, Santa Fe, Southern Pacific, Chicago & North Western, and Duluth, South Shore & Atlantic. In the East the Pennsylvania, Erie, Norfolk & Western, and Lackawanna studied possibilities, and in the South the Atlantic Coast Line and the Louisville & Nashville used combinations to expand single-line service and simplify operations.

From 1955 to the end of that decade more than twenty merger applications were filed with the Commission. The mergers involved thirty-eight major railroads and about 90 percent of the country's 218,000 miles of track.[40] Viewing such combinations to be in the public interest, the Commission approved most of the them. As Gregory S. Prince, vice president of the Association of American Railroads (AAR), said, "Students of transportation now know that the major competition of the railroads is not with each other but with other modes of transportation."[41]

In each case carriers cited a host of advantages anticipated from union. These included extended single-line service, more efficient use of freight cars, and elimination of superfluous routes. Examples of expected annual financial savings from such coordination included $3.3 million annually for the Louisville & Nashville, $12 million annually for the Norfolk & Western, $3 million annually for the Chicago & North Western, and $1.2 million annually for the Duluth, South Shore & Atlantic.[42]

A report completed in 1960 by the AAR summarized the benefits that the industry attributed to intercarrier combinations. It noted that mergers "may result in more efficient and more economical use of motive power in the longer hauls thereby made possible, and in faster, more dependable service to the public."[43] Benefits specifically included improvement of facilities, strengthening of weaker constituent roads, discontinuance of duplicate service, more efficient car utilization, and a reduction in employement.

The notion that combinations would improve rail service was welcomed throughout the nation in the 1960s. As in the 1920s and 1930s, most experts believed that the establishment of a limited number of large systems was the only available means to ensure the future health of the industry.[44] A wide variety of interests concerned with rail operations, moreover, shared this sentiment. For example, a spokesperson for the United States Department of Agriculture noted, "Any improvement in service resulting from mergers, with no accompanying increase in rates, would be welcomed by many shippers of agricultural products."[45]

Many railroad officials, however, still believed that the combinations that were approved were not extensive enough. As Walter J. Tuohy, president of the Chesapeake & Ohio, noted, "There are too many railroads in the country as evidenced by the fact that too many are not making money."[46] Another eastern railroad president expressed the same idea more succinctly when he complained, "We've got too damned many railroads in the country and not enough traffic."[47]

The crux of the problem was that the Interstate Commerce Commission's case-by-case evaluation of proposed combinations was excessively time consuming. President John F. Kennedy blamed ICC shortcomings on "a chaotic patchwork of inconsistent and often obsolete legislation."[48] Kennedy sought to reduce bureaucratic delays and Commission inconsistencies by offering a number of suggestions to the Commission. Those included creating more specific guidelines for those carriers requesting merger—the tool through which railroads hoped for "a sharp cut in costs, a big increase in speed and efficiency of service, and a great deal of modernization."[49]

Throughout the 1960s, however, there was little progress in overhauling the ICC's regulation of the railroads. The Department of Transportation, created in 1966, criticized the Commission and transportation policy in general, but the new body did not change ICC standards. The nation was too preoccupied with civil rights and Vietnam to concern itself with transportation policy. Additionally, some groups believed that change within the industry would have to provide the impetus for policy change. The Department of Commerce noted, "By reducing the number of companies and the diversity of their individual interests, consolidation would permit a more rapid development of policy and a more flexible and adaptive response to rapidly changing conditions."[50]

If policy followed practice, then regulatory changes would be forthcoming, since combinations were just as common during the 1960s as in the 1950s. Systems that operated parallel as well as those that connected end-to-end sought the benefits of combinations. In the Northeast, three carriers were especially aggressive in seeking the advantages of unification—the Chesapeake & Ohio, the Norfolk & Western, and the Pennsylvania.

The Chesapeake & Ohio began this next round of combinations on July 14, 1960, when it submitted its application to acquire stock control of the Baltimore & Ohio.[51] While maintaining operations as distinct corporate entities, the two companies expected to enhance operational coordination. Moreover, the financial strength of the C&O was expected to remedy severe deferred maintenance problems on the B&O resulting from deteriorating rolling stock and inadequate maintenance of roadway.

One year after the C&O-B&O transaction, the Norfolk & Western began an effort to become a major eastern system. In applications filed in 1961 and 1962, the N&W absorbed the New York, Chicago & St. Louis (Nickle Plate) and purchased stock control of the Wabash and Akron, Canton & Youngstown as well as lesser subsidiaries of the Pittsburgh & West Virginia. The combinations were expected to enhance N&W's competitiveness against its primary rival, the Pennsylvania Railroad, by reducing the number of connections, improving schedules, and consolidating facilities.[52]

For similar reasons, the Commission permitted the Pennsylvania and the New York Central to merge in 1966, while four other systems merged into the Norfolk & Western.[53] In the former transaction, the new Penn-Central (PC) consolidated the operations of the two struggling eastern giants in the hopes that efficiencies of line rationalization would permit rehabilitation. In the latter transaction, the Norfolk & Western, PC's competitor absorbed the Erie-Lackawanna (EL); Delaware & Hudson (D&H); New York, New Haven & Hartford (New Haven); and the Boston & Maine (B&M). Decided upon during Commission hearings on the Penn-Central merger, incorporation of the four carriers was designed to preclude certain bankruptcy resulting from expected PC traffic diversions.

While the details of the N&W transaction were still being worked out, the C&O and its new B&O affiliate sought to enhance their competitive position once again. In 1967 they were permitted to obtain stock control of the Western Maryland Railway. The B&O family lines already interchanged 70 percent of all Western Maryland interline traffic. Moreover, the additional equipment owned by Western Maryland was expected to alleviate the B&O's deferred maintenance problems while creating operational efficiencies.[54]

As carriers were improving their competitive positions in the Northeast, carriers in the South and West also sought the benefits of unification. In 1962 the Southern Railway was permitted to obtain stock control of the ailing Central of Georgia (C of G). The combination was expected to modernize C of G facilities, improve its cash position, rationalize its trackage, and provide increased single-line service.[55]

In December 1963, the Seaboard Air Line merged with the Atlantic Coast Line.[56] The ICC considered both carriers to be financially healthy, but it believed the combination would help meet the challenge of ever-increasing intermodal competition. In addition, the new Seaboard Coast Line expected to solve the problems of excess capacity and inadequate traffic, problems that each line suffered as separate companies serving Richmond and south Florida. Other advantages included the elimination of interchanges and in-transit traffic delays and the creation of more flexible schedules and more direct routes.

For similiar reasons, several carriers in the western district were permitted to combine. In the most important case, the age-old dream of James J. Hill and Northern Securities was finally realized. After three previous attempts at merger over a seventy-year period, a Northern Lines transaction joined the parallel Great Northern and Northern Pacific lines with the complimentary lines of the Chicago, Burlington & Quincy. The new Burlington Northern (BN) was now dominant in the Northwest.[57]

A CONTINUING TREND

The pursuit of efficiency and competitive advantage through combination continued following the BN and PC combinations in the late 1960s. Moreover, several other unification requests in the 1960s, involving such carriers as the Rock Island and the Missouri Pacific, continued into the early 1970s. The process of unification was not interrupted by the Vietnam imbroglio or the domestic civil unrest that marked the close of the decade.

The Commission continued to apply "public interest" standards to combinations, and it continued to promote consolidation. History had taught the ICC that a decentralized industry was not the solution to the financial troubles of railroads. Regulators could only hope that an increasingly centralized industy was.

Through the following two decades the benefits of combinations would become more clearly evident. Unifications would facilitate the elimination of unproductive lines and the opening of more productive routes. They would rationalize operations to markets and maximize utilization of equipment and facilities. Combinations would also permit corporate diversification into other modes of transportation, thus giving rise to "total" transportation systems. These comprehensive transportation systems, in turn, would diversify into a variety of business ventures outside the transportation field. Consequently, modern-day railroads would become parts of giant multifaceted conglomerates.

Railroad freight transportation would lose its distinctiveness while preserving its usefulness. It would become one of many elements in the new worldwide network of cargo shipment. The benefit to the railroads would be greater financial security, something rail executives had been seeking since the merger movement began.

NOTES

1. Association of American Railroads, *Mergers—Efficiency is the Target*, Background paper on mergers: Association of American Railroads, undated [Washington, D.C.], 2.

2. Jeffrey Orenstein, *United States Railroad Policy: Uncle Sam at the Throttle* (Chicago: Nelson–Hall, 1990), 54.

3. Gabriel Kolko, *Railroad Regulation, 1877–1916* (Princeton: Princeton University Press, 1965), 335; Roy V. Scott, *Railroad Development Programs in the Twentieth Century* (Ames: Iowa State University Press, 1985), 4.

4. Stuart Dagget, *Railroad Reorganization* (New York: August M. Kelly, 1967), 335.

5. *Mergers—Efficiency is the Target*, 2.

6. Joseph Nimmo, Jr., is quoted in Kolko, *Railroads and Regulation*, 8, 19, 26. Among eastern carriers a similar mechanism know as a "community-of-interest" sought to eliminate rate competition. The Pennsylvania and New York Central were prime examples of railroads that used this tool. Through stock control and interlocking directors, these two carriers were able to eliminate a lot of intercarrier friction.

7. John D. Hicks, *The Populist Revolt: History of the Farmer's Alliances and the People's Party* (Minneapolis: University of Minnesota Press, 1931), 54–95, 405; Richard Stone, *The Interstate Commerce Commission and the Railroad Industry: A History of Regulatory Policy* (New York: Praeger, 1991), 3.

8. Keith L. Bryant Jr. (ed.), *Encyclopedia of American Business History and Biography* (New York: Facts on File, 1988), xviii; Theordore Saloutos and John D. Hicks, *Twentieth Century Populism: Agricultural Discontent and the Middle West, 1900-1939* (Lincoln: University of Nebraska Press, 1951), 32. As Roy V. Scott pointed out, however, many railroads took an active role in promoting agricultural advancements at their own expense. See Roy V. Scott, "American Railroads and Agricultural Extension, 1900–1914," *Business History Review* 39(Spring 1965), 74–98; "Railroads and Farmers: Educational Trains in Missouri, 1902–1914,"

Agricultural History 36 (January 1962), 3–15.

9. Stone, *Interstate Commerce Commission and the Railroad Industry*, 5.

10. Austin Godfrey Aaron, *Government Operation of the Railroads, 1918–1920* (Austin: Jenkins Publishing Company, 1974), 5–6.

11. Stone, *The Interstate Commerce Commission and the Railroad Industry*, 11; Martin, *Enterprise Denied*, 38, 40.

12. Stone, *The Interstate Commerce Commission and the Railroad Industry*, 12; Kolko, *The Railroads and Regulation, 1877–1916*, 132–144.

13. Martin, *Enterprise Denied*, 228; Kolko, *Railroads and Regulation*, 173.

14. Henry Cabot Lodge is quoted in Stone, *Interstate Commerce Commission and the Railroad Industry*, 13.

15. *The Nation* 121 (August 12, 1925), 185.

16. As a result of a 1906 investigation of E. H. Harriman's empire, the ICC requested that Congress make illegal any combination that reduced competition. Richard Saunders, *Railroad Mergers and the Coming of Conrail* (Westport, Conn.: Greenwood Press, 1978), 32.

17. Martin, *Enterprise Denied*, 17. See also Derek C. Bok, "Section 7 of the Clayton Act and the Merging of Law and Economics," *Harvard Law Review* 74 (December 1960), 233.

18. Martin, *Enterprise Denied*, 338–339; Stone, *Interstate Commerce Commission and the Railroad Industry*, 17.

19. Austin K. Kerr, *American Railroad Politics, 1914-1920: Wages, Rates, and Efficiency* (Pittsburgh: University of Pittsburgh Press, 1968), 67–69; I. L. Sharfman, *The Interstate Commerce Commission: A Study in Administrative Law and Procedure*, 5 vols. (New York: The Commonwealth Fund, 1931–1937), I, 151–153; Stone, *Interstate Commerce Commission and the Railroad Industry*, 19.

20. Stone, *The Interstate Commerce Commission and the Railroad Industry*, 19; Sharfman, *Interstate Commerce Commission*, I, 157–158.

21. *Traffic World* 25 (January 31, 1920), 185. This view represented a break with Cummins's traditional concept that "big was bad" in the world of business. In *Enterprise Denied*, Albro Martin portrayed Cummins as one of the progressive leaders who destroyed the vitality of the railroad industry. Saunders, *Railroad Mergers and the Coming of Conrail*, 38.

22. Stone, *The Interstate Commerce Commission and the Railroad Industry*, 20; Frederick Lewis Allen, *Only Yesterday: An Informal History of the 1920s* (New York: Harper and Brothers, 1931), 47.

23. Kerr, *American Railroad Politics*, 175, 206–7; Robert E. Cushman, *The Independent Regulatory Commissions* (New York: Oxford University Press, 1941), 117.

24. Orenstein, *United States Railroad Policy, 63.*

25. Stone, *Interstate Commerce Commission and the Railroad Industry*, 22.

26. Kolko, *Railroads and Regulation*, 35.

27. *Annals of the American Academy of Political and Social Science* 171 (January 1934), 169.

28. Ibid., 55.

29. *In the Matter of Consolidation of the Railway Properties of the United States into a Limited Number of Systems* 159 ICC 522.

30. Stone, *The Interstate Commerce Commission and the Railroad Industry*, 38; Robert C. Fellmeth, *The Interstate Commerce Commission: The Public Interest and the ICC* (New York: Grossman, 1970), 8–9.

31. Phillip D. Locklin, *Economics of Transportation*, 7th edition (Homewood, Ill.: Irwin, 1972), 264–265; Stone, *Interstate Commerce Commission and the Railroad Industry*, 40.

32. *Mergers–Efficiency is the Target*, 2.

33. *Gulf-Merger-Mobile & Ohio* 236 ICC 61. This was the only major merger case, as distinguished from acquisition of control cases, that affected southern railroads between 1920 and 1940. U.S. Interstate Commerce Commission, Bureau of Transport Economics and Statistics, *Railroad Consolidations and the Public Interest: A Preliminary Examination* (Washington, D.C.: U.S. Interstate Commerce Commission, Bureau of Transport Economics and Statistics, 1962), 20–21.

34. William M. Leonard, *Railroad Consolidation under the Transportation Act of 1920* (New York: Columbia University Press, 1946), 256; Saunders, *The Railroad Mergers and the Coming of Conrail*, 57.

35. Saunders, *The Railroad Mergers and the Coming of Conrail*, 57.

36. Bryant, *Encyclopedia of American Business History and Biography*, xxiii.

37. Interstate Commerce Commission, Bureau of Transport Economics and Statistics, *Statistics of Railways in the United States* (Washington, D.C.: Interstate Commerce Commission, 1940), 89–91; ICC, *Statistics of Railways in the United States*, 1945, 81–82; Orenstein, *United States Railroad Policy*, 64.

38. *Gulf, Mobile & Ohio-Purchase- Chicago & Alton* 261 ICC 405; *Nickel Plate-Control-Wheeling & Lake Erie* 267 ICC 163; *Pennsylvania-Control-Detroit, Toledo & Ironton*, 275 ICC 455; *Central of Georgia-Control-South Western* 282 ICC 359; *Central of Georgia-Control-Savannah & Atlanta* 282 ICC 39.

39. Orenstein, *United States Railroad Policy*, 87.

40. *Mergers—Efficiency Is the Target*, 3.

41. Gregory S. Prince is quoted in *Business Week*, November 29, 1958, 47.

42. U.S. Interstate Commerce Commission, *Railroad Consolidations and the Public Interest: A Preliminary Examination*, appendix, 3–6. Also see *Louisville & Nashville Railroad Company et al. Merger, Etc.* 295 ICC 457; *Norfolk & Western-Merger-Virginian Railroad* 307 ICC 806; *Chicago & Northwestern-Purchase-Minneapolis & St. Louis* 312 ICC 285; *Duluth, South Shore & Atlantic et al. Merger, Etc.* 312 ICC 341.

43. Association of American Railroads, *Consolidations and Mergers in the Transportation Industry*, Report to the Transportation Study Group under S. Res. 29, February 1960, pp. 17–18; U.S. Interstate Commerce Commission, *Railroad Consolidations and the Public Interest: A Preliminary Examination*, 9–10.

44. *Barron's* 40 (September 26, 1960), 11–13; *Railroad Consolidations and the Public Interest: A Preliminary Examination*, 11.

45. U.S. Economic Research Service, "Recent Railroad Merger Activity," *The Marketing and Transportation Situation* (Washington, D.C.: U.S. Department of Agriculture, 1961), 31.

46. *Newsweek*, May 30, 1960, 70.

47. *U.S. News & World Report* 49 (April 18, 1960), 90.

48. Stone, *Interstate Commerce Commission and the Railroad Industry*, 53; George W. Wilson, "Economic Analysis of Transportation: A Twenty-Five Year Survey," *Transportation Journal* (Fall 1986), 269.

49. *U.S. News & World Report* 49 (July 18, 1960), 91.

50. U.S. Department of Commerce, *Rationale of Federal Transportation Policy* (Washington, D.C.: U.S. Department of Commerce, 1960), 69–70.

51. *Chesapeake & Ohio-Control-Baltimore & Ohio* 317 ICC 261; U.S. Interstate Commerce Commission, Rail Services Planning Office, *Rail Merger Study: Initial Paper* (Washington, D.C.: U.S. Interstate Commerce Commission, 1977), 49–50.

52. *Norfolk & Western-Merger-St. Louis Railroad Company, Etc.* 324 ICC 1; Interstate Commerce Commission, *Rail Merger Study: Initial Paper*, 71–72.

53. *Pennsylvania-Merger-New York Central* 327 ICC 475; 328 ICC 304; 330 ICC 328; 331 ICC 754; *Norfolk & Western and New York, Chicago & St. Louis-Merger, Etc.* 330 ICC 780.

54. *Chesapeake & Ohio and Baltimore & Ohio-Control-Western Maryland* 328 ICC 684; Saunders, *Railroad Mergers and the Coming of Conrail*, 251–252.

55. *Southern-Control-Central of Georgia* 317 ICC 557.

56. *Seaboard Air Line-Merger-Atlantic Coast Line* 320 ICC 122. See also Saunders, *Railroad Mergers and the Coming of Conrail*, 202–204.

57. *Great Northern Pacific-Merger-Chicago, Burlington & Quincy-Merger-Great Northern* 328 ICC 460; 331 ICC 228.

3

The Financial Imbroglio:
Impetus for Change

"Railroading has been a profoundly troubled industry for many decades."[1] This assessment by the Federal Railroad Administration in 1979 succinctly and accurately described the health of the nation's first big business by the 1970s. The nostalgia for the past faded amid challenges to railroads by alternative transportation modes—challenges which illuminated the debilitating effects of federal regulation and the intrinsic failures of rail operations. Signs of decay were everywhere to be seen. Returns on net investment remained at low levels, market share of freight hauled and numbers of passengers transported decreased, and trackage and equipment deteriorated.

LEGACY OF DEGENERATION

Since the late 1920s, with the exception of the years of World War II, the operational and financial verve of the railroad industry had been on the decline. According to the U.S. Department of Transportion, the national railway network reached its maximum size between 1907 and 1930. The number of operating railroads peaked at 1,564 in 1907; miles of track operated crested at 429,000 in 1930; and the work force climaxed at 2,076,000 in 1920. The number of freight cars in service reached a high of 2,414,083 in 1925. After 1930, all of these statistics declined.[2]

The industry was in poor financial condition during the 1920s. The Transportation Act of 1920 included provisions to ensure a 6 percent rate of return on net investment for individual carriers, but railroads still earned an average return of only 5.3 percent in 1929. This capital intensive industry could not maintain adequate earning levels. Considering that the trucking industry was still in its infancy, railway operating results did not portend a promising future.

Between 1940 and 1970, railroad financial statistics spiraled downward. In constant 1972 dollars, net railroad investment declined from $79.6 billion in 1940 to $30.9 billion in 1970. Net railway operating income decreased from $2.3 billion to $531.8 million over that same span of time, using the same statistical base. Only during 1942 and 1943, in the middle of World War II, did Class I railroads have a rate of return on average net investment (based on current dollars) near or above the 6 percent promised in the Act of 1920.[3] In 1940, the railroad industry's rate of return on average net investment was 2.95 percent. By 1970, that figure was down to 1.73 percent. Revenues per ton-mile (in constant 1972 dollars) decreased from 3.2 cents in 1940 to 1.6 cents thirty years later.[4] Technological innovation had increased car capacities, but inadequate rate increases minimized the impact of increased efficiency.

Adding to the railroad industry's financial ills was the increasing loss of freight market share to other modes of transportation, especially the motor-carrier industry. Between 1940 and 1970, the rise of the trucking industry dealt the single greatest blow to railroad intercity freight traffic statistics.[5] In 1940, railroads hauled 61.3 percent of all intercity freight traffic or 379.2 billion ton-miles, while motor vehicles hauled 10.3 percent or 62 billion ton-miles. By 1970 the railroad share had eroded to 39.8 percent, while that of motor vehicles rose to 21.3 percent.

Water carriers, air carriers, and oil pipelines also either maintained or increased their share of the intercity freight market. The water-carrier share remained relatively static, fluctuating between 13 percent and 19 percent during the three decades from 1940 to 1970, while the oil pipeline share increased from 9.6 percent to 22.3 percent. The air-carrier freight share was statistically insignificant in 1940, but it grew dramatically after World War II.

Between 1947 and 1977, the economy (real GNP) rose 185 percent, and the nation's industrial production grew 250 percent. That growth translated into a 91 percent increase in the amount of intercity freight traffic, but railroads actually carried 9 percent fewer tons of freight in 1977 than they had thirty years earlier.[6]

Paralleling the loss in the railroad market share of freight tons hauled was the decline in the percentage of freight revenue earned by railroads. It declined from 76 percent in 1940 to 38 percent by 1976. Over that same span, the motor-carrier revenue share increased from 17 percent to 53 percent. According to the Transportation Association of America, regulated and nonregulated intercity trucking earned revenues estimated at $56 billion by 1976. That figure represented three times the total of railroad freight revenues at that time and demonstrated the fact that motor carriers were hauling a larger share of the higher-rated goods.[7]

While the railroad share of freight tonnage was declining, so too was railroad passenger traffic. The primary provider of intercity passenger transportation prior to World War I, railroads gradually yielded their passengers to the lure of automobile transport for relatively short trips and to air transport for the longer ones. In 1940, trains carried 452,921,000 passengers. Thirty years later passengers transported by rail decreased to 283,894,000.[8] Although rail carriers recaptured a segment of the passenger market between 1946 and 1955 with new equipment and operating innovations, it became increasingly apparent that they would lose passenger traffic in the future.

The increase in the number of air carriers and bus lines after the late 1940s added to the loss of rail passenger traffic. In 1947, there were 474 air carriers and 46 bus lines in the nation. By 1970, those numbers rose to 679 and 106, respectively.[9] Since railroads monopolized the passenger traffic market before World War I, these increases by other modes suggested the capturing of rail traffic or potential rail traffic. The growth of these alternate forms of passenger travel in combination with the proliferation of automobile ownership led many railroads to abandon passenger service altogether by the 1970s.

As the decline in passenger traffic led to neglect of passenger service, static or declining operating revenues resulted in the deterioration of rail infrastructures between 1940 and 1970.[10] Capital expenditures for roadways (in constant 1972 dollars) were relatively static, rising from $934.4 million to $1.1 billion, but equipment expenditures over the same period fell from $540.3 million to $392.2 million. Meanwhile, the cash base of railroads dropped sharply from $2.1 billion to $229.8 million, while capital lost to retirment benefits and equipment and roadway depreciation increased from $707.2 million to $889.5 million.

THE CONSEQUENCES

In the 1970s, the long-term direction of the industry changed little. Return on net investment remained low, tonnage of revenue freight hauled remained static, and capital lost to railroad retirement and depreciation of roadway and equipment remained at high levels. Railroad return on average net investment declined from 1.7 percent in 1970 to 1.2 percent by 1975. Tonnage of revenue freight originated, which had fluctuated between 1 billion and 1.4 billion since 1940, declined from 1.5 billion in 1970 to 1.4 billion in 1975.[11] Meanwhile, capital lost to depreciation and retirement (in 1972 dollars), although declining from $889.5 million to $683.2 million between 1970 and 1975, still reflected the financial burden of a capital intensive industry.[12] Finally, in 1972 dollars, capital expenditures for equipment declined from $1.1 billion in 1970 to $1 billion in 1975, and capital expenditures for roadways declined from $392.2 million to $382.5 million.

The poor rate of return on net investment, the decline in revenue-tons originated, the high level of depreciation and retirement costs, and the decline in expenditures for roadway and equipment maintenance generated unhealthy consequences. As a result of these factors, the railroad industry started to crumble. Important Class I carriers fell into bankruptcy, abandonment of routes increased, and car shortages generated bottlenecks that discouraged shippers and railway managers.

During the first half of the 1970s, numerous rail systems, encumbered by financial setbacks, no longer had the capital to continue operations. Most of these carriers were located in the northeastern district of the nation where rail systems thrived off large shipments between industrial centers. In late 1970 and early 1971, the Boston & Providence completed a bankruptcy reorganization plan under Section 77 of the Bankruptcy Act, while the Lehigh Valley went into reorganization of its own. Three northeastern systems already in reorganization, the Penn Central, the Jersey Central, and the Boston & Maine, complained that they could not generate sufficient cash to remain operational and threatened to shut down.

The federal government, already attentive to the difficulties of northeastern systems, used the Emergency Rail Services Act of 1970 to forestall further decline of at least two systems. The U.S. Department of Transportation guaranteed a loan of $100 million to Penn Central and $6 million to Jersey Central to ensure maintenance of basic operations.[13] These infusions, however, only temporarily eased the companies' difficulties, and, at the same time, increased their debt burdens.

Northeastern problems became more acute as the decade progressed. Four additional northeastern carriers went into reorganization in 1971. These were the

Reading, Cadillac & Lake City, Lehigh & Hudson River, and the Erie-Lackawanna. Meanwhile, the Jersey Central, unable to continue service on its Pennsylvania routes, turned those lines over to the Lehigh Valley. In July 1973, Penn Central showed signs of its impending collapse when fifteen of its subsidiaries went into reorganization under Section 77. In October, the Ann Arbor made it sixteen. Over the next two years, the New York, New Haven & Hartford, the New Hope Ivyland, and the New York, Susquehanna & Western joined the band of northeastern bankrupts. Meanwhile, a midwestern carrier, the Chicago, Rock Island & Pacific, also filed for reorganization.

The federal government struggled to find solutions for these problems. Federal administrators continued to offer individual lines moderate loan guarantees to facilitate rehabilitation to a level that would permit them to maintain basic line services. Officials hoped this effort would suffice until the railroads recovered during some future cyclical upswing in the economy. Unfortunately, however, the moderate guarantees provided no long-term recovery, and bankrupt carriers slipped into liquidation. Finally realizing the scope of the problem, the Interstate Commerce Commission began an extensive investigation in 1973 into the financial imbroglio entangling the Northeast and the effect of bankruptcies there on the industry nationwide. In the meantime, the bankrupt companies languished.

Augmenting the financial and traffic difficulties of bankrupt railroads were rail car shortages. Although technological improvements permitted the handling of greater tonnage, improvements did not keep pace with the growth rate of railroad traffic volume. Even the new 90-ton capacity cars, introduced in the mid-1970s to replace the 60-ton models, were insufficient.[14] The volume of traffic moving over the railroads had risen by 25 percent during the previous fifteen years. At the same time, the number of rail cars being retired from service outpaced the number of new cars being put in service. In 1974, for example, freight car retirements included 12,282 box cars, 16,964 open-top hoppers, and 5,880 gondolas. Acquisitions were 9,579 covered hoppers and 4,083 specially equipped boxcars.[15] The amount of capital available for investment and the capacities of car manufacturers were factors in this disparity.

Several factors contributed to the problem of car shortages. A changing economy altered the geographic demand for rail cars depending where the shipment of natural resources, grain products, heavy industrial goods, and light commodities were in the greatest demand at a given time. In addition, flooding and blizzards frequently brought the operations of certain lines to a halt and prevented the interregional movement of rail cars. Finally, intercarrier operating agreements, which involved the lending of rail cars, created shortages when carriers failed to return borrowed cars in a timely manner after a given shipment was delivered.

The Commission attacked these problems by increasing the per diem charges which carriers paid for the use of cars owned by other carriers.[16] In 1972, that charge was $5 per day. The Commission also increased demurrage charges on shippers who did not release unloaded cars promptly. Starting at from $5 to $15 a day, these charges were raised in 1971 to $30.[17] Additional charges were levied when cars were not completely emptied at terminals or left in such a condition as to delay their use.[18]

Despite the positive results arising from such steps, car shortages still existed, generated at times by other factors. Strikes by railroad employees were especially devastating. For example, in July 1971, work stoppages resulting from selective strikes and lasting more than two weeks shut down the operation of ten major railroads. Since many of these systems held the cars of numerous other carriers, the car shortage was made worse.

Another major factor contributing to car shortages was rail car variety. Most railroads maintained numbers of box cars, open or covered hopper cars, and gondolas, among other types, depending on the markets they served. If demand for a particular product increased dramatically, a given carrier encountered a shortage of a particular kind of car and had to lease cars from other carriers. The fact that ICC regulation required the shipment of certain commodities in specific types of cars exacerbated such shortages.

Such was the case following the sale by the United States of 83 million tons of grain to the Soviet Union in 1972. Covered hoppers loaded with grain jammed port facilities. This concentration left regular traffic at interior points short of cars and port facilities clogged. As a result of these unusual circumstances, Class I railroads experienced daily freight car shortages of 29,000 units, peaking at 44,000 during the month of February.[19]

Fuel shortages during the winter of 1973–1974, arising from the Arab oil embargo, exaccerbated these shortages. As part of a conservation effort, electric power plants began converting from oil to coal, and the railroads had to adjust to changing demand for cars. The sudden increased need for open top hopper cars led to shortages between January and April 1974 of from 2,000 to 7,000 cars daily.[20]

By late 1975 the general car shortage came to an end as a result of two factors, a decline in the demand for rail service and remedial action by the ICC. The decline in demand stemmed from a general economic downturn, a decline in manufacturing and agricultural output, and a coal strike. The remedial action taken by the Commission included regulation revisions and the formation of a rail car company to pool rail cars. The Commission revised rail services orders restricting the number and model of cars used for certain products and over certain routes in case-by-case instances. For example, in the fall of 1975 the Commission authorized the Union Pacific and the Rock Island to intercept 200 hopper cars owned by other railroads and to use those cars to handle promptly a sugar beet crop in an effort to prevent loss from freezing.[21]

The newly formed rail car company, American Rail Box Car Company (Railbox), also helped resolve the nation's car shortages. The company operated a pool of 10,000 new 50-foot, wide-door box cars. Costing the railroads $230 million, the company's cars were to supplement the national boxcar fleet and to relieve car shortages wherever they arose.[22] Revenue came from rental fees charged to railroads using the cars.

While the industry threatened to deteriorate under the pressures of bankruptcies and car shortages, many carrier executives sought to contract overextended systems. By the 1970s, managers attempted to adjust trackage to market demand through planned line abandonments. Generally, railroads considered abandoning a particular line when the earnings from that line fell below the cost of operating it. After a carrier filed an application to abandon trackage, the ICC had to weigh the proposal against "public convenience and necessity" tests. This meant that the Commission had to consider the needs of the public and firms on a particular line against the carrier's need to limit unprofitable operation. In the year ending June 30, 1971, railroads filed 241 applications with the ICC to abandon lines, and they filed 304 the following year.[23]

In 1972, the Commission tried to facilitate the abandonment of unprofitable lines by introducing procedures to reduce the time and cost of processing applications. A study of more than 1,000 abandonments over a ten-year period showed that the public did not oppose a majority of them.[24] The study also showed that proposed discontinuances usually involved trackage that was little used and in poor condition. Accordingly, the Commission decided to exempt from review abandonment applications covering track that handled fewer than 34 carloads per mile annually. Only in special circumstances would discontinuances under such conditions be denied.

Abandonment proceedings for lines over which more than 34 carloads moved per mile per year were approved almost as easily. An example was an application by Missouri-Kansas-Texas and its subsidiary, the Beaver, Meade & Engelwood Railroad, which proposed abandoning 335 miles of line in northwestern Oklahoma. The Commission simply concluded that "the cost of rehabilitating the lines could not be justified in terms of present and potential traffic revenues and that adequate substitute transportation service was accessible to meet the needs of the shipping public."[25]

From this case came the criteria used to evaluate future abandonment proceedings. Those criteria were designed to determine whether the line proposed for abandonment was "marginally profitable, operated at a deficit, or would have been operated at a deficit were it not for the deferral of maintenance and rehabilitation costs; and . . . whether the carrier's available funds for maintenance and rehabilitation are required for those portions of line within its system for which a greater public need had been demonstrated and which offer a larger profit potential for the carrier."[26] These criteria were applicable not only for struggling systems but also for those systems which used the deferral of maintenance on less profitable lines as a way of cutting losses and of maintaining service on the lines.[27]

In 1973, the Regional Rail Reorganization Act altered abandonment regulations. The new law restricted railroads in reorganization from filing abandonment applications with the Commission. Pursuant to Section 304(f) of the Act, the United States Railway Association was authorized to consider turning such lines in the northeast over to a new federally run system, Consolidated Rail Corporation.[28] This new legislation was the single most important factor in the general reduction in abandonment applications thereafter filed with the Commission. In 1975 and 1976, the number of abandonment applications that came before the Commission declined by 40 percent.[29] Nevertheless, between 1976 and 1979 average yearly abandonments averaged over a hundred.

The Commission continued to aid railroads in finding the most efficient means of filing abandonment applications. To achieve its goal, the ICC modified procedures in 1976 and again in 1978. The Railroad Revitalization and Regulatory Reform Act of 1976 (4R Act) altered abandonment procedures in three different ways. First, the law required the Commission to process abandonments and conduct related proceedings under strict time constraints (i.e., within 35 days).[30] This stipulation simply legalized the Commission's new commitment to speed the railroad's ability to rationalize operations. The 4R Act also expanded the scope of public notice that railroads had to provide when proposing an abandonment. This stipulation was designed to reduce the negative impact of impending abandonments and limit public objections during processing. An abandonment expected in advance was less likely to stir additional opposition. Finally, the 4R Act gave interested parties the opportunity to provide the operating railroad with financial assistance to keep the targeted line operational.

To ensure that railroads fulfilled their public notice obligations, the 4R Act required rail carriers to file maps with the Commission outlining abandonment projections.[31] Railroads had to indicate, where feasible, those lines operating under subsidy, those lines undergoing abandonment proceedings, those lines that they might abandon within three years, and those lines that they might consider abandoning sometime in the future. This stipulation was expected to provide the Commission and the public with a better understanding of the railroads' plans for contraction and permit them to cope better with the impact of discontinued service.

As railroads disclosed their abandonment projections, the public was given the opportunity to intervene. Businesses or public agencies offering assistance to a railroad to maintain operations over a given line were evaluated by two criteria. The ICC first determined whether or not the offer met the acquisition cost of a line. Then the Commission tried to determine if the offer covered the difference between revenues of the line and avoidable cost of providing rail freight service while generating a reasonable return.

The new abandonment stipulations represented the growing federal commitment to address rail problems in detail. That fact, however, did little to slow the rate of abandonments. An analysis of system diagram maps in 1977 revealed that railroads (excluding Conrail) throughout the country were planning at some point to abandon 16,663 miles of track. This was 8.3 percent of the 200,391 total line-haul miles in operation in 1975.[32]

ALLOCATING BLAME

The decline of the railroad industry after World War II and the consequences that culminated in the 1970s were clear. Equally evident were those factors responsible for the difficulty the industry had in adjusting to a changing marketplace. Three elements bear responsibility for the problems—management, labor, and federal regulation.

Management is a crucial element in the performance of all businesses. Managers are responsible for the operation of a firm and for ensuring its profitability. For those systems that fared poorly in the decades following World War II, management failed to meet its responsibility. This failure stemmed in part from incompetent staffing in the managerial structure. The inept leadership pursued policies that undermined the health of railroads. Too many officials emphasized volume of traffic at the expense of profit; they focused on improving productivity rather than on controlling costs and improving service quality; and they operated in the short term at the expense of long-term stability.

Traditionally, rail managers emphasized volume over profit in shaping rail operations.[33] Traffic officers, lacking reliable cost and profit analysis, sought to increase their railroads' traffic volume by generating new traffic or attracting traffic from other railroads or modes. If the traffic officers could not achieve their carload or revenue goals through sales of service, they resorted to service improvements or rate reductions at the expense of overall profitability.

Service improvements often meant promising individual shippers improved car service at the expense of the company's overall system. Usually such agreements were not accompanied by the reorganization of the system's overall car utilization. These commitments, moreover, could not always be altered after the short term, because the shipper's only tie to a particular railroad might be the availability of a certain number and type of car at demand. The result was high cost to the railroad.

Rate adjustments created similar problems for railroads. Carriers often offered rate reductions in an effort to attract new traffic. However, since contracts providing reduced rates in exchange for tying future shipments to a railroad were illegal, all a railroad could depend on with rate reductions were informal agreements by shippers to favor the routes of the given line. This practice tended to encourage circuitous routing and limit the rationalization of operations needed to generate efficiency and savings and to pay for the reductions in the first place. Shippers, moreover, could renege on their agreements at any point, leaving railroads with overextended circuitous routes requiring more costly rationalization in the future. Nevertheless, as a result of such arrangements, the volume of traffic often increased, thereby suggesting that railroads reached their goals.

While managers emphasized volume over profit, they also promoted productivity at the expense of cost and service quality. Rail executives tended to focus on aggregate operating statistics as a measure of performance rather than on unit costs.[34] For example, managers might point to the operation of longer trains as a means to increase tonnage of freight without considering that the factors of time, empty mileage, and equipment availability might generate increased costs per unit shipped. While greater tonnage may have been transported on a given shipment, the cost of that larger movement may have been proportionally higher.

Concomitantly, railroad management failed to emphasize the importance of quality standards and performance—elements of primary importance in most large businesses.[35] Managers often neglected to compare unit costs at varied levels of quality service, so they could not make adjustments in quality service factors based on hard evidence. They simply were unable to determine the cost effectiveness of making operational adjustments to meet the needs of specific shippers whose business railroads solicited through offers of specialized service.

While railroad managements emphasized volume over profit and productivity over cost and service quality, they also held short-term rather than long-term economic perspectives.[36] This view was particularly evident with regard to the impact of depreciation and inflation on equipment and roadway expenditures. Specifically, inflation greatly influenced railroad investment in maintenance or improvement of equipment and roadways. Managers frequently measured depreciation in the short term. They used current or actual expenditure statistics on roadway and equipment as a variable in measuring depreciation over short spans, such as five years, without adjusting for inflation each year or for the increased depreciation rate resulting from that yearly inflation. The result was that capital lost to depreciation appeared less than it was in reality. This distorted accounting meant that railroad financial statistics gave an unrealistic picture of a company's financial health.

Several logistical characteristics peculiar to railroading also explained the outmoded business perspectives of managers. Rail systems were so vast that gradual deterioration in the aggregate was difficult to detect by any manager. Fixed right-of-ways and facilities inhibited speedy route adustments once the need for change was identified. Finally, it was difficult for rail managers, themselves engaged in obsolete practices, to identify outdated policies.[37]

The background of rail officials often limited a railroad's ability to maximize efficiency. The specialized training and experience needed to be a railroad manager made it difficult for carriers to appoint to upper management positions individuals with service in other industries. Consequently, railroads did not benefit from operational innovations and new management techniques that "new blood" was introducing in other businesses.[38]

In addition, railroad directors, drawn almost exclusively from upper management, sought to ensure the security of primary stockholders who were often shippers or financial leaders of other industries. These investors were interested in short-term profits on investment in an industry that required long-term attention. Consequently, the directors avoided high risk overhauls of operations—a vital necessity for many systems.[39]

Another element contributing to railroad decline was railroad labor costs. These consumed approximately 65 percent of railroad operating revenues by the mid-1970s.[40] Railroads suffered at the hands of labor because of the complexity of labor organization in the industry, efforts of labor to ensure job security regardless of cost, and rising wage levels.

More than two dozen separate unions represented the interests of railroad labor. Twenty-one of these were exclusively railroad unions. They were divided into three general categories: operating unions, nonoperating craft unions, and nonoperating industrial unions. So many different labor interests absorbed a great deal of the time of railway managers who were often forced to work out agreements with each union and settle disputes between them.[41]

The lack of cooperation between unions often intensified labor-management disputes, sometimes to the detriment of labor as well as to management. For example, the Brotherhood of Locomotive Engineers refused to combine with the other main operating craft union, the United Transportation Union. All major rail unions rejected suggestions that they join with the AFL-CIO, preferring instead to maintain their independence.

As a result, compartmentalization of problems at times generated imbalanced work forces within a system. Too many of one skill or not enough of another produced waste. While measuring the "wasted" hours as a result of dealing with so many unions individually was impossible, railroad management recognized the problem.

While railroad labor unions absorbed enormous amounts of the time of railroad managers, they also limited managerial innovation in railway operations in order to preserve rail employment. Technological innovation affected shopcraft, nonoperating craft, and operating crafts in similar ways.

Between 1944 and 1976 shopcraft employees involved with the maintenance of equipment declined in number from 390,000 to 103,000.[42] Many of these job losses occurred in the late 1940s and 1950s when diesels replaced steam locomotives. The operation of diesels made blacksmiths and boilermakers superfluous, and the engines' fewer parts and ease of maintenance reduced the need for repairmen. Finally, diesel engines and higher capacity cars eliminated the need for so many carmen.

Some threatened union members were able to obtain employment elsewhere in the postwar boom, but others chose to fight railroad changes. In particular, labor fought against the growing railroad practice of contracting its shopcraft work to locomotive manufacturers. By 1964, labor received protection against this and other railroad practices with the Employee Protection Agreement of that year. The legislation prohibited railroads from cutting costs through subcontracting unless the railroad could not do the work in question in its own shops.

Nonoperating crafts also took action against railroads to forestall employment cuts induced by innovation. The nonoperating crafts—which included maintenance-of-way employees, signalmen, dining car workers, telegraphers, and clerks—suffered heavy employment losses following World War II. Between 1945 and 1976, maintenance-of-way employment fell from 301,000 to 87,000 as a result of improved roadway maintenance machinery, reduced trackage, and use of continuous welded rail which required less maintenance than standard rails. Numbers of clerical workers dropped from 231,000 in 1945 to 99,000 in 1976 partly because of increased use of electronic data processing.[43] Moreover, telegraphers, whose numbers declined by half after 1955, lost jobs because of the rise of alternate forms of communication, such as radio and microwave, and the emergence of centralized traffic control, a system that permitted remote operation of switches and signals.

Because of resistance among the unions comprising the nonoperating crafts, however, railroads were not permitted to eliminate positions to the extent that they desired. Railroads had to comply with agreements ensuring accommodation of such employees for years at a time. For example, the National Employment Stabilization Agreement of 1965 permitted railroads to eliminate superfluous positions only through attrition. Barring a massive business decline, a railroad could be required to maintain such employees until retirement.

The operating crafts were just as determined when employment loss resulted from innovation. The number of operating craft employees—engineers, switchmen, conductors, and trainmen—was reduced from 478,000 in 1944 to 178,000 in 1976. Diesel engines permitted the operation of longer trains with smaller crews and completely eliminated the need for firemen.[44]

Operating crafts first obtained some security against job loss arising from innovation with the National Diesel Firemen's Agreement of 1937. That agreement with rail managements guaranteed the firemen's position on all diesel engines on yard and road service. At that time, officials of many railroads thought that diesels would not be commonly used in road service and they expected the diesels to replace no more than 10 percent of the steam engines. Had they foreseen what did occur, they would never have made such a concession to labor. The change to diesels became more complete after 1945 than could have been imagined ealier.

After serious controversy in the 1950s over the employment of firemen, the ICC recommended to a Presidential Railroad Commission that those jobs be eliminated. Once negotiations through the National Mediation Board failed, Congress passed a law that called for the elimination of 90 percent of the firemen positions. Termination of employment would depend on years of service. Firemen with less than two years of service were terminated immediately. Through the 1960s and into the early 1970s, court appeals and further negotiations revised the method of termination for the remaining firemen. In addition to attrition, the carriers agreed to help reduce the pool of firemen by drawing apprentice engineers from the firemen ranks. The cost to railroads was substantial.

Another important cost to railroads was the insurance required for employees whose jobs were threatened by reorganizations or mergers. Railroads literally had to pay off employees whom they no longer needed. According to various pieces of legislation from 1933 to 1980, railroad employees had to be compensated in some fashion.[45]

Adding to railroad costs for labor protection were labor wages. By the estimates of the National Railway Labor Conference in 1977, road enginemen received $29,000 annually, road conductors $26,000, and road brakemen $21,000. Although working irregular hours, many of the employees earning those wages were not required to work more than 35 hours per week.[46]

Railroad workers were well paid in comparison to employees in other industries. In 1975, the base pay for railroad employees was 21 percent higher than for workers in the trucking and warehousing industries and 41 percent higher than for all industry. If the benefits of railroad retirement were included, railroad employees made 32 percent more than trucking employees and 55 percent more than all workers.[47] Such wage levels resulted from decades of increases. Between 1947 and 1976, the average rail employee quintupled his income.

Two policies that augmented labor costs were arbitraries and basis of payment. Arbitraries represented extra payments made to employees for unforeseen difficulties or unexpected overtime. Ultimately, that meant higher outlays by rail carriers. Adding to arbitraries was the standard by which operating crews were paid. Wages of train crews were based on eight hours of operation or distance traveled, whichever was most beneficial. If a train went beyond a certain distance, the crew was paid by mileage. Otherwise, they were paid for a standard eight-hour day. Unfortunately, the nature of the payment system eliminated incentives for rail crews to handle a train as rapidly as possible so as to ensure the preferable eight-hour pay standard. The reverse occurred for crews operating high-speed trains. The dual pay system often allowed them to obtain a full week's pay for working only two days a week.[48]

Like labor and management, federal regulation contributed to the decline of the railroad industry—the most regulated of all forms of transportation through the

1970s.[49] Specifically, federal regulation of railroad rates was fundamental in preventing railroads from earning the capital necessary to function profitably in an increasingly competitive environment.

Rate regulation became increasingly restrictive over the years. The Interstate Commerce Act (1887) required that rates be "just and reasonable." The Hepburn Act (1906) gave the ICC the power to prescribe maximum rates where they were found "unjust and unreasonable," and the Mann-Elkins Act (1910) empowered the Commission to suspend rates for ten months pending investigative hearings. In 1920, the Transportation Act augmented ICC control with the authority to prescribe minimum and maximum rates and to adjust joint rates with other rail or water carriers.[50] In 1933, the Emergency Transportation Act eliminated the railroad revenue adequacy provision of the 1920 legislation, leaving revenue adequacy of railroads to the discretion of the Commission.

By the end of the decade, new legislation included umbrella rate-making provisions. Under the Transportation Act of 1940, rates set for one mode of transportation had to account for the effects on competing modes. Nearly always used to preserve the competitive health of other modes, these provisions contributed to the decline of railroads in the face of motor-, water-, and air-carrier competition. The umbrella provisions were later abandoned as a result of stipulations in the Transportation Act of 1958 and the Railroad Revitalization and Regulatory Reform Act of 1976. By then, however, railroads had already suffered greatly.

Overall, ICC rate regulation was harmful to rail carriers in two important ways. First, the time lag between carrier requests for rate increases and their approval cost railroads millions in revenue. According to the Association of American Railroads, regulatory time-lags cost carriers $2.2 billion between 1967 and 1975.[51] That amount represented almost one quarter of the total amount of rate increases permitted during the same span. Second, umbrella ratemaking hurt the ability of railroads to compete against other modes. With rate competition removed from the picture, modes could only compete on the basis of quality of service. Since they had the ability to deliver freight door-to-door, motor carriers had a distinct advantage in the area of service quality.

By the 1970s, rail carriers were embroiled in the rate issue as much as ever. As the primary variable in determining the earnings of a carrier per shipment, rate flexibility represented an important element in the growth or decline of railroad earnings. Since railroads were prohibited from contracting with shippers for a given rate, railroads had to establish general rates within Commission parameters. Carriers generally desired rate levels that were "sufficiently competitive to induce shippers to purchase transportation services and sufficiently profitable to permit a feedback of capital for improvement of such services."[52] However, the ICC measured proposed rates against a host of standards to "guard the public against the possibility that the rates are unreasonable, preferential, prejudicial or discriminatory."[53] The wording of the stipulations was reminiscent of the era in which they were enacted more than three-quarters of a century earlier.

In order to compensate for inflation in the 1970s, the Commission approved rate increases for carriers.[54] These increases were generally instituted or broadly applied to specific regions of the country. On March 4, 1971, for example, the Commission approved general increases amounting to 29 percent in the Northeast, 18 percent in the West, and 12 percent in the South and interterritorially.[55]

While the Commission permitted some increases in rates, it undertook a comprehensive investigation of the railroad rate structure. The stimulus for this investigation was concern that the Commission's policy of periodically issuing general rate increases across the industry was fundamentally unsound. Across-the-board increases were thought to have caused "a misalignment of rate relationships and a distortion of proper rate levels."[56] As during the Progressive era, industry regulators had been applying measures that were not specific enough to accommodate the complexities of individual markets.

In 1972, after receiving dozens of suggestions from railroads, shippers, and senators and congressmen, the Commission worked on a remedy. By early 1974, Commission investigators adopted a proposal intended to provide "a workable frame of reference for consideration of millions of freight rates on file with the Commission."[57] According to the proposal, the major commodities shipped by rail would be divided into 126 separate groups. Each of these groups was then investigated to find a standard rate for shipping that commodity. Once a standard rate was found, the prevailing rates were to be adjusted.

The investigation of each commodity group was both thorough and extensive.[58] By mid-1975 studies of lumber, iron ore, and coal rate structures were still taking place. These investigations crossed a plethora of transportation variables with the costs of service. Rate adjustments made on the basis of these studies helped preclude the disparity between rates and costs of service and prevented some commodities from carrying an improper burden in the overall rate structure.

While investigators analyzed commodity rate structures, railroads began asking the Commission for increased regulatory flexibility in the shipment of food products. Railroads wanted permission to increase charges on freight that required refrigeration. Refrigerated products such as fruits, vegetables, and meats required special cars and treatment by carriers, and railroads believed that fact should factor into the rate structure.[59] The railroads also sought to eliminate the lower charges that regulators maintained on the transport of non-frozen perishables. To the dismay of the railroads, however, the ICC rejected the increases because they would be unjust and unreasonable to shippers dependent on refrigerated rail shipments.[60]

The fear that motor carriers might capture the traffic of food products continued to be a major concern of the Commission and railroads alike. In 1975, for example, the Commission investigated a request by railroads to raise rates on the shipment of fresh fruits and vegetables moving between western, eastern, and southern territories.[61] Board officials argued that the proposed increases "would largely eliminate the use of railroad transportation on many of the considered commodities with extreme hardship to the producers and consumers of such commodities."[62] The fresh fruits and vegetables markets would not sustain a mode of transportation that absorbed too great a share of their value.

Juxtaposed to limitations on rate increases in the shipment of fresh fruits and vegetables were restrictions on rate slashing. In 1960, for example, high capacity "Big

John" grain cars created a competitive advantage for Southern Railway which sought to use them to cut rates on grain shipments to the Southeast. After a Supreme Court ruling in 1965 overturned an ICC decision, Southern obtained its desired rate cuts. Consequently, a tremendous amount of wheat flour moved from midwestern points to terminals in the South. The influx stimulated a burgeoning milling industry.

By the early 1970s, several railroad companies that suffered competitive disadvantages from systems that owned the new grain cars sought relief. These systems asked the Commission for permission to cut rates by 20 percent on their own wheat flour shipments into the South in order to draw traffic from those carriers that controlled the market with their Big John cars.

To the dismay of the requesting carriers, the Commission would not approve the rate reductions. The Big John cars of 1960 had altered the structure of the grain and milling industry nationwide. Rate reductions would significantly affect grain and milling firms. Those that advocated the 20 percent reduction and those that opposed it included competing millers. Additionally, the rates for shippers and receivers at intermediate points would suffer rate increases if such reductions were allowed. The initial rate reduction would attract traffic, thus leaving less space for those at intermediate points. With greater demand comes higher rates. The same scenario applied to connecting carriers.

During the late 1970s, rate flexibility continued to be one of the industry's foremost concerns. From 1976 to 1979, the Commission implemented broad rate increases based on geography or commodity type. In 1976, the Commission permitted a 2.8 percent increase to offset increased tax liability as a result of new railroad retirement laws. At the same time, a 5 and a 2.5 percent rate increase was granted to compensate for increased labor costs. Additionally, a temporary 10 percent rate increase enacted in 1974 was extended through 1977. In 1977, that rate increase was extended to 1978 while two other rate increases, a 5 and a 4 percent, were authorized to offset labor costs that occurred after 1976. The following year the Commission sanctioned four separate increases, and in 1979, the ICC permitted fuel surcharges, both general and specific, to offset increased fuel costs.[63]

While general rate increases helped offset fluctuations in the general economy, the ICC deemphasized them, preferring investigations into individual rate structure increases. For example, researchers argued for the greater use of demand-sensitive grain rates, separate rates for district grain rail services, and a rate relationship between domestic and export grains. Commission examiners contended that such modification would facilitate railroad alignment with the fluctuation in the grain market. Better alignment translated into more efficient service to grain shippers and greater potential earnings for railroads.

Commission authorities conducted rate investigations on several other commodities shipped by rail. These included paper products, recyclables, and coal.[64] In each case, the ICC determined the rate structure to be sound and claimed that rates were not unreasonably high. The rate structure on the shipment of iron ores, scrap iron, and steel was also found to be nondiscriminatory.[65] Finally, an investigation into the rate structure for the shipment of other commodities, such as fruits and vegetables, generated an unusual determination. The Commission finally decided to deregulate those shipments. Rates could be set by railroads without the constrictions of rate minimums or rate caps. Considering that motor carriers were becoming the dominant mode in the shipment of such products, regulators believed that rail carriers required unlimited flexibility to save this important market.[66]

Rate adjustments, both general and customized, helped the industry survive increasing rail costs. The Commission finally understood the need for such rate flexibility, and it was willing to facilitate it. Unfortunately, however, by the 1970s that flexibility was not sufficient to save many ailing systems from the quagmire of economic stagnation. Only a dramatic revision of regulatory policies could forestall further deterioration of the weaker systems.

ASSESSMENT

The decades following World War II represented a period of growth and prosperity for most industries but not for the business of railroading. From the 1940s through the 1970s, the railroad industry experienced unprecedented decline. The vanguard of transportation in the nineteenth century, railroads in the 1970s were struggling to survive the evolution of transportation markets and alternate modes of transportation. If the industry was to survive the shakeout, three facets of railroading would have to be overhauled as rapidly as possible—management, labor, and federal regulation. Rail executives had already started the transformation of management and labor, using corporate combinations as a tool of restructuring. In 1970, the federal government would begin to revamp regulation.

NOTES

1. U.S. Department of Transportation, Federal Railroad Administration, *The Railroad Situation: A Perspective on the Present, Past and Future of the Railroad Industry: Final Report* (Washington, D.C.: GPO, March 1979), 1.

2. U.S. Department of Commerce, Bureau of the Census, *Historical Statistics of the United States, Colonial Times to 1957* (Washington, D.C.: GPO, 1960), 427–430, 437. See also Association of American Railroads, *Railroad Transportation, A Statistical Record, 1921–1959* (Washington, D.C.: Association of American Railroads, 1960).

3. U.S. Department of Transportation, *Railroad Situation*, 77–80.

4. Ibid.

5. *Moody's Transportation Manual* (New York: Moody's Investor's Service, Inc., 1993), a-4 and a-5. See also *Staggers Rail Act, Legislative History*, U.S. Code, vol. 10A, secs. 7453–7454 (1980).

6. Ibid., 7454.

7. Transportation Association of America, *Transportation Facts and Trends*, 14th edition (Washington, D.C.: Transportation Association of America, 1978), 4.

8. *Moody's Transportation Manual*, 1993, a-2 and a-3.

9. Transportation Association of America, *Transportation Fact and Trends*, 15.

10. U.S. Department of Transportation, *Railroad Situation*, 79–80.

11. Ibid.

12. Ibid., 78.

13. U.S. Interstate Commerce Commission, *Annual Report, 1971* (Washington, D.C.: GPO, 1971), 72.

14. ICC, *Annual Report, 1976*, 37; *1975*, 25.

15. ICC, *Annual Report, 1974*, 34.

16. *Chicago, Burlington & Quincy Railroad Company v. New York, Susquehanna & Western Railroad Company* 332 ICC 176; *United States v. Florida East Coast Railway Company* 410 U.S. 224; *Incentive Per Diem Charges-1968* 337 ICC 217.

17. *Demurrage Rules and Charges, Nationwide* 340 ICC 83; ICC, *Annual Report, 1972*, 25–26.

18. Investigation and Suspension Docket 8701, *Notification of Unloaded Car, by Consignee to Railroad*, December 19, 1972.

19. ICC, *Annual Report, 1974*, 34.

20. Ibid., 35.

21. ICC, *Annual Report, 1976*, 36. See also Directed Service Order No. 1237, *Regulation for the Return of Hopper Cars*; Directed Service Order No. 1171, *Regulation for the Return of Open Top Hopper Cars*; Directed Service Order No. 1182, *Substitution of Stock Cars for Hopper Cars*.

22. ICC, *Annual Report, 1975*, 225.

23. ICC, *Annual Report, 1971*, 35; *1972*, 10.

24. *Abandonment of Railroad Lines and Discontinuances of Service* 354 ICC 129; ICC, *Annual Report, 1972*, 10; *Abandonment of Railroad Lines, Commonwealth of Pennsylvania, et al. v. United States Report* 414 U.S. 1017.

25. ICC, *Annual Report, 1972*, 12.

26. Ibid.

27. Ibid.

28. *Regional Rail Reorganization Act Cases* 419 U.S. 102; ICC, *Annual Report, 1975*, 16.

29. ICC, *Annual Report, 1976*, 21.

30. Ibid.; *Procedures for Pending Rail Abandonment Cases*, Notice decided March 24, 1976, served March 31, 1976.

31. Ex Parte No. 274 *Abandonment of Rail Lines and Discontinuance of Service* 354 ICC 129.

32. ICC, *Annual Report, 1977*, 40.

33. U.S. Department of Transportation, *Railroad Situation*, 195.

34. D. Daryl Wyckoff, *Railroad Management* (Lexington, Mass.: Lexington Books, 1976), 171–173.

35. Ibid., 172.

36. U.S. Department of Transportation, *Railroad Situation*, 199–200.

37. Wyckoff, *Railroad Management*, 103–104.

38. U.S. Department of Transportation, *Railroad Situation*, 194. See also W. Frederick Cottrell, *The Railroaders* (Stanford: Stanford University Press, 1940), 7, 16; Paul C. Dunn, *Selection and Training of Railroad Supervisors* (Cambridge, Mass.: Harvard University Press, 1942), 37.

39. Morris Stuart, "Stalled Professionalism: The Recruitment of Railway Officials in the United States, 1885–1940," *Business History Review* 47 (Autumn 1973): 322; Wyckoff, *Railroad Management*, 89, 174.

40. U.S. Department of Transportation, Federal Railroad Administration, *The Crew Size Dispute in the Railroad Industry* (Washington, D.C.: U.S. Department of Transportation, Federal Railroad Administration, 1979), 29.

41. Ibid., 32. See also Edward Shils, "Industrial Unrest in the Nation's Rail Industry," *Labor Law Journal* 15 (February 1964): 81–110; Robert C. Lieb, *Labor in the Transportation Industries* (Washington, D.C.: U.S. Department of Transportation, 1973), 37–40.

42. U.S. Department of Trasportation, *Railroad Situation*, 204.

43. Ibid.

44. Ibid., 206.

45. This compensation is detailed in Chapter 4.

46. U.S. Department of Transportation, *The Railroad Situation*, 209. See also Transportation Association of America, *Transportation Facts and Trends*, 13th edition (Washington, D.C.: Transportation Association of America, 1977), 24.

47. Ibid.

48. Ibid., 212.

49. Transportation Association of America, *Transportation Facts and Trends*, 14th edition (Washington, D.C.: Transportation Association of America, 1978), 9; *Staggers Rail Act of 1980, Legislative History*, U.S. Code, vol. 10A, 7380.

50. Richard Stone, *The Interstate Commerce Commission and the Railroad Industry: A History of Regulatory Policy* (New York: Praeger, 1991), 13–14, 31–32. See also George E. Mowry, *The Era of Theodore Roosevelt, 1900–1912* (New York: Harper, 1958), 260; Albro Martin, *Enterprise Denied: Origins of the Decline of the American Railroads, 1897–1917* (New York: Columbia University Press, 1971), 362–364.

51. U.S. Congress, House of Representatives, Committee on Interstate and Foreign Commerce, Subcommittee on Transportation and Commerce, Staff Report, *Materials Concerning the Effects of Government Regulation on Railroads and an Economic Profile of Railroads in the United States* (Washington, D.C.: GPO, 1975), 1.

52. ICC, *Annual Report, 1971*, 17.

53. Ibid.

54. Ex Parte No. 262, *Increased Freight Rates, 1969; Increased Freight Rates, 1970* 339 ICC 125; *Increased Freight Rates 1970 and 1971* 339 ICC 125; *Increased Freight Rates and Charges, 1972* 340 ICC 358; *Increased Freight Rates 341 ICC 288*; Ex Parte No. 303 *Increased Freight Rates-Nationwide*; Ex Parte 305, *Nationwide Increase of 10% in Freight Rates and Charges, 1974*; Ex Parte No. 313, *Increased Freight Rates and Charges-Labor Costs, 1975*; Ex Parte No. 318, *Increased Freight Rates and Charges, 1976*.

55. ICC, *Annual Report, 1971*, 18.

56. Ibid, 17.

57. ICC, *Annual Report, 1974*, 33; *Net Investment - Railroad Rate Base* 344 ICC 55.

58. *Inspection in Transit, Grain and Grain Products* 339 ICC 364; *Wheat and Wheat Flour, Westbound* 337 ICC 858.

59. *Provisions on Vegetables and Melons, Transcontinental* 340 ICC 807; *Citrus Arizona and California to Eastern States* 341 ICC 622.

60. *Protective Service Charges-1972* 341 ICC 573.

61. ICC, *Annual Report, 1975, 23*.

62. Ibid.

63. Ex Parte No. 313 *Increased Freight Rates and Charges-Labor Costs-1975*; Ex Parte No. 318 *Increased Freight Rates and Charges-1976*; Ex Parte No. 343 *Nationwide Increase in Freight Rates and Charges-1977*; *Increased Freight Rates and Charges- Nationwide* 359 ICC 740; Ex Parte No. 374 *Increased Freight Rates and Charges-Western Railroads-2 percent-1980*; Ex Parte No. 375 *Increased Freight Rates and Charges-Nationwide-1980*.

64. *Investigation of Railroad Freight Rate Structure-Coal* 345 ICC 493; *Investigation of Railroad Freight Rate Structure-Paper and Paper Products* 345 ICC 2092; Ex Parte No. 319 *Investigation for the Transportation of Recyclable or Recycled Commodities* 3 ICC 2d 65.

65. *Investigation of Railroad Freight Rate Structure-Iron Ores* 345 ICC 548; *Investigation of Railroad Freight Rate Structure- Scrap Iron and Steel* 345 ICC 867.

66. ICC, *Annual Report, 1979*, 39; *Rail General Exemption Authority- Fresh Fruits and Vegetables*, March 21, 1979.

4

The Federal Initiative:
Tale of Consolidation

Between 1970 and 1980, Congress passed four major pieces of legislation in a continuing attempt to forestall further decline of the railroad industry. These new laws initiated a large-scale consolidation of passenger and freight operations. The National Rail Passenger Service Act of 1970 relieved railroads of an enormous financial burden by consolidating responsibility for nationwide rail passenger service under a federally operated system. The Regional Rail Reorganization Act of 1973 rescued the railroad freight industry in the Northeast from imminent liquidation by combining ailing systems under federal operation. The Railroad Revitalization and Regulatory Reform Act of 1976 reconciled newly unified federal passenger and freight operations to the market through subsidization and regulatory adjustments. The Staggers Rail Act of 1980 transferred the benefits of consolidation and regulatory relaxation to the private sector.

PASSENGER CONSOLIDATION—AMTRAK

The National Rail Passenger Service Act of 1970 rescued the nation's railroads from the burden of passenger service. The new law created a pseudo-public firm, the National Rail Passenger Corporation (Amtrak), to take responsibility for passenger rail transportation routes where private carriers sought to abandon service. The new corporation, under federal direction, was intended to rejuvenate travel by rail, attract investors, and become profitable after being provided with new equipment and initial funding.[1]

Starting in the late 1920s, rail passenger service in the United States began a general decline. At that time, the motor vehicle and airline industries were just gaining a foothold in the passenger transportation market. The market share for these two industries rose markedly in subsequent decades at the expense of rail passenger service, and that trend would not reverse itself.

In 1929, approximately 20,000 passenger trains served citizens in all parts of the country. By 1946 more than 9,000 of those trains had vanished. In 1970, there were fewer than 500 passenger trains left, and more than one-fifth of those were in the process of being discontinued. In addition, most of the remaining systems operated under the burden of growing deficits. The Secretary of Transportation reported that the rail passenger deficit for 1969 was approximately $200 million. Considering that total rail net income for that year was only $500 million, the rail passenger deficit was a serious concern. Observers expected most passenger trains to be eliminated at some point in the future.[2]

Despite the discouraging prospects for rail passenger service, regulators believed that some form of intercity rail passenger transportation was worth saving. Noisy airports and congested highways suggested that some travelers might turn to rail transportation. Railroads were capable of providing great numbers of people with urban and interstate mobility. In terms of fuel use and environmental impact, moreover, rail transportation had an advantage over both the automobile and airline industries.

The newly established National Rail Passenger Service Corporation was expected to preserve the inherent advantages of passenger rail service. The system was to receive direct federal financing of not more than $40 million, and the Secretary of Transportation was to guarantee more than $100 million but less than $200 million in loans to finance the upgrading of roadbeds and the purchase of rolling stock.[3] Contracts were then offered to railroads through 1974.

Once under contract with a given railroad, Amtrak provided rail passenger service between major points on that line. In return, the carrier paid Amtrak in one of three ways. It could pay 50 percent of its passenger deficit as recorded for the 1969 calender year; it could pay 100 percent of the avoidable loss of all rail passenger service based on figures for 1969; or it could pay 200 percent of the avoidable loss of intercity rail transportation over routes between basic points based on the 1969 system. These sums would be paid to Amtrak in cash, equipment, or future service. In return, the carrier received (unless otherwise waiving this right) common stock in Amtrak. Those railroads that chose not to contract with Amtrak were required to continue basic passenger service until July 1, 1974. Thereafter, service could be discontinued if Amtrak rejected an opportunity to consider continued service at the request and financing of state, regional, or local agencies.

Amtrak began service with heavy subsidies. It started operations on May 1, 1971, with $40 million in federal grants and $197 million from railroads contracting with the new passenger system. From that time to 1975, federal subsidies amounted to $5.3 billion, and Amtrak obtained another $860 million in federal loan guarantees.[4]

The result of such support was improved passenger service. In 1974, Amtrak transported 18.5 million passengers, a 10 percent increase over the previous year and one of the best records since the 1950s. It operated 240 trains daily over 24,315 miles of route. Amtrak appeared to be prospering, and such crises as the oil embargo of 1974–75, which threatened other forms of transportation, only enhanced that prosperity. With federal dollars annually pouring into the system, Amtrak was expected to maintain a high level of passenger service in subsequent years.[5]

Despite huge traffic gains, the passenger rail system required annual infusions of capital through the next two decades, a circumstance that caused some legislators to rethink the prospect of a profitable passenger system.[6] The first infusion came in 1975 when Congress passed the Amtrak Improvement Act appropriating $1.1 billion to the National Rail Passenger Corporation through 1977.[7] That funding was designed to meet inflation costs generated by the recession of 1974-75, offset wage increases for labor, and help Amtrak accommodate seven newly acquired routes.

With the subsidies it received, Amtrak embarked on a program to modernize its rolling stock. It purchased a fleet of F-40 diesel locomotives and retired a number of old units. It also acquired new passenger coaches and two-level cars. Despite such improvements, more than 20 percent of Amtrak's fleet was between 30 and 40 years old.[8]

In 1979, Amtrak required another infusion of funds. The Amtrak Reorganization Act of 1979 helped the National Rail Passenger System to replace aging equipment, rehabilitate deteriorating right-of-way, overhaul the scheduling system, and establish cost control procedures.[9] The legislation authorized three separate capital infusions between 1980 and 1982 aggregating $1.7 billion.

Following the massive funding at the beginning of the 1980s, annual assistance from the federal government fell off rapidly, and between 1985 and 1989 it averaged less than $32 million.[10] During the second term of President Ronald Reagan and the first part of the Bush administration, federal support for Amtrak waned. The government's passenger railroad project became the object of spending cuts; Amtrak was left largely to its own devices.

As a result, the passenger system wore out much of its rolling stock. The National Railroad Passenger Corporation simply did not have the capital to replace aging equipment, a factor that threatened the system's long-term viability. By the early 1990s, Amtrak reported that it needed 420 new passenger cars and over 250 new locomotives.[11]

During the second half of the Bush administration, Congress again took action to aid Amtrak when it enacted the Amtrak Reauthorization and Improvement Act of 1990. The legislation drew up a four-year funding package appropriating $2.7 billion for the years 1989 through 1992.[12] Once again, the system's future seemed secure.

By 1992, however, Amtrak was again in trouble, so Congress passed the Amtrak Authorization and Development Act. This legislation authorized total appropriations of $1.1 billion in each of fiscal years 1993 and 1994.[13] It appeared that Congress would continue to support the National Rail Passenger Corporation. At least, Amtrak's short history supported such a projection.

Despite repeated requests for financial assistance, Congress continued to see benefits in the service that Amtrak provided. Two improvements often cited by supporters of the passenger system were higher employment and higher revenue levels. When operations commenced in 1971, the National Rail Passenger Corporation employed 1,522 workers and generated $163 million in revenues. By 1992, the system employed 23,000 people, generated $1.4 billion in annual revenues, and operated over 24,000 miles of line.[14] Moreover, the carrier was transporting more than 40 million passengers per year. In addition, despite facing a $67 million shortfall in 1992, the National Rail Passenger Corporation planned to eliminate federal subsidization by the year 2000. It claimed, however, that it could not achieve financial independence without federal funds for equipment modernization and plant improvements in the immediate future.

Despite its heavy investment over the years, Congress foresaw increased passenger operations in the future. According to a report issued by the Office of Technological Assessment, the population of the United States was expected to increase by 30 million by the year 2010, and highway traffic was projected to double.[15]

In turn, such increases were predicted to generate greater petroleum consumption and carbon monoxide pollution. By the 1990s, transportation accounted for 67 percent of all oil consumption in the United States, and 70 percent of that was used by highway transportation. Since diesel locomotives could transport passengers with considerably less fuel consumption than other modes, the train was an important transportation alternative for the future.

In addition to fuel savings, railroad service was relatively cheaper to maintain than air service, especially for short distance travel such as between Boston and New York City. An investment of $51 million dollars in rail service improvements between those cities was expected to attract some three million passengers to three-hour express service. Airport costs to handle growing traffic over the same route was projected to be upwards of $1 billion. Cost advantages of this sort ensured congressional support for the rail passenger service industry.[16]

The Rail Passenger Service Act of 1970 drastically altered one aspect of rail transportation. Passenger service had long been an unprofitable venture for rail carriers, and by the 1960s they were seeking to discontinue such service on a massive scale. Most rail executives believed passenger service could never be profitable, so the federal government assumed responsibility for what it perceived to be an important transportation resource. Over the next two decades, the attitude of Congress changed little. Federal legislators, however, came to realize what railroads had learned years earlier—passenger service had no short-term prospect of generating enough revenue to cover costs of service. The market had identified passenger operations as an enormous category of "dead wood," and the railroads were belatedly allowed to discontinue service. By the 1990s, the federal government still had not accepted the fact that without miraculous innovation, passenger service would remain an unprofitable venture.

FREIGHT CONSOLIDATION—CONRAIL

While the Rail Passenger Service Act of 1970 changed the nature of passenger service, the Regional Rail Reorganization Act of 1973 transformed freight service in the northeastern United States. The purpose of the legislation was to rescue the operations of seven insolvent Class I systems in that district. This was to be accomplished through the establishment of a United States Railway Association, created to plan and finance a new northeastern system, Consolidated Rail Corporation (Conrail). The new corporation would assume control of the insolvent rail systems, modernize and rehabilitate their operations, and ensure crucial freight service to that portion of the nation.[17]

The need for such drastic measures in the Northeast stemmed from a precipitous decline in the financial condition of the carriers in the preceding decades. A variety of factors contributed to the decline, including inadequate public policies, increased competition from other modes, and managerial failures to meet changing economic conditions.[18] Attempts to counter the general decline, such as the merger of the Pennsylvania Railroad and the New York Central into the Penn Central Transportation Company in 1968, provided little relief to the region and actually accentuated financial difficulties. In 1970, the largest carrier in the Northeast, the Penn Central, collapsed, thereby devastating the entire freight industry. By 1973, eight railroads were still in reorganization proceedings under Section 77 of the Bankruptcy Act, and many others were in a dubious financial condition.[19]

Shortly after the collapse of the Penn Central, the United States Senate Committee on Commerce began an investigation into the causes of the disaster, and in December 1972, it published its findings. The Committee reported that Penn Central suffered from a variety of problems, some of which were shared by railroads nationwide. Overall, the Committee found that railroads were losing market share, even with those products that were traditionally moved by rail. These included agricultural, mining, and nondurable goods. Additionally, with industrial growth, factories were increasingly being built closer to consumer markets, thus reducing the need for transportation services. Railroads in the late 1940s and early 1950s, moreover, lost much of their less-than-carload (LCL) service. This loss contributed to the decline in the railroads' share of total intercity freight traffic from 44 percent in 1960 to 41 percent in 1969 and their share of freight revenues from 28 percent in 1960 to 22 percent in 1969.[20]

These declines reflected to some extent the changes in the economies of the Northeast and Midwest. Those regions contained 65 percent of American manufacturing in 1950, but only 54 percent in 1969. Similarly, in 1957, the regions produced 71 percent of the nation's coal, but only 62 percent in 1970. One factor that contributed to the decline in coal transport was that by 1970 three times the amount of coal mined in 1957 was being used to generate power at or near the mine, thus requiring little or no rail transportation.[21]

Adding to the decline in the shipment of certain products by rail was the carriers' lack of capital. Heavy debt burdens and meager earnings resulted in deferred maintenance and increased dependence on leased equipment, both of which produced higher operating costs, operational delays, and accidents. Deferred maintenance costs in 1972 alone amounted to $25 million.

Another factor accentuating the financial problems in the Northeast was management. Corporate leadership of Penn Central Transportation was a prime example. When the system began experiencing serious financial difficulties, management hid losses through a policy known as "earnings maximization," a deceptive term which meant that earnings were inflated and losses were deemphasized.

The practice was designed to deceive stockholders. For example, in 1968 after the Pennsylvania and the New York Central merged operations, the new company suffered a $2.8 million operating loss but paid dividends amounting to $5.5 million. The next year the company lost $82.8 million, but stockholders received dividends totalling $43.4 million.[22] The intention of this practice was to prevent the sale of company stock by investors who would have dumped their shares had they been fully informed as to the company's prospects. Meanwhile, real estate ventures like Penn Central's Great Southwest Corporation were used to distort earnings by emphasizing the paper profits generated by such investments.

The Senate Committee on Commerce realized financial declines among northeastern carriers were a serious concern to the nation. The elimination of Penn Central services alone was expected to generate a 5.2 percent decline in economic activity in the Northeast and produce a 2.7 percent decline in the GNP after the eighth week of suspended operations. Even more ominous were the projected effects on local economies. The Indiana Department of Commerce estimated that the closing down of Penn Central would generate 24 percent unemployment in the state within the first month.[23] The geographic zone served by the northeastern bankrupt companies, moreover, represented the nation's center for the auto, steel, and machine industries. A cataclysmic loss in transportation in the Northeast had the potential to paralyze these industries.

By 1973, Penn Central's financial situation was precarious. Continued operations under reorganization status depended on "its ability to generate sufficient positive cash flow to sustain working capital needs, cover maturing equipment obligations, and pay for essential maintenance and capital expenses."[24] The company was unable to sustain such a cash flow, and it continued to deteriorate. Congress, therefore, passed the Regional Rail Reorganization Act (3R Act) of 1973 to remedy the problem.

The 3R Act was divided into six titles detailing federal remedial action for the mounting railroad crisis. The first title explained the seven goals of the new legislation, the most important of which was to identify a rail service system in the Northeast that could adequately meet the needs of the region and those of the national rail system.[25] The legislation also established a Federal Railway Administration to help govern rail operations and a Consolidated Rail Corporation (Conrail) to assume control of the restructured regional system. Finally, funding provisions were included to enable states and local authorities to finance continued service to specified areas, to provide individual systems with loan guarantees for rail equipment acquisition and utility improvements, and generally to assist the railroads at the lowest feasible cost to the public.

The newly established United States Railway Association (USRA) was the agency responsible for detailing the Northeast's restructuring.[26] This body had to identify those specific rail lines which would compose Conrail. It also received the power to make loans to Amtrak, Conrail, or other railroads in need and was responsible for the financial assistance allocated to states and local authorities. Another responsibility of the USRA was the preparation of various ongoing operational and financial studies of rail service in the region.

Conrail, the pseudo-public corporation created under the auspices of the United States Railway Association, was the tool through which northeastern rail restructuring was implemented. Authorized to engage solely in activities related to transportation, Conrail assumed control of those systems operating under the reorganization status established by Section 77 of the Bankruptcy Act. The specific properties to be acquired were outlined in the final system plan created by the USRA bureaucrats. Conrail was then expected to rehabilitate and modernize those properties in order to maintain adequate and efficient rail service in the region. The new system would conduct operations, thereafter, in much the same fashion as any Class I rail carrier.

One way in which the system was different, however, was that for two years after the implementation of the final system plan, the new railroad had the power to purchase and abandon lines without approval.[27]   Nevertheless, in certain circumstances the intent to preserve transportation was not lost.   In certain circumstances, the Secretary of Transportation was authorized to subsidize service by Conrail or other carriers over specified lines in order to preserve local rail service. Considering the energy crisis facing the nation in the early 1970s, Congress believed that such a provision was important to preserve "one of the most energy-efficient modes of transportation for the movement of passengers and freight and [one that] caused the least amount of pollution."[28]

Congress also included provisions in the 3R Act to protect adversely affected employees.   As a general rule, employees of railroads in reorganization that were transferred to Conrail negotiated new collective bargaining agreements for each class and craft of employees governing pay rates, rules, and working conditions.   The employees who lost compensation or were displaced were entitled to monthly allowances. Such allowances were limited to $2,500 per month and continued until the age of 65. The aggregate of the allowances and other expenses provided to employment protection was not to exceed $250 million, the amount the U.S. Treasury deposited in the Regional Rail Transportation Protective Account. Like other labor arrangements in the past, the protection provided by the 3R Act was costly.

In the end, the Regional Rail Reorganization Act of 1973 preserved the integrity of the nation's freight service in the northeastern United States.   The inability of bankrupt lines, like the great Penn Central, to stave off impending liquidation indicated a need for federal intervention. Without it, numerous industries dependent on rail service would have been devastated, and the nation as a whole would have suffered.

Ironically, salvation came to the Northeast via corporate combinations.   Conrail represented a government-sponsored consolidation of northeastern railroads.   Under the auspices of the United States Railway Association, financially weak railroads were combined and operations coordinated to create a gigantic railway system. The fact that Conrail still existed as one of the largest private Class I carriers in the nation by the mid-1990s was indicative of the benefits of combination and the value of the subsidization that made such rationalization possible.

RATIONALIZING THE INITIATIVES

In 1976, the federal government again sought to remedy railroad ills with the Railroad Revitalization and Regulatory Reform Act of 1976 (4R Act). In this case, however, revitalization and reform measures would be applicable to carriers nationwide. As indicated by its title, the legislation was designed to "provide the means to rehabilitate and maintain the physical facilities, improve the operations and structures, and restore the financial stability of the railway system of the United States, and to promote the revitalization of such railway system, so that this mode of transportation will remain viable in the private sector of the economy and will be able to provide energy-efficient, ecologically compatible transportation services with greater efficiency, effectiveness and economy."[29]

The 4R Act was the culmination of regulation and financing changes that began with the Rail Passenger Service Act and the Regional Rail Reorganization Act. Also, it was the prelude to the Staggers Act of 1980.

As in 1973, regulators in 1976 continued to argue the need for government intervention in the railroad industry. Adjusted for inflation, railroad earnings in the mid-1970s were 75 percent of their 1947 level, and revenue miles for passenger traffic had declined 80 percent since World War II.[30] Many federal regulators and legislators in Congress believed that federal regulation of the industry needed to be overhauled drastically.

Legislation that promoted the development of various modes of transportation was one area where revamping was needed. During the twentieth century, the railroad and pipeline industries represented the only two forms of transportation not substantially subsidized. Between 1946 and 1975, railroads obtained only 1 percent of direct federal aid to transportation, while their chief competitor, truck transportation, received 69 percent.[31] The automobile, barge, and airline industries consumed the remainder of public assistance.

This large-scale federal financial support was designed to develop transportation technologies that boosted traffic. Subsidization of highway systems along with advances in the motor-carrier industry, for example, permitted trucking companies to capture 23 percent of total intercity freight ton-miles. According to the United States Railway Association, the federal government during the 1970s allocated $20 million per year for highways, about $500 million per year for the airline industry, $1 billion for mass transit, $16 million through 1971 for inland waterways, and another $500 million for the maritime industry.[32]

Meanwhile, federal aid to rail carriers was minimal. Railroads had to construct, repair, and pay taxes on their own rights-of-way. The fact that the federal government paid for the rights-of-way of other modes put railroads at a competitive disadvantage. Nevertheless, complaints by rail executives were all but ignored by the Commission.

By the 1970s, however, collapsing railroads in the Northeast and the general deterioration of rail transportation elsewhere awakened regulators to the needs of this neglected mode. Federal financial assistance bailed out bankrupt carriers and prevented further industry decline. Between July 1, 1969, and June 30, 1975, $1.5 billion in aid went to the industry. But estimates indicated that such funding had to continue to ensure the future of railroading.[33]

In 1976, the federal government was ready to fund the rejuvenation of the industry. This time, however, lawmakers sought assurances that financing would not be wasted. They did not want to subsidize an industry that would continue to require periodic capital infusions. Instead, they hoped that federal assistance would pump prime the industry into financial independence. To accomplish this, Congress proposed a package that combined subsidization with regulatory modification. The result was the Railroad Revitalization and Regulatory Reform Act of 1976 which addressed the issues of railroad rates, mergers and consolidations, rehabilitative financing, high-speed intercity passenger service, and local rail service.

Title II of the 4R Act amended Part I of the Interstate Commerce Act to revamp ICC railroad rate regulation. Essentially, provisions in the 4R Act created new criteria for determining whether a given railroad rate was "just and reasonable." According to the new standards, a railroad rate could not be deemed unreasonably high if it contributed to a carrier's attainment of revenue levels that met or exceeded variable costs and if the ICC found no indication of market dominance.

Moreover, without a finding of market dominance, the ICC was not allowed to suspend any proposed rate for two years. If a proposed rate did not represent more than a 7 percent increase or decrease over the existing rate and was not destructive or unfair, it could be approved. These stipulations were expected to promote more competitive pricing.

Amendments to Title II required the ICC to establish standards for the implementation of railroad rates based on seasonal, regional, or peak-period demand; resolve disputes between carriers involved in joint rates more rapidly; and use the "public interest" test before canceling a joint rate. [34] The amendments also ordered the Commission to establish parameters for determining adequate revenue levels of railroads, draw up rules covering demurrage charges, and modify standards governing freight car leases.

In addition to the modification of rate regulations, the new legislation altered rules governing mergers and consolidations. During the previous fifteen years, railroad merger proceedings suffered from a number of problems that legislators wanted to remedy. First, the ICC generally conducted unification proceedings without considering fully the effects of a merger on the national system. This practice tended to incite subsequent mergers by carriers seeking to adjust to changes wrought by previous combinations. Railroad mergers also suffered excruciating delays in processing. Between 1955 and 1970 fifty-nine merger applications came before the Commission. Twenty-two took a year to process; twelve took more than two years; eight took more than three years; six took more than four years; four took more than five years; three took more than six years; two took more than seven years; and one took more than eight years.[35] Moreover, the last one resulted in a rejection of the merger, and the carrier involved, the Rock Island, went into bankruptcy.

Title III contained provisions "designed to expedite and rationalize Commission action on applications for mergers and consolidation of rail services." First, the legislation sought to eliminate ICC delays in processing merger applications. To accomplish this objective, the legislation established time deadlines for each stage of the processing. Second, the legislators expedited merger procedures by limiting the initial review of merger proposals to the secretary of the ICC rather than allowing analysis by the entire ICC board.

Finally, the law reasserted the ICC's commitment to the "public interest" standard established by the Transportation Act of 1940. When deciding whether or not to approve a combination, the Commission had to assume that the general consolidation of the industry was in the public interest. In addition, requests by third parties for inclusion in proposed unifications were not to be factors in measuring public interest but were to be treated as separate issues.

While the 4R Act modified rate and merger regulations, it also provided for the financial rehabilitation of targeted systems. Under Title V of the legislation, the Secretary of Transportation administered financial aid to needy systems, drawing from the Treasury Department's $600 million Railroad Rehabilitation and Improvement

Fund. Those railroads seeking funding were to submit to the Secretary of Transportation an application outlining proposed improvements and rehabilitation projects along with a five-year operating history. If an application was in the public interest, the Secretary would offer to purchase nonvoting shares of the company's stock. Further assistance from the Secretary of Transportation might be available in the form of loan guarantees. The Secretary had the power to approve amounts up to $1 billion.

In addition to the arrangement with the Secretary of Transportation, another form of financing was established under the United States Railway Association. The USRA was authorized to purchase up to $2.1 billion of Conrail securities. Moreover, the USRA could issue up to $230 million in loans to Conrail for the purchase of materials and supplies to aid in Conrail's acquisition of bankrupt and other targeted carriers. The idea behind the financing of Conrail was to ensure orderly development in the Northeast with as little disruption of service as possible.

Adding to the support of rail transportation in the Northeast, the 4R Act provided for the establishment of a $1.75 billion Northeast Corridor Project.[36] The project called for the establishment of high-speed intercity rail passenger service along the densely populated eastern seaboard in the states of Massachusetts, Rhode Island, Connecticut, New York, New Jersey, Pennsylvania, Delaware, and Maryland and the District of Columbia. One goal of the venture was to establish within five years a dependable intercity rail passenger service operating on a 3-hour-and-40-minute schedule between Boston and New York City and a 2-hour-and-40-minute schedule between New York City and Washington, D.C. Improvements were also to be made on routes from Harrisburg, Pennsylvania; Albany, New York; and Springfield, Massachusetts, to Boston, Massachusetts, and New Haven, Connecticut.[37]

In addition to helping finance passenger service in the Northeast, the 4R Act authorized the federal government to allocate up to $360 million to states that desired to preserve local rail service. These provisions provided states with a means to cope with abandonments that railroads wanted and which the ICC sanctioned. The provision represented essentially an extension of the $180 million authorized for such purposes under the 3R Act of 1973.

After February 1976, the federal government continued the deregulatory trend fostered by the 4R Act. In August of that year, the Commission adopted market dominance guidelines for accepting or rejecting rates which shippers complained were unreasonably high. Shippers could only object on the grounds of "market dominance" to block increases if three conditions were present: the carrier hauled 70 percent or more of the involved traffic the previous year; the proposed rate exceeded variable costs by 60 percent; and the protesting shipper had no alternative mode of transportation. This stipulation limited the ability of shippers to interfere with rail rate-making.[38]

The reduction of regulation continued at the end of the decade. In November 1978, the Commission permitted carriers to establish rate contracts with shippers without ICC involvement.[39] Contract disputes were in the jurisdiction of the courts. Shortly thereafter, the Commission virtually ended its regulation of fresh fruits and vegetables shipped by rail. In December, officials eased merger stipulations that required the Commission to do its utmost to freeze traffic patterns and thereby preserve the financial integrity of carriers that would have to compete with the merged system. The following year, restrictions governing the abandonment of lines were modified to make it easier for a carrier to dispose of unprofitable routes. Finally, regulators proposed reducing the Commission's role in the control of rail car service and sought to reduce regulatory delays by placing even stricter limits on proceedings related to railroad transactions.

By the end of the 1970s, the regulatory structure governing the railroad industry was far different from that of a decade earlier. Moreover, the industry itself had changed considerably. Instead of being on the brink of collapse, the industry was proceeding with recovery and rehabilitation. The Rail Passenger Service Act consolidated passenger operations and sustained them through subsidies. The Regional Rail Reorganization Act of 1973 used federal funds to rescue bankrupt railroads in the Northeast from corporate liquidation and to consolidate ailing systems under a new potentially profitable corporation, Consolidated Rail. The Railroad Revitalization and Regulatory Reform Act of 1976 attempted to rationalize federal consolidation actions by combining further financial assistance with regulatory restructuring.

Considering the changes generated by the 4R Act, it became necessary for Congress to rewrite legislation only four years later. Officials in Washington were becoming increasingly aware that the railroad industry could be revitalized if the regulatory structure permitted carriers to exploit rationalization strategies in the way Amtrak and Conrail had been permitted to do from their inception.

REACHING THE PRIVATE SECTOR

In 1978, the Department of Transportation, complying with Sections 504 and 901 of the 4R Act, submitted a report to Congress assessing the capital needs of the railroad industry. In that report, entitled "A Prospectus for Change in the Freight Railroad Industry," the DOT predicted that between 1976 and 1985 the railroad industry would have a capital shortfall of between $13.1 and $16.1 billion.[40] The agency pointed out that railroad earnings were insufficient to cover existing and future capital needs, and there were no indications of a reversal under the existing regulatory structure.

By 1980, the House Interstate and Foreign Commerce Committee noted that unless the industry could overcome this ominous shortfall, rail operations would continue to deteriorate. The consequences of inadequate revenue for railroads was clear, as exemplified by the collapse of the industry in the Northeast. Despite the changes made by the Rail Passenger Service Act, the 3R Act, and the 4R Act, financial difficulties prevailed.

In 1980, financially weak carriers handled almost 30 percent of rail business. At the same time, rail traffic continued to decrease. For example, the transportation of grain, once dominated by the railroads, was moving to other modes. Fifty-eight percent of U.S. grain was transported by rail in 1973. By 1977, that number had fallen to 43 percent. Rail shipment of fresh fruits and vegetables declined from 31 percent in 1970 to 11 percent in 1977.[41] After the 1960s, the rail industry also experienced declines in the shipment of textiles, leather products, paints, drugs, chemicals, fabricated metal products, and meat and dairy goods. The House Interstate and Foreign Commerce Committee ascertained that the decline in business and inability of railroads to earn adequate revenue stemmed from inflexibility in the federal regulatory system.

It seemed clear that, in comparison with other modes, rail transportation was overregulated. While 100 percent of railroad business (measured in intercity ton miles) was regulated, only 40 percent of truck intercity ton miles and 10 percent of barge intercity ton miles were so controlled. Moreover, those federal agencies that had a voice in the regulatory process were so numerous as to create difficulties in reconciling their different agendas.

As of 1980, twelve different federal bodies were making decisions that directly affected rail operations. They included the Council on Wage and Price Stability, the Environmental Protection Agency, and the Securities and Exchange Commission. Among those strictly involved in transportation were the Federal Railroad Administration, Railroad Retirement Board, National Transport Safety Board, and the Interstate Commerce Commission. Other regulators of finance and employment of railroads were the Internal Revenue Service, Federal Trade Commission, Equal Employment Opportunity Commission, National Bureau of Standards, and the Department of Labor.[42]

According to the House Interstate and Foreign Commerce Committee, even the 4R Act of 1976 failed to provide adequate rate flexibility for the industry. Before 1976, any attempt by carriers to raise rates generated protests of "unreasonableness" from shippers. Railroads had to battle constantly with the ICC for rate hikes. With the 4R Act, however, Congress hoped to remove most railroad traffic from regulation by instituting the "market dominance tests." Unfortunately, the new legislation only liberated about 30 percent of rail traffic from rate regulation. Laws governing rail operations were still too restrictive.

Railroads continued to be viewed as monopolistic institutions by the Commission and were regulated accordingly. By using case-by-case analysis of railroads' requests for financial or operational change, the ICC quashed any substantial freedom that the 4R Act might have afforded. The "market dominance" test for railroads seeking rate or operational changes was usually interpreted in such a way as to justify rejection of the railroads' requests. The ICC argued that railroads held "market dominance" over shippers in nearly every market in which railroads sought changes.

In the three years between the enactment of the 4R Act and 1980, ICC officials and other federal administrators began to redefine their views on regulation. Many within President Jimmy Carter's administration began to see the 4R Act as a stumbling block to efficient market operations, and they wanted remedial action. The administration had already been seeking deregulatory measures in the airline and motor carrier industries, so there appeared to be no reason why the railroad industry should not be deregulated as well. As early as 1977, President Carter's newly created National Commission for the Review of Antitrust Laws & Procedures promoted an easing of transportation regulation. Secretary of Transportation Brock Adams saw deregulation of both the railroad and motor-carrier industries as the most plausible way to solve the nation's transportation problems.

The Staggers Rail Act, signed into law by President Carter on October 14, 1980, gave railroads greater latitude in managing their own affairs. The law was designed "to provide for the restoration, maintenance, and improvement of the physical facilities and financial stability of the rail system of the United States."[43] To accomplish this goal, the Staggers Act was carefully constructed. It was designed "(1) to assist the railroads of the nation in rehabilitating the rail system in order to meet the demands of interstate commerce and the national defense; (2) to reform federal regulatory policy so as to preserve a safe, adequate, economical, efficient, and financially stable rail system; (3) to assert the rail system to remain viable in the private sector of the economy; (4) to provide a regulatory process that balances the needs of carriers, shippers and the public; and (5) to assist in the rehabilitation and financing of the rail system."[44]

The new law consisted of seven titles addressing a variety of issues. Seven provisions within these titles were of particular importance. They addressed rate setting, rate contracts, collective rate-making, revenue adequacy, joint rates and surcharges, and abandonments and mergers. The most important of these concerned regulations governing rates. First, the Staggers Act eliminated general rate increases; the last one came December 12, 1980. Thereafter, increases designed to offset inflation were accomplished through the use of a cost recovery index. This index included provisions to measure the degree to which inflation affected a given geographical or commodity market.

Additionally, the new legislation revised the use of maximum rate levels. According to Staggers, maximum rate levels would be established only in those markets where the shipper proved that it did not have an alternative transportation mode and where the railroad in question charged rates above a fixed level.[45] That level was established at 160 percent of the variable cost of providing the rail service. To allow for alterations in the market and inflation, Staggers increased that threshold by 5 percent a year until 1984. Meanwhile, during those four years, rates in various markets would be permitted to fluctuate within a zone of flexibility that would allow railroads to raise rates up to 6 percent a year (to a total of 18 percent) above the cost recovery index. After 1984, compensation for market changes and inflation would be included in a cost recovery percentage that ranged from between 170 percent and 180 percent of variable costs of providing the service. Moreover, annual increases would be restricted to 4 percent and permitted only among carriers not attaining "revenue adequacy" levels.[46]

Unfortunately, the new stipulations brought the ICC's desire to protect "captive" shippers into conflict with its intent to allow differential pricing. In the early years following the enactment of Staggers, these conflicts were usually settled in favor of shippers. Sixty-five of the first eighty-two market dominance cases brought before the Commission were resolved to the satisfaction of the shippers.

Over the years, the maximum percentage of rail freight rates and the formula for determining the rail cost adjustment factor (RCAF, variable for determining the zone of rate flexibility) changed. By 1989, productivity gains and interest expenses were included in determining rail cost adjustment factors. Unfortunately, the inclusion of productivity gains lowered the index and thereby reduced the level of maximum allowable rates for railroads.[47] As a result, RCAFs became useless as a tool to aid railroad ratemaking. By 1990, several Class I railroads disassociated themselves from RCAFs. The Commission made no objection.

Subsequently, rate increases were simply subject to Commission discretion following shipper protests. The RCAF had already become defunct in light of a 1986 Commission ruling that required railroads to roll back rate increases based on RCAF when costs declined. Moreover, by that time railroads had become more dependent on rate contracts.

Staggers also addressed collective ratemaking. Traditionally, railroads sometimes joined together to set rates collectively over given routes. Rate bureaus (permitted by the Reed-Bulwinkle Act of 1948) established these rates and helped facilitate order and cooperation between railroads. The existence of rate bureaus proved to be no threat to competition as the Commission strictly regulated rates. With the regulation of rates being liberalized, however, Congress included provisions in Staggers to eliminate much of the power of rate bureaus. Specifically, Staggers prohibited collective ratemaking except among those lines engaged in a joint rate over a specific route.

Ultimately, collective ratemaking yielded to contract ratemaking. Staggers included provisions that allowed railroads to negotiate contracts with individual shippers involving freight movements by rail. The industry embraced rate contracts, and their use spread rapidly. Besides allowing railroads and shippers to be directly involved in determining rates, the ICC rid itself of a tremendous responsibility. The Commission left the burden of contract enforcement with the courts. The Commission, henceforth, merely approved or disapproved contract implementation after the two parties filed an application. If a contracted shipper or railroad reneged on an agreement, the concerned parties went to court.

Included among Staggers's provisions permitting rate adjustments were new rules governing joint rates. According to the legislation, railroads that were involved in joint rates and which failed to earn 110 percent of the variable costs of service were allowed to cancel those joint rates or, for three years, apply surcharges.[48] The variable cost threshold was determined by weighing capital, maintenance, and equipment replacement costs. This provision represented another attempt to help railroads meet the costs of operation and facilitate rationalization of the market.

While allowing rate adjustment, Staggers also permitted service adjustments by means of abandonments. Although the Commission did not alter standards for abandoning rail lines, it shortened the length of time for processing abandonment requests. Abandonment proposals that faced no objections from shippers or the public were to be sanctioned within 75 days of the application. In cases where protests did arise, the Commission was required to investigate and resolve the issue within 225 days. In some cases, the ICC could decide not to hear a case and simply exempt an abandonment from ICC proceedings. In such instances, the Commission automatically approved applications within 120 days.[49]

Although Staggers saddled the Commission with strict time constraints in its processing of abandonments, it did little to change merger policy. The traditional public interest test, as established by the Transportation Act of 1940 and reiterated in the 4R Act of 1976, was the standard on which the Commission based its decision to approve or disapprove unifications. Nevertheless, the 1980 Act included provisions requiring that the Commission analyze the effects of such unions on competitors.

Meanwhile, the Commission applied a different standard when analyzing combinations among smaller carriers. For smaller railroads (i.e., Class II or Class III), the public interest test yielded to competitive impact analyses as the basis of ICC decisions.[50] Under this policy, regulators promoted increased competition. Shortlines were less critical to the national transportation system, so the Commission worried less about protecting them from the debilitating effects of intercarrier rivalries.

The Staggers Rail Act of 1980 represented a major attempt by the federal government to remedy the operational and financial ills plaguing the railroad industry. The new legislation was the result of changing outlooks on the part of federal officials. By the mid-1970s, they recognized their inability to ensure the viability of every major railroad operating throughout the nation. The multiplicity of economic variables made that prospect unfeasible. The only alternative was to decentralize the regulatory structure.

The ICC and other federal bodies understood the importance of governing the industry. However, they also realized that if regulations were not shaped specifically to the complex interaction of financial forces, they would inhibit the efficiency of operation and growth. Outdated rules could not be applied to the complexities of modern transportation without generating waste.

FEDERAL ILLUMINATION

By the end of the 1970s, the federal government had become a student of railroading. Since the Transportation Act of 1920, officials in Washington had envisioned a highly consolidated railroad transportation network. With the Transportation Act of 1940 Congress had encouraged unifications as being in the public interest. Not until the 1970s, however, did legislators become aware of the logistics behind ensuring the benefits of railroad combinations.

Rail unifications prior to the 1970s taught regulators that combinations, in and of themselves, would not necessarily improve the financial state of struggling systems. In some cases, such combinations simply created larger struggling systems. Not until the federal government assumed the role of railroader following the Rail Passenger Service Act of 1970 and the Regional Rail Reorganization Act of 1973 were legislators able to identify the shortcomings of consolidation. When federal funds were on the line, government officials educated themselves on the intricacies of railroading. The lesson was reminiscent of those learned during World War I, when members of Congress became more aware of the capital needs of railroads.

After assuming the role of railroader, the federal government awakened to the fact that inadequate regulations were a primary factor in the inability of railroads to prosper or reap the full benefits that combinations afforded. Subsequently, adustments were made. First, the Railroad Revitalization and Regulatory Reform Act of 1976 began the process of overhauling railroad regulation using the experiences of running Amtrak as a basis for modification. The Staggers Rail Act of 1980 picked up where the 4R Act left off. The result was a loose regulatory structure which permitted railroads the flexibility to adjust operations to an amorphous market without losing the benefits of that flexibility to outdated policies.

NOTES

1. U.S. Congress, House, Committee on Interstate and Foreign Commerce, *Passenger Train Service: Report to Accompany H.R. 17849*, H. Rept. 91-1580, 91st Cong., 2nd sess., 1970, 1, 3; U.S. Congress, House, *Passenger Train Service*, Supplemental Hearings before the Subcommittee on Transportation and Aeronautics of the Committee on Interstate and Foreign Commerce, on H.R. 17849 and S. 3706, 91st Cong., 2d sess., 1970, 76.

2. *Rail Passenger Service Act of 1970, Legislative History*, U.S. Code, vol. 3, 4736–4737 (1970).

3. See Lloyd Musolf, *Uncle Sam's Private, Profitseeking Corporations* (Lexington, Mass.: Lexington Books, 1983), 51.

4. *Amtrak Improvement Act of 1975, Legislative History*, U.S. Code, vol. 1, 166 (1975).

5. Ibid., 167.

6. Musolf, *Uncle Sam's Private, Profitseeking Corporations*, 56; see comments of Senator Thomas Eagleton, U.S. Congress, Senate, *Department of Transportation and Related Agencies Appropriations for Fiscal Year 1977*, Hearings before a Subcommittee of the Committee of Appropriations on H.R. 14234, 94th Cong., 2d sess., 1976, 576; see comments of Representative B. F. Sisk, U.S. Congress, House, *Amtrak Discontinuance Criteria*, Hearings before the Subcommittee on Transportation and Commerce of the Committee on Interstate and Foreign Commerce, 94th Cong., 2d Sess., 1976, 112.

7. Amtrak Improvement Act of 1975. U.S. Code 89 STAT 92.

8. *Amtrak Authorization & Development Act, Legislative History*, U.S. Code, vol. 5, 3058 (1992).

9. *Amtrak Reorganization Act of 1979*, U.S. Code 93 STAT 538; U.S. Congress, House, *Amtrak Reorganization Act of 1979: Conference Report to Accompany H.R. 39961*, H. Rept. 96-481, 96th Cong., 1st sess., 1979, 34–35.

10. *Amtrak Authorization & Development Act, Legislative History*, 3058; U.S. Congress, Senate, Committee on Commerce, Science and Transportation, *Amtrak Improvement Act of 1981: Report to Accompany S. 1199*, S. Rept. 97-96, 97th Cong., 1st sess., 1981, 6.

11. *Amtrak Authorization & Development Act, Legislative History*, 3060.

12. *Amtrak Reauthorization and Improvement Act*, U.S. Code 104 STAT 295.

13. *Amtrak Authorization & Development Act*, U.S. Code 106 STAT 3517.

14. *Amtrak Authorization and Development Act, Legislative History*, 3060. For an economic analysis of Amtrak operations between 1970 and 1995 see Jean Love, Wendell Cox, and Stephen Moore, "Amtrak At Twenty-Five: End of the Line for Taxpayer Subsidies," *Policy Analysis*, December 19, 1996.

15. Ibid., 3062.

16. Ibid., 3063.

17. *Regional Rail Reorganization Act of 1973, Legislative History*, U.S. Code, vol. 1, 3242 (1973); Mulsolf, *Uncle Sam's Private, Profitseeking Corporations*, 72.

18. Paul W. MacAvoy and John Snow (eds.), *Railroad Revitalization and Regulatory Reform: Ford Administration Papers on Regulatory Reform* (Washington, D.C.: American Enterprise Institute for Public Policy Research, 1977), 15–24.

19. Richard Stone, *The Interstate Commerce Commission and the Railroad Industry* (New York: Praeger, 1991), 55; MacAvoy and Snow, *Railroad Revitalization and Regulatory Reform*, 25–26; Musolf, *Uncle Sam's Private, Profitseeking Corporations*, 71.

20. *Regional Rail Reorganization Act of 1973, Legislative History*, 3247.

21. Ibid., 3247–3248.

22. Ibid., 3248.

23. Ibid., 3248–3249.

24. Ibid., 3250.

25. *Regional Rail Reorganization Act of 1973*, U.S. Code 87 STAT 1103–1104.

26. *Regional Rail Reorganization Act of 1973, Legislative History*, 3261–3262; Musolf, *Uncle Sam's Private, Profitseeking Corporations*, 72.

27. U.S. Congress, House, *United States Railway Association Preliminary System Plan*, Hearings before the Subcommittee on Transportation and Commerce of the Committee on Interstate and Foreign Commerce, on Oversight on the Implementation of the Rail Reorganization Act of 1973 and a Review of the Preliminary System Plan of the USRA, 94th Cong., 1st sess., 1975, 380.

28. *Regional Rail Reorganization Act of 1973*, 1133.

29. *Railroad Revitalization and Regulatory Reform Act of 1976*, U.S. Code 90 STAT 33.

30. *Railroad Revitalization and Regulatory Reform Act of 1976, Legislative History*, U.S. Code, Vol. 2, 16.

31. *Staggers Rail Act of 1980, Legislative History*, U.S. Code, vol. 10, 7470.

32. *Railroad Revitalization and Regulatory Reform Act of 1976, Legislative History*, 16.

33. Ibid., 16–17.

34. Stone, *Interstate Commerce Commission and the Railroad Industry*, 76–77.

35. *Railroad Revitalization and Regulatory Reform Act of 1976, Legislative History*, 33.

36. *Railroad Revitalization and Regulatory Reform Act of 1976*, U.S. Code 90 STAT 120.

37. Ibid., 121.

38. Stone, *Interstate Commerce Commission and the Railroad Industry*, 86; ICC, *Annual Report, 1977*, 41; *Special Procedures for Making Findings of Market Dominance as Required by the Railroad Revitalization and Regulatory Reform Act of 1976* 353 ICC 874.

39. ICC, *Annual Report, 1979*, 6; *Railway Age* 179 (May 8, 1978), 10; *Railway Age* 179 (November 27, 1978), 12; *Railway Age*, 180 (February 26, 1979), 50.

40. *Staggers Rail Act of 1980, Legislative History*, 7439.

41. Ibid., 7455.

42. Ibid., 7472.

43. *Staggers Rail Act of 1980*, U.S. Code 94 STAT 1897.

44. Stone, *The Interstate Commerce Commission and the Railroad Industry*, 116–117; Martin T. Farris, "The Multiple Meanings and Goals of Deregulation: A Commentary," *Transportation Journal* 21 (Winter 1981), 45–49.

45. Stone, *The Interstate Commerce Commission and the Railroad Industry*, 120; See also *Market Dominance Determinations and Consideration of Product Competition* 365 ICC 118; *Rail Market Dominance* 365 ICC 116.

46. Stone, *Interstate Commerce Commission and the Railroad Industry*, 119.

47. *Traffic World* 217 (March 27, 1989), 35; *Traffic World* 217 (March 6, 1989), 20–21.

48. *Staggers Rail Act of 1980*, 94 STAT 1916; Stone, *Interstate Commerce Commission and the Railroad Industry*, 126.

49. Stone, Interstate Commerce Commission and the Railroad Industry, 126; *Staggers Rail Act of 1980*, 94 STAT 1941; *Railway Age* 181 (December 29, 1980), 4; ICC, *Annual Report, 1981*, 37–38.

50. Stone, *Interstate Commerce Commission and the Railroad Industry*, 131.

5

Private Sector Combinations:
Assessing Rationalization

While congressional initiatives such as the Rail Passenger Service Act and Regional Rail Reorganization Act promoted public consolidation of the railroad industry, the Interstate Commerce Commission continued to promote combinations in the private sector. On February 2, 1977, the ICC announced that its Rail Services Planning Office (RSPO) was initiating a study of rail mergers in order to "review the advantages and disadvantages of such arrangements, to identify the principal problems involved and to propose solutions to the problems identified."[1]

The study was designed to aid the Commission in its assessment of future merger applications. The analysis addressed a variety of issues including the impact of mergers on rail service, other rail carriers, and railroad labor. Also included was a section addressing possible alternatives to merger. In August 1977 the RSPO published its findings.

IMPACT ON SERVICE

In its first report, the RSPO examined the impact of rail mergers on overall rail service by measuring changes in the adequacy, efficiency, and economy of rail operations following combinations. Adequacy represented the availability of rail service—the number of railroads and routes, car supply, and switching frequency—provided to territories directly impacted. Efficiency measured the quality—the speed, reliability, extent of loss and damage, and support services—in the same region. Economy translated into costs measured in rates to shippers and savings to the merging carriers.

The Commission often measured the adequacy of rail service by the number of carriers, car supply, and switching frequency in a particular market. In terms of availability, shippers preferred to have at least two railroads serving their markets to ensure the inherent benefits of competition. On the other hand, railroads favored pooling their operations to minimize intercarrier competition. Carriers wanted to concentrate their efforts on fending off other modes rather than on preserving rail competition. By abandoning service on targeted lines and merging operations with other systems, railroads were able to reduce competition.[2]

Railroads abandoned lines in markets where traffic levels were not adequate to support continued service. The abandonment of such lines, usually branch or secondary main line, resulted in a larger number of the nation's shippers losing access to direct rail service. In some cases, motor carriers or water carriers served those markets, but in other instances, geography made even that possibility impractical.[3]

Railroads reduced competition through parallel mergers. Carriers serving the same regions over parallel routes found that they could reduce destructive rail competition by joining operations with their rail competitors. With the post–World War II growth of the trucking and water carriers adversely affecting railroads, the ICC usually permitted the combinations. Prime examples included mergers resulting in the births of the Burlington Northern, the Seaboard Coast Line, and the Illinois Central Gulf.[4] The result, however, was a loss in transportation options for shippers, many of which became captive customers of a single railroad.

Like railroad availability, rail car supply remained an important issue in merger proceedings. In most cases, merger applicants claimed potential improvement in car supply to be one motivation to merge operations. The Chesapeake & Ohio and the Baltimore & Ohio argued that greater financial strength resulting from combination would permit greater car utilization in their operations. The Missouri Pacific and the Chicago & Eastern Illinois cited improved fleet planning and car allocation as a reason for enhanced car service following their union.

Despite the arguments of applicants, however, there was doubt as to the control that carriers actually had over car supply. For example, by stipulations in the Interstate Commerce Act, the ICC had the power to "change car service rules, fix freight car compensation, require joint or common use of terminals, impose embargoes, reroute traffic, or direct railroads to operate service for a carrier that has ceased operations for a period not to exceed 240 days."[5]

Switching service, like car supply and rail availability, was an integral factor in measuring the adequacy of rail service. Without adequate switching, improvements in rail access and car supply were incidental. However, switching operations received relatively little attention from the Commission in its review of merger applications because of the difficulty in predicting the advantages or disadvantages that a merger had on this operation. Management philosophy was a key determinant in switching efficiency. A market-oriented management might improve the switching of a newly acquired and traditionally conservative railroad. On the other hand, the complexities of joining too many railroads or the nature of conservative marketing might reduce switching efficiency. Nevertheless, railroads continued to cite huge reductions in costs as a result of merging switching districts and combining rail yards.

While railroad adequacy was a major issue in rail combination, so too was efficiency or the quality of service. As noted by the RSPO, measuring service efficiency was difficult because railroads and shippers often viewed service quality from two different perspectives.[6] Nevertheless, the RSPO used four factors to analyze service quality—speed, reliability, loss and damage, and support services.

The average speed a given train moved from origin to destination depended in part on the commodity being shipped. For example, when railroads were handling traffic that was unconsigned, a slow steady speed was usually preferred. In moving large inventories, speed was a minor factor as long as the movement was steady. On the other hand, the shipment of perishables or valuable market-sensitive merchandise required high-speed service.

As noted by the 1973 Task Force on Railroad Productivity, end-to-end combinations should increase the speed of movements by rail.[7] The growth of major transcontinental systems, aided by end-to-end combinations, reduced the expensive and time-consuming delays created by traffic interchanges between different systems. Single system service was more efficient.

Parallel mergers also could increase speed of freight shipment. Increased speed would be achieved by reducing switching service and forcing shippers into specific shipping routes. The extra time taken in the switching process would be eliminated, so transit time would decrease.

Notwithstanding, if a carrier downgraded one of its parallel lines, an increase in transit time could result for shippers on that line. Moreover, downgraded systems could force too much traffic on the remaining line, thereby creating traffic jams. The fact that carriers often sacrificed speed for maximum tonnage shipped per train did not help in such cases.

Reliability was another service factor affected by mergers, and like speed it was critical for some shipments but not for others. As with speed, reliability was expected to improve when operations were merged. By the 1970s, unfortunately, most railroads were unable to study local shipments en route to assess in-transit problem areas. Railroads did not have access to origin-destination interline performance data. Ironically, the only group that had access to this information were large shippers that owned computerized vendor performance systems. These systems tracked purchase orders from time of purchase to receipt of purchase and could determine the time an order was in transport.[8]

Another element in measuring efficiency was loss and damage to freight. According to the RSPO, mergers would theoretically preclude much of the loss and damage to shipments through reduced interchanges, improved car handling, better utilization of freight equipment, and modernization of rail yards. Despite the numerous mergers since World War II, however, loss or damage to shipments continued to be a major problem for railroads as late as the 1970s.[9]

In addition to reducing the damage to shipments in transit, mergers expected to result in more efficient and coordinated support services. Car tracing, billing, accounting, and other such departments would logically become more efficient following mergers. Lacking the complexities of extensive switching between carriers, one set of service departments could effectively serve a larger region.[10]

On the other hand, as executives of combining carriers admitted, the merging of railroad computing systems often provided managements with their greatest difficulties. The complexities involved in their union frequently created a period of chaos and delay before the benefits of increased efficiency were realized.

Like adequacy and efficiency, economy or cost was an important issue in determining the impact mergers had on service. To shippers, the degree of success of a merger was measured by rate reductions or the avoidance or postponement of rate increases. To railroads, the success of a combination was reflected in "increase[d] traffic and revenue, decrease[d] costs, and increase[d] profits, cash flow, and return on investments."[11]

Unfortunately for the railroads and shippers expecting cost benefits from mergers, several studies cited by the RSPO pointed to tenuous cost savings from such transactions. In his 1968 dissertation, *Railroad Mergers: Cost, Competition and the Future Organization of the American Railroad Industry*, Robert Gallamore argued that very little actual cost savings resulted from railroad mergers. A 1972 study by the Senate Committee on Commerce entitled *The American Railroads: Posture, Problems and Prospects* pointed out that railroads exaggerated estimated cost savings when submitting merger applications.[12] In 1973, a presidential Task Force on Railroad Productivity produced a report entitled *Improving Railroad Productivity* which noted, "In sum, merger savings have been elusive and offer a tenuous justification for mergers." The report went on to say,"Large mergers have done less well than small mergers in realizing cost savings. On the basis of cost savings, [moreover,] there appears to be no evidence for favoring parallel mergers over end-to-end mergers."[13] In 1975, the Massachusetts Institute of Technology published a work that also questioned the cost advantages of merging railroad operations. It noted that although mergers enhanced the finances of some carriers, "improvement was neither as great nor as widespread as might have been expected on the basis of projections."[14] In his 1976 *Railroad Management*, D. Daryl Wyckoff argued that existing railroad management technology and organization were not capable of fully realizing the cost benefits that rail combinations might afford.[15]

Overall, the Commission was faced with a serious problem in its attempt to evaluate the effect of mergers on service. The impact of mergers on railroad adequacy, efficiency, and economy was difficult to determine with any certainty. Speed and reliability, two factors of adequacy, varied in importance from market to market. The efficiency or quality of service was difficult to measure as railroads, which lacked computerized vendor performance systems, did not systematically measure those variables. Moreover, this variable could not be examined from a "total transportation system" perspective because a railroad, at best, could offer quality measurements only over the lines it served.

Finally, cost savings generated by mergers were hotly debated throughout the industry. The Commission usually restricted its measurements of cost savings to the analysis of projected revenue gains from traffic diversions, fuel savings, routing rationalization, and other such variables. The ICC depended heavily on the projections made by the merger applicants, and the Commission often failed to include long-range projections, such as from five to ten years, or to maintain a database to test its pre-merger projections with post-merger actualities.[16]

IMPACT ON OTHER CARRIERS

One of the most important issues facing the ICC when presented with a merger application was the potential effect that the given transaction would have on carriers not involved in the combination. As noted by the RSPO, the high level of interdependence among the nation's rail operations created a phenomenon in which every unification had some impact on other carriers.

Mergers could impact the operating income of other carriers. The diversion of traffic as a result of an attractive combination could reduce the revenue earnings of other systems. Without a comparable reduction in costs, an affected railroad might lose its ability to serve a given market profitably. Moreover, investment predictions that a given railroad would be negatively affected as a consequence of a merger might result in the sale or decline in the value of its securities.

Parallel mergers could be the most damaging type of combination for third-party carriers. Merged parallel lines frequently used abandonments to rationalize their respective systems. The abandoned segments often were important to third-party carriers dependent on such lines for access to interchanges, markets, or terminals. Moreover, depending on whether the unified system decided to downgrade or upgrade given lines determined whether or not a third-party system would gain or lose advantages in the movement of traffic. Finally, the merger of railroads serving the same routes represented loss in competition. The Commission determined the importance of that loss on an individual case basis.[17]

The threat posed by end-to-end unifications was slightly different from that of parallel mergers. End-to-end combinations provided the greatest threat to third-party carriers, because they provided the merging systems with market penetration. Newly merged systems could often offer shippers new single-line service over routes where single-line service had not existed previously. Since single system service was less subject to delays, lost or damaged freight, or misroutings, it represented an enticing lure to shippers.[18]

That some mergers affected third party carriers negatively did not mean that all combinations had the same result. A merger could potentially bring more traffic to outside carriers, thereby increasing the operating income and securities value of the third party. Third parties also could avoid losses by adequately compensating for market diversions through route adjustments of their own. Shippers satisfied with the service of a third-party system, moreover, did not always switch operations to newly merged railroads serving their markets. Finally, some unifications did not threaten the traffic flow of third parties at all, while those which did were often delayed in achieving diversions for many years.

In measuring the potential impact of a merger on a given carrier, the ICC depended largely on in-house estimates of traffic diversion by the applicants seeking to unify and the opponents trying to block the transaction. In these studies, actual traffic samples were usually analyzed against the networks of the third-party carriers. Three different types of traffic were measured for the evaluation—bridge traffic, received traffic, and forwarding traffic.

Bridge traffic, measured in carloads, neither originated nor terminated with the third-party carriers. Nevertheless, it provided an important source of revenue for third-party systems. Bridge traffic was usually subject to diversion as a result of combinations. Without specified routings by shippers, moreover, the merging carriers often gained the capability to extend hauls over a given route at the expense of a third-party carrier by moving interchange points closer to third-party loading points.[19]

Received traffic was also subject to diversion by a newly merged system. The impacted carrier terminating the shipment, however, could not always be circumvented if the shipper sought the most direct route to a given point. In those cases, the merged forwarding carrier would often convince shippers to allow full transport of a given shipment over a more circuitous route in return for the security of single-system service.[20]

Forwarded traffic was the least likely to be diverted. Whatever the affected carrier's relationship with a given shipper vis-à-vis other diversions, it usually did not impact the routing of outbound traffic over the carrier's lines. The carrier still needed the traffic and the shipper still needed the transportation.

In trying to assess the impact of a proposed merger on surrounding rail systems, the ICC had a number of problems. The Commission depended largely on projections made by applicant carriers and by opponents who claimed a given combination impacted them negatively. Moreover, although the Commission established regulations concerning the type and method of data analysis to be used in merger studies, the ICC maintained little post-merger data to assess the true effect unifications had on impacted carriers. Finally, in earlier merger cases, the Commission often failed to analyze the long-term impacts of combinations on other systems. According to the RSPO, affected carriers usually did not experience the effects of a merger for from five to ten years following its approval by the ICC. Failure to include long-term studies meant that the Commission did not know the true impact of mergers on carriers and the national transportation system in general.[21]

While it had its shortcomings, the Commission did maintain a policy to compensate for the impact of mergers on other systems. Since 1950 that policy consisted of a group of remedies known as the DT&I (Detroit, Toledo & Ironton) Conditions. The Commission designed these conditions to help preserve the premerger relationships between combining parties and third-party carriers.

The DT&I conditions were the result of an application submitted by the Pennsylvania and Wabash railroads in 1950 to acquire stock control of the DT&I.[22] The Nickle Plate, New York Central, and Baltimore & Ohio protested that such a combination would harm their respective traffic flows. All depended on the DT&I to some extent. Although the Commission ultimately approved the acquisition, it drew up conditions that "insured that the independence of the DT&I be maintained under [the] applicants' control."[23]

The DT&I Conditions started with six basic stipulations. Routes and channels of trade through existing gateways and junctions would remain open following combination unless the Commission determined otherwise. The same operating neutrality regarding routing, shipping, or scheduling would continue. The Commission maintained previous traffic relationships where possible and prompt car handling without discrimination. The ICC prevented carriers from restraining businesses desiring to route traffic over existing avenues, and the Commission established provisions for the future modification of such conditions.

The industry received these conditions with open arms. The ICC applied them to combinations involving the Louisville & Nashville, the Norfolk & Western, Burlington Northern, and Penn Central; and they served as the basis for subsequent conditions.[24] Moreover, their modification in the Chesapeake & Ohio-Baltimore & Ohio and in the Seaboard Coast Line merger cases revealed their adaptability.

In addition to the DT&I conditions, the Commission often imposed several other conditions when it approved merger applications. These included granting trackage rights to impacted carriers over various lines of a merged system, opening terminal markets to reciprocal switching for the negatively affected railroads, providing joint use of terminals, allowing impacted carriers access to new routes or participation in joint rates, and requiring that merged carriers absorb weak systems. These conditions would provide solutions that the DT&I conditions, by themselves, could not.

IMPACT ON LABOR

Just as combinations affected the service of applicant railroads and surrounding carriers, they impacted the labor forces of the merging systems. Specifically, the unification of two railroads often required the adjustment of the respective labor forces to the newly created system. Such accommodation included the elimination of superfluous employees.

According to Section 5(2)(c) of the Interstate Commerce Act, the ICC was responsible for drawing up a fair and equitable arrangement to protect the interests of employees affected by mergers.[25] Consequently, the Commission required railroads to include labor protection proposals in their plans to merge with other carriers. The specifics of these proposals were usually hammered out in collective bargaining with the employees involved.

Unfortunately, working out a satisfactory agreement was often complex and sometimes impossible. Labor feared that management might not include equal provisions for every class or craft in a protection arrangement. Management might create the least costly and least favorable arrangement with its employees. These two factors often generated friction between labor and management and among different labor classes and crafts, so collective bargaining frequently broke down. The only alternative was for the Commission to mandate labor protection in unification proceedings prior to the approval of merger applications.

This federal involvement in labor arrangements was unique. In other industries, the National Labor Relations Board involved itself in management-labor negotiations only to the extent of ensuring an atmosphere conducive to healthy bargaining. In the railroad industry, however, the federal government assumed an active role in formulating the terms and conditions of management-labor arrangements. Reliance on collective bargaining was therefore reduced, and management leverage weakened.[26]

In its new role, the Commission mandated a variety of labor protective conditions on merger applications as they arose. From the 1930s to the 1990s, the Commission formed a collective body of protective conditions that could be applied to most combinations with only minor modifications from case to case.

One of the earliest attempts to reduce the adverse impact of combinations on labor came when Congress passed and President Frankilin D. Roosevelt signed the Emergency Transportation Act of 1933. The legislation was part of Roosevelt's broader effort to combat unemployment. The law essentially placed a moratorium on job reductions that occurred as a result of railroad attempts to use consolidation as a remedy for the economic ills generated by the Great Depression. The law all but eliminated consolidations during the 1930s.[27]

The Washington Job Protection Agreement of 1936 represented the next attempt by the federal government to lessen the impact of combinations on employees.

According to this law, employees who lost their positions as a result of mergers would be compensated with 60 percent of their latest year's average monthly earnings, the payments to continue from six months to five years, depending on length of service.[28]

In 1944, another set of labor arrangements emerged from an abandonment proceeding involving the trustees of the Oklahoma Railway. The Oklahoma conditions, as they were called, went further than earlier legislation in protecting labor against the adverse effects of combination and were considered the first standard set of protective conditions. They comprised the major tenets of the subsequent New Orleans conditions mandated by an ICC decision in 1952 involving the New Orleans Union Passenger Terminal.[29] Essentially, they required monthly railroad allowances equal to the latest year's average monthly earnings of employees displaced into a lower position as a result of an approved transaction. Employees dismissed from service received a dismissal allowance under similar terms. Labor was also assured of protected fringe benefits, reimbursement for moving expenses and related losses on sale of homes, and arbitration of disputes. Their compensation could continue for up to four years.

The Amtrak conditions, established by the Rail Passenger Service Act of 1970, raised from four to six years the maximum period of employment protection, and monthly compensation resulting from displacement allowances was increased. Also, the burden of proof was placed on the carrier to show that an employee who claimed displacement benefits did not deserve them. Finally, employees who held displacement status received priority rights and retraining rights for other crafts or classes of employment.[30]

Employee protective conditions were augmented again in 1979, long after the RSPO study, as a result of the Commission's review of the New York Dock Railway's acquisition of controlling interest in the Brooklyn Eastern District Terminal.[31] Among the provisions, no changes in operations, facilities, services, or equipment were permitted before labor notification and arbitration.

Because much of the labor litigation failed to address employees displaced as a result of the bankruptcy of carriers (as opposed to combinations), the Milwaukee and Rock Island conditions were adopted. Growing out of the Milwaukee Railroad Restructuring Act of 1979 and labor agreements between the bankrupt Rock Island and its employees in 1980, the new conditions provided compensation for employment loss and protection for employees effected by the division and sale of segments of bankrupt carriers. The new conditions assured employees of 80 percent of base income for a maximum of three years. Employees also received supplemental benefits, moving and sale-of-home compensation, preferential hiring, and retraining. Those obtained through acquisitions would maintain the same three-year monetary protection, receive preferential hiring, fall under the labor agreements of the acquiring carrier, and submit to arbitration in seniority disputes.

In sum, the ICC applied labor protective conditions to defend employees against the adverse effects of combinations in much the same way it protected the markets of third-party carriers. Although the Interstate Commerce Commission was expected to assure labor of compensation against the negative impact of mergers by provisions in the Interstate Commerce Act, regulations were not specific enough to be effective.

From 1933 through the 1980s, however, the level and quality of that compensation changed as the ICC developed a practice of applying standard labor protective conditions to combinations on an individual basis. The peculiarities of individual cases generated slightly different conditions until nearly all the possibilities concerning labor protection were addressed. These cases comprised a collective body of labor conditions which continued to grow with each new combination and which applied the lessons of past transactions to new proposals.

ALTERNATIVES TO MERGER

Since the end of World War I, numerous rail experts have suggested that rail mergers could provide the solution to most, if not all, of railroads' financial problems. According to these analysts, combinations "could either reduce costs through the consolidation of fixed plant, equipment, administrative support, and personnel or increase revenues by offering better service."[32] Either way, combinations were expected to aid carriers in their attempts to overcome traditionally low profits and general financial instability.

By the mid-1970s, however, the ICC sought to identify alternatives that could permit railroads to achieve reduced costs, increased revenues, and improved service. Ultimately, the Commission found nearly two dozen ways that railroads could achieve some of these goals in varying degrees short of merger.

Trackage rights arrangements and joint use of facilities provided two possibilities. The first allowed one carrier to operate over the lines of another in accordance with rules and charges agreed to by the participating systems. There were benefits and disadvantages to these tools. On the one hand, trackage rights could increase market access, allow for the elimination of duplicate facilities, lower facility maintenance, and improve equipment utilization in much the same way as mergers. On the other hand, these arrangements could increase rail-to-rail competition, raise service costs, and affect profit levels of participants.[33]

Similarly, by sharing the use of facilities and equipment, carriers could realize capital savings, reach new markets, and even attract intermodal shipments. However, this sharing might also lead to congestion, coordination problems, and increased competition. The sharing of facilities, moreover, often required new contracts with labor, something that was often difficult to obtain.

Labor also tended to object to another rationalization tool, joint use of service functions. This arrangement involved joint or collective use of revenue accounting, cost accounting, car accounting, freight sales, pricing, and marketing and freight claims departments. The advantages included reduction of labor force and corresponding costs, more efficient utilization of equipment, and better coordination through operation standardization. The primary reason that such rationalization did not frequently result outside of mergers was that it threatened exclusive control of functions by individual carriers.[34]

Equipment pooling, on the other hand, was a widespread practice despite the reduction of operational control by participating railroads. Equipment pooling essentially involved leasing cars to another railroad or to a shipper. The shipper would control the cars used for its shipments and the contributing carriers would be compensated with a fraction of the revenue earned over routes where the "contributed" car was utilized. This arrangement provided increased service capabilities, reduced the need for increased car investments, and enhanced competition between carriers. Unfortunately, pooling equipment sometimes resulted in carrier-shipper disputes and inefficient car utilization, problems usually avoided through mergers.

An alternative to equipment pooling also intended to enhance car utilization was centralized car control. Under such a system, an authority, such as the Association of American Railroads's "Train II" program, would monitor the location of rail cars throughout the nation and allocate them in accordance with traffic and coordination data. Unfortunately, although such a system could potentially reduce car shortages and car fleet investment, it also would reduce in-house car staffs, affect incentives for the development of new car technologies, and create disputes with carriers regarding individual contributions of new cars and efficiency of car service.[35]

Many of the same advantages of centralized control could also be gained through the consolidation of special services. Companies specializing in trailer-on-flat car, equipment supply, or maintenance services might be consolidated for service to all railroads. This type of arrangement would generate many of the same advantages of efficiency that consolidating railroads offered, such as a reduced labor force and increased operating efficiency.

Operating authority agreements, joint ownerships, and reciprocal switching offered other means to gain the benefits of mergers short of combination.[36] In the first arrangement, a carrier might obtain access to a remote market via a connecting carrier for a fee or some reciprocal service. Service access into remote areas was often acquired through purchases of individual lines. Unlike a full-scale merger, purchases that extended a line permitted penetration into new markets and reduction in interchange costs without the major challenges to competition. An example of this was the purchase of the Pennsylvania's Sandusky Line by the Norfolk & Western as a prerequisite to the Norfolk & Western-Wabash-Nickel Plate combination.[37] When more than one carrier wanted to purchase the same bridge or terminal line, joint ownerships often solved the problem. This assured equal access to markets over a given route while preserving competition elsewhere.

Reciprocal switching arrangements provided similar benefits. Under these constructs, a carrier with access to the same market as another would agree to interchange the cars of the requesting carrier in return for a switching charge. The charge often equaled that price set in other markets where the requesting carrier controlled switching operations. Reduced costs and increased rail efficiency normally resulted from such arrangements.

Efficiency was also enhanced with a greater use of run-through trains. These were fully loaded trains that moved directly from origin to destination without stops at intermediate points. Reclassification generally entailed crew changes and car exchange as the train transferred from one railroad to another—a consequence of industry growth through the rise of a private patchwork of small roads. A 1971 survey revealed that a major southeast terminal was able to cut transit time from fifteen hours to three through the use of run-throughs.[38] Greater use of these trains would allow for the elimination of superfluous interchange points throughout the nation.

Another method of improving the financial condition of a railroad short of merger was asset manipulation. A carrier could acquire stock control of another carrier, thereby obtaining many of the benefits of outright merger, without fully integrating every aspect of the acquired system. The acquired system would remain operationally independent but would become more cooperative in generating efficiency between the two systems. The federal government used a similar strategy when establishing the Consolidated Rail Corporation.

Like stock acquisitions, the efficiencies of centralization could also be achieved through nationalization, the establishment of holding companies, or the creation of multimodal transportation systems. The first method had been considered since World War I when President Wilson used emergency measures to nationalize the nation's railroads for purposes of coordination and efficiency. While the option offered advantages of centralized control as revealed by the systems of Great Britain, Japan, and Germany, nationalization had its drawbacks. Federal operation of the railroads between 1917 and 1919 generated a loss to the government in excess of $2 billion. In addition, nationalization placed other modes of transportation in direct competition with the federal government.

Holding companies, on the other hand, provided a form of centralized control in the private sector. Holding companies had the potential to infuse railroads with capital while promoting coordination and efficiency through their control of multiple railroad subsidiaries. Acquisition of stock control of railroads was often more advantageous than rail-on-rail purchases, because the former permitted carriers to circumvent certain federal regulations. While rail-on-rail acquisitions required ICC approval, holding company acquisitions of multiple railroads were generally exempt from Commission jurisdiction. Only when a holding company sought control of two Class I systems was ICC review necessary.

Conglomerate holding companies also could benefit railroads through the acquisition of multiple modes of transportation.[39] By controlling multiple modes, rail companies could provide shippers with a "total transportation" package. They could receive new traffic from door-to-door trucking services and from container ships at the nation's ports. Conversely, railroads would gain the ability to serve motor-carrier markets throughout the nation and water-carrier markets around the world.

Overall, the alternatives to mergers represented facets of combinations in isolation, and railroads nationwide commonly engaged in such transactions to acquire these benefits. More desirable than obtaining one or some of the benefits of merger, however, was the attainment of all the advantages that unifications offered. Aside from the advantages generated by the creation of multimodal conglomerates, the combination of two rail systems provided most of the benefits outlined by these alternatives.

Mergers generally provided market access, direct routing, employment reduction, single-line service, centralized car control, fuel and equipment savings, and an attraction to intermodal shipping. Despite studies citing meager cost savings, officials of merged systems often claimed savings from their transactions long after combination.   Such advantages not only explained the widespread use of this reorganization tool but also federal support of unifications industry-wide.

THE VERDICT

After completing its year-long study, the RSPO discovered that there were differences of opinion on the use of mergers in the railroad industry. Parties favoring some form of merger were shippers, railroads, financiers, and various states. Leading the attack on the use of merger as a restructuring tool of the industry was railway labor.

Shippers generally supported the use of mergers as a restructuring tool of the railroad industry. According to shippers, combinations aided them by providing greater access to single-line service, a simplification in rate structures, and assurance of a strong railroad structure in the future.

Shippers, however, also wanted the Commission to be cautious when making decisions about combinations. They argued that mergers should not be used as a panacea for marginal carriers; end-to-end combinations were generally preferable to parallel unifications; and mergers should continue to be decided on a case-by-case basis. Shippers were most concerned when combinations made them captive to a single railroad.[40]

Finance companies like Merrill Lynch, Salomon Brothers, and Morgan Stanley also supported the industry's use of mergers as a rationalization mechanism. Such companies pointed out that rail combinations, like unifications in other types of business, "can lead to substantial gains in operating, marketing, planning and financing efficiencies."[41] Salomon Brothers further recommended that if the federal government needed to aid marginal carriers, it should assist them with one massive infusion of capital rather than with smaller periodic grants. The finance company also believed the cost of labor protective provisions arising from a unification proceeding should be borne by the public rather than by the merged system.

Railroads were somewhat divided on the issue. The Class I systems, although highly supportive of mergers, were apprehensive about using combinations as a remedy for smaller marginal systems. They adamantly opposed the Commission practice of requiring merging carriers to include smaller systems in their combinations.

Many of the smaller carriers, on the other hand, believed their inclusion in larger combinations could remedy many of their own financial ills. The primary concern of smaller lines, however, was that the Commission adequately measure traffic diversion in merger proceedings. They feared that the emphasis on end-to-end combinations might undermine the importance of the smaller systems serving the same regions as newly merged carriers.

Various states also provided a perspective on the railroad merger issue. New York and Arizona supported the use of combinations as a restructuring tool. Like large carriers and shippers, however, they warned against the use of unifications as a panacea for the ills of smaller systems. In contrast, smaller states like Massachusetts and Vermont questioned the benefits of mergers. They worried that larger carriers might become less responsive to their shippers' needs.

Labor was the interested party most critical of using mergers as a rationalization tool in the railroad industry. The Railway Labor Executives' Association (RLEA) bashed the Commission's recommendation of restructuring through mergers and in particular its encouragement of end-to-end combinations. The RLEA claimed that such recommendations "prejudge the merits of individual consolidations yet to be filed."[42] The RLEA also believed that the claim that mergers should not be used to solve the ills of marginal systems was inappropriate. According to RLEA, the marginal road problem was "too indefinite and [such a generalization] creates unnecessary uncertainty regarding the preservation of essential services."[43] Finally, labor contended that the ICC should not emphasize the case-by-case method of trying unifications at the expense of considerations about the national transportation system. The shock that mergers tended to cause labor was sufficient to explain the RLEA's adamant stand on such issues.

After considering the views of various participants in its study, the RSPO study group made several recommendations to the ICC that outlined the sentiments of the industry and federal officials. The RSPO recommended restructuring through mergers, emphasizing the benefits of end-to-end mergers over parallel combinations. The RSPO recognized that mergers would not be used as a remedy for the ills of marginal systems and that in such cases adequacy of service should take precedence over preservation of corporate entities. Moreover, labor protection would be maintained.

Finally, the RSPO made several recommendations to improve the Commission's processing of mergers. The RSPO suggested that the ICC streamline its merger process, perform post-merger analyses, search for new ways to quantify merger data, and continue with the case-by-case method of examining merger proposals. Such action was expected to facilitate a smoother merger process and to provide hard data on the long-term effects of mergers on service and competion.

NOTES

1. U.S. Interstate Commerce Commission, Rail Services Planning Office, *Rail Merger Study: Initial Paper* ([Washington, D.C.]: U.S. Interstate Commerce Commission, 1977), 1.

2. U.S. Interstate Commerce Commission, Rail Services Planning Office, *Rail Merger Study: Service* ([Washington, D.C.]: Interstate Commerce Commission, August 1, 1977, 28–30.

3. Benjamin J. Allen, "The Economic Effects of Rail Abandonment on Communities: A Case Study," *Transportation Journal* 15 (Fall 1975), 52–61; Leigh B. Boske and Mark J. Wolfgram, "A Social Decision-Making Framework for Analyzing Rail Service Abandonment Impacts," *Transportation Journal* 16 (Summer 1977), 78–85.

4. ICC, *Rail Merger Study: Initial Paper*, 37, 53, 74.

5. Ibid., 31; *Interstate Commerce Act of 1887*, Statutes at Large, Vol. 24, 379 (1887); U.S. ICC, Bureau of Transport Economics and Statistics, *Railroad Consolidations and the Public Interest: A Preliminary Examination* (Washington, D.C.: U.S. Interstate Commerce Commission, 1962), 17–18.

6. ICC, *Railroad Consolidations*, 65.

7. Task Force on Railroad Productivity, *Improving Railroad Productivity: Final Report of the Task Force on Railroad Productivity* (Washington, D.C.: The National Commission on Productivity and the Council of Economic Advisers, November 1973), 258.

8. ICC, *Rail Merger Study: Service*, 39.

9. *Railway Age* 172 (March 27, 1972), 40–41; *Railway Age* 170 (June 28, 1971), 29–30; *Railway Age* 174 (March 26, 1976), 14–16.

10. ICC, *Railway Merger Study: Service*, 39–40.

11. Ibid., 41; ICC, *Railroad Consolidations*, 44.

12. *ICC, Railroad Consolidations*, 44–50; Robert E. Gallamore, "Railroad Mergers: Costs, Competition and the Future Organization of the American Railroad Industry" (Ph.D. diss., Harvard University, 1968), 276; U.S. Congress, Senate Committee on Commerce, Staff Report, *The American Railroad: Postures, Problems and Prospects*, 92nd Cong., 2d sess., August 28, 1972, 75. See also James T. Kneafsey, *Transportation Economic Analysis* (Lexington, Mass.: D.C. Heath, 1975).

13. Task Force on Railroad Productivity, *Improving Railroad Productivity*, 256; see also James C. Nelson, *Railroad Transportation and Public Policy* (Washington, D.C.: The Brookings Institution, 1959), 183.

14. ICC, *Rail Merger Study: Service*, 48–49; James Sloss et al., "An Analysis and Evaluation of Past Experiences in Rationalizing Railroad Networks," *Studies in Railroad Operations and Economics* (Cambridge, Mass.: MIT Press, 1975), 123.

15. Daryl D. Wyckoff, *Railroad Management* (Lexington, Mass.: Lexington Books, 1976), 173.

16. ICC, *Rail Merger Study: Service*, 69–73.

17. U.S. Interstate Commerce Commission, Rail Services Planning Office, *Rail Merger Study: Impacts on Other Carriers* (Washington, D.C.: Interstate Commerce Commission, August 12, 1977), 12–13.

18. Ibid., 14.

19. Ibid., 15.

20. Ibid., 15–16.

21. Ibid., 22–26.

22. *Detroit, Toledo & Ironton Railroad Company et al.-Control, Etc.* 275 ICC 455–494.

23. Ibid., 492; ICC, *Rail Merger Study: Impacts on Other Carriers*, 32.

24. ICC, *Rail Merger Study: Impacts on Other Carriers*, 33–34; *Pennsylvania Railroad Company-Merger-New York Central Railroad Company* 327 ICC 569; *Norfolk & Western Railway and New York, Chicago & St. Louis Railroad-Merger, Etc.* 324 ICC 6; *Great Northern Pacific & Burlington Lines-merger-Great Northern Railway* 328 ICC 481.

25. For a legal discussion of this issue, see Norton N. Newborn, "Protection of Employees in Railroad Consolidations Under the Interstate Commerce Act," *Labor Law Journal* 23(April 1972), 207–231.

26. U.S. Interstate Commerce Commission, Rail Services Planning Office, *Rail Merger Study: Labor*, (Washington, D.C.: Interstate Commerce Commission, August 26, 1977), 19–20.

27. *Emergency Transportation Act of 1933*, Statutes at Large, Vol. 48, sec. 214 (1933).

28. *Staggers Rail Act of 1980, Legislative History*, U.S. Code, vol. 10, 7484 (1980); ICC, *Rail Merger Study: Labor*, 14, 52.

29. *Oklahoma Railway Trustees Abandonment* 257 ICC 177; *New Orleans Union Passenger Terminal Case* 282 ICC 271. Modifications were made to these conditions in *Southern Railway-Control-Central of Georgia* 317 ICC 577; 317 ICC 729; and 331 ICC 151, 164.

30. *Rail Passenger Service Act of 1970*, U.S. Code, vol. 1, 1557 (1970); ICC, *Rail Merger Study: Labor*, 63–83.

31. *New York Railway-Control-Brooklyn Eastern District* 360 ICC 60.

32. U.S. Interstate Commerce Commission, Rail Services Planning Office, *Rail Merger Study: Alternatives to Merger* (Washington, D.C.: Interstate Commerce Commission, August 18, 1977), vii.

33. Ibid., 2–4.

34. Ibid., 8–10.

35. Ibid., 11–13.

36. Ibid., 17–23.

37. Ibid., 35–37.

38. Ibid., 29. Norfolk Southern believed run-throughs were essential to increasing on-time or improved performance, *Railway Age* 172 (February 26, 1973), 37.

39. W. Graham Claytor, Jr., "A Single Intermodal Transportation Company," *Transportation Journal* 11 (Spring 1972), 31–38.

40. ICC, *Rail Merger Study: Service*, 22; Simat, Helliesen & Eichner, Inc., *Competition in the Railroad Industry*, prepared for the United States Railway Association (Washington, D.C.: February 1975), 51–53

41. U.S. Interstate Commerce Commission, Rail Services Planning Office, *Rail Merger Study: Final Report* (Washington, D.C.: Interstate Commerce Commission, February 1, 1978). See also Baruch Lev and Gershon Mandelker, "The Microeconomic Consequences of Corporate Mergers," *Journal of Business* 45 (January 1972), 85–104.

42. ICC, *Rail Merger Study: Final Report*, 16.

43. Ibid.

6

Rise of the Eastern Giants

In the two and a half decades between 1970 and 1995, the railroad network in the eastern United States experienced enormous consolidation. While the federal government actively promoted combinations with the creation of Amtrak and Conrail, carriers in the private sector continued with their own agendas of horizontal expansion. At the beginning of 1970, some forty-six Class I carriers crisscrossed the nation east of the Mississippi River. For various reasons, including reclassification, bankruptcy, and combination, that number had already decreased to five by 1995. The five carriers that survived the shakeout were very different from those that existed when the period opened. These survivors were systems created or regenerated through major combinations with or among lesser railroads in the 1970s and 1980s.

The modern Illinois Central, a subsidiary of IC Industries, was born in 1972 when the old Illinois Central Railroad merged with the Gulf, Mobile & Ohio to form the Illinois Central Gulf. Consolidated Rail Corporation (Conrail) emerged in 1975 as the product of the United States Railway Association's consolidation of the failing Penn Central with five other bankrupt railroads in the northeastern United States. Grand Trunk Western, a subsidiary of the Canadian National, grew through the acquisition of two major systems, the Detroit, Toledo & Ironton in 1980 and the Detroit, Toledo & Shoreline in 1981. CSX Transportation resulted from a combination in 1980 of the Chessie System and the Seaboard Coast Line Industries. Finally, the primary competitor of CSX, the Norfolk Southern Corporation, emerged in 1980 from the merger of two large Class I carriers, the Norfolk & Western and the Southern Railway.

ILLINOIS CENTRAL

The modern Illinois Central was incorporated as the Illinois Central Gulf Railroad on December 30, 1971, to implement the merger of the old Illinois Central and the Gulf, Mobile & Ohio. In 1972, the ICC approved the combination which had been pending since the application was filed with the Commission four years earlier on May 16, 1968.[1]

The Illinois Central, an Illinois corporation founded in 1851, was controlled prior to 1972 by Illinois Central Industries, a Delaware corporation created in 1962. The latter was established so that the Illinois Central might diversify into noncarrier enterprises, a practice becoming increasingly popular among larger railroads after World War II. Overall, the railroad owned about 8,000 miles of main line track. Although 60 percent of that track lay within the borders of Illinois and Mississippi, the system spanned thirteen central and southern states. Its principal lines stretched from Chicago to New Orleans, but others reached St. Louis, Missouri, and Louisville,

Kentucky; Indianapolis, Indiana; and Birmingham, Alabama. From Chicago lines extended west to Omaha, Nebraska; Council Bluffs and Sioux City, Iowa; Sioux Falls, South Dakota; Albert Lea, Minnesota; and Madison, Wisconsin. A line also connected Meridian, Mississippi, and Shreveport, Louisiana.[2]

Like the Illinois Central, the Gulf, Mobile & Ohio ran an extensive system in the Mississippi Valley. Originally organized under Mississippi laws in 1838, the railroad owned some 2,400 miles of mainline track, 62 percent of which was in Illinois and Mississippi. The system spanned seven states and served such industrial centers as Chicago, New Orleans, St. Louis, and Birmingham while providing service to Mobile and Montgomery, Alabama, and Memphis, Tennessee.[3]

The ICC considered the Illinois Central and the Gulf, Mobile & Ohio to be financially sound carriers. Both had impressive earnings, and both maintained adequate levels of working capital.[4] Traditionally, the Commission was hesitant to approve the merger of two healthy carriers. Ideas about combinations detracting from competition were still pervasive among regulators. Nevertheless, the Commission adopted a different approach in this case. The ICC pointed out that there "is not provision in the [Interstate Commerce] act which expressly or by implication prohibits the merger of financially strong railroads. The act draws no distinction as between strong and the weak, between competitive and non-competitive railroads. There is no requirement in either the statute or judicial precedent which limits the Commission's authority to approve mergers to those involving carriers which are insolvent or on the brink of bankruptcy."[5]

The desire of the Illinois Central and the Gulf to merge operations was based on projected financial savings and traffic increases. Service improvements were expected to "assure the adequacy of future transportation services in midwestern and southern states; and render a more coordinated economical efficient and expeditious service to the public."[6] Single-line service to major terminals like Kansas City and Montgomery, served exclusively by the Gulf in the past, would offer new markets to shippers operating over the Illinois Central's system. Moreover, superfluous routes could be eliminated, and Gulf stations would utilize the Illinois Central's high grade data system which provided instantaneous car location information to shippers. This type of car tracing would provide greater efficiency in car allocation and service runs. In addition, the applicants projected that shorter routes would reduce elapsed time for shipments between Chicago and Montgomery by more than 25 hours and from Chicago to Mobile by more than 23 hours.[7] Moreover, a combined fleet of 66,861 cars would reduce car shortages throughout the system. Authorities in both the Central and the Gulf estimated an annual savings of $12.1 million.

The ICC ultimately approved the transaction, agreeing that the combination would "provide the means for the growth and development of a better rail transport system in mid-America."[8] This approval came despite the vigorous protests of competitors concerned with traffic diversions. The strongest criticism came from the Missouri Pacific, St. Louis-San Francisco, Kansas City Southern, Milwaukee, and Rio Grande. As with most merger cases, the protestors estimated diversions far above those of the applicants. For example, the Rio Grande claimed that it would lose more than $835,597 in revenue, while the applicants estimated the loss at only $50,590.

Recognizing that the applicants and the protestors generally used different variables to calculate estimates, the Commission regulary conducted its own diversion analyses. In the case of the Rio Grande, the Commission estimated losses to be about $238,462 annually.[9]

Despite complaints about traffic diversions, the issue of competition was not a major factor in the Illinois Central-Gulf combination. Only thirteen of thirty-four points served by both carriers would be without competitive rail service following the merger. Also, despite ICC estimates of $6 million in added annual revenue from diversions, the Commission believed that no more than 10 percent of total rail competition in the region provided by Central and Gulf would be eliminated after unification.[10]

The ICC explained that shippers in the Illinois Central-Gulf service area had adequate access to other modes of transportation. Of the 224 cities served by the Mississippi River system the Illinois Central served only 59, and the Gulf served 24.[11] A loss in rail service to any of those points as a result of combination would be of relatively little importance to shippers. In addition, the 14-state area served by the two applicants was also served by more 912 Class I and Class II motor carriers in the 1970s.[12]

The Commission, nevertheless, mandated protective conditions in the approval of the merger, one of the more important ones requiring that Illinois Central Gulf absorb three shortlines, the Bonhommie & Hattiesburg Southern; the Fenwood, Columbia & Gulf; and the Columbus & Greenville. The Commission contended that without such a condition, the three rail systems might be irreparably damaged since they depended heavily on the Central and Gulf as separate systems.[13]

After the conditions were established, the ICC approved the combination. According to the terms of the unification, stockholders of Gulf, Mobile & Ohio common stock received three-fourths of a share of newly issued IC Industries $6 cumulative first preferred stock for each common share held. Meanwhile, IC Industries also issued 367,677 common shares in order to acquire Illinois Central common stock held by a variety of minority interests.

The Illinois Central Gulf (ICG) underwent little expansion over the next two decades. Its management spent most of its time simplifying the system it controlled. In 1983, the company absorbed a subsidiary, the New Orleans Great Northern Railway, and it sold another, the Gulf Transport Company. In 1989, the Illinois Central sold 75 percent of its ownership in Trailer Train Company for $13 million, and a year later it sold some industrial park property for $17 million.[14]

By 1995, the Illinois Central Gulf was a smaller but still vigorous railroad providing common carrier service over 2,700 miles of mainline road, 200 miles of secondary mainline road, and 1,700 miles of miscellaneous road. Operating in six southern and midwestern states, the system had important yard facilities in Chicago, Illinois; Memphis, Tennessee; Jackson, Mississippi; New Orleans and Baton Rouge, Louisiana; and Mobile, Alabama. With 397 diesel locomotives and 15,767 freight cars, Illinois Central Gulf's 3,268 employees provided transportation for the movement of chemicals, paper products, coal, grain, and milled grain products. Among its subsidiaries were the Chicago Intermodal Company, Kensington & Eastern Railroad,

Mississippi Valley Corporation, and the Waterloo Railway.[15]

CONRAIL

While the Illinois Central Gulf was forming, other carriers in the eastern district were undergoing enormous change via corporate combinations. One of these was Penn Central Transportation, whose collapse was the most widely remembered railroad event of 1970. Hauling 20 percent of the nation's passenger and freight traffic, Penn Central was the flagship of the Northeast. Its fall into bankruptcy shocked the industry.

Initial financial turmoil led to a readjustment, starting at the top. The board of directors discharged Chairman Stuart T. Saunders and Finance Committee Chairman Alfred E. Perlman. Paul A. Gorman, who had been president of Penn Central since the previous December, was appointed chairman. But such a last minute shift of officers was too late to change the company's prospects. On June 21, the directors informed the public that due to "a severe cash squeeze and having been unable to acquire from any source additional working capital," Penn Central had requested and received reorganization status from a district court in eastern Pennsylvania.[16]

During the reorganization, four trustees were appointed to oversee rehabilitation. Among the four were Jervis Langdon Jr., former chairman and president of the Rock Island Railroad, and W. Willard Wirtz, the nation's former secretary of labor.[17] This quartet appointed William H. More of the Southern Railroad as president and began planning steps to revive the company. First, the managerial structure was simplified in order to eliminate overlapping functions and to concentrate responsibilities in fewer administrators. Although the railroad continued to employ thousands more workers than did the second largest railroad, more than 5,500 jobs were eliminated.[18] Additionally, Penn Central purchased new locomotives and freight cars for greater efficiency. Finally, like all carriers in financial trouble, Penn Central established an extensive program to abandon lines that were the least profitable or that required the most maintenance.

Despite such efforts by Penn Central executives, the prospects for the system's survival remained dismal. While maintaining operations in the hope of recovery, one of the railroad's four trustees admitted, "No one can really bring himself to recognize the fact that Penn Central railroad may actually have to stop running."[19]

By 1972, the concern over the imbroglio in the Northeast increased. Twelve carriers were seeking reorganization under Section 77 of the Bankruptcy Act. They included the Penn Central, Central of New Jersey, Erie Lackawanna, Reading, Lehigh Valley, and the Boston & Maine. The region contained 55 percent of America's manufacturing capacity, and the railroads that serviced many of the manufacturing centers were financially strained. By July 1973, fifteen of Penn Central's subsidiaries went into bankruptcy. They included the Beech Creek; Cleveland, Cincinnati & St. Louis; Cleveland & Pittsburgh; Connecting Railway; Delaware; Erie & Pittsburgh; Michigan Central; Northern Central; Penndel Company; Philadelphia & Trenton; Philadelphia, Baltimore & Washington; Pittsburgh, Fort Wayne & Chicago; Pittsburgh, Youngstown & Ashtabula; Union of Baltimore; and United New Jersey

Railroad & Canal Company. In October, the Ann Arbor Railroad made it sixteen.

Congress, already attentive to the problems of the Northeast, passed the Regional Rail Reorganization Act of 1973 to remedy the problem. Authored by Richard G. Shoup, a Montana Republican, and Brock Adams, a Washington Democrat, the Regional Rail Reorganization Act sought to restructure in stages the entire railway system in the Northeast. Federal judges investigated financially struggling railroads to determine the feasibility of their reorganization. Federal administrators then decided whether to sell the reorganized railroad to a profitable system, release it to operate under its own management, or include it in a new, publicly funded system, Consolidated Rail Corporation. Those included in Conrail were operated as a single system that received periodic capital infusions from the federal government. Those not included in Conrail had to face market forces alone.

After two and a half years of reorganizing systems in the Northeast according to a plan established by the United States Railway Administration, Conrail officially started operations on April 1, 1976. The Railroad Revitalization and Regulatory Reform Act of 1976 helped Conrail complete its restructuring of the Northeast with allocations in excess of $2 billion. Subsequently, Conrail, like its Amtrak counterpart, started the quest for self reliance.

To compensate for Conrail's financial inadequacies, Congress included special stipulations in the Staggers Rail Act of 1980 and the Northeast Rail Services Act of 1981. These provisions gave Conrail "new rate freedoms and special advantages, including wage concessions, tax exemptions, and relief from operating unprofitable freight and commuter services."[20] These stipulations, combined with the extraordinary efforts of Stanley Crane, the system's chief executive, resulted in the Consolidated Rail Corporation posting its first annual operating profit in 1981. Subsequently, Conrail continued to prosper, producing profits approaching $250 million by 1983.[21]

According to other stipulations in the Northeast Rail Services Act, the federal government was required to begin a search for buyers for Conrail once profitability was reached. Shortly after Conrail's 1981 profits were posted, therefore, Secretary of Transportation Elizabeth Dole began the long and tedious process of locating more than 100 potential buyers.[22] By June 1984, after careful study and extensive negotiations, she had identified fifteen viable offers to purchase the northeastern giant. The following year, she chose a candidate.

Dole presented her findings to the Senate Committee on Commerce, Science and Transportation in February and April 1985. She had chosen Norfolk Southern as the purchaser of Conrail. Members of the Senate Committee had to decide whether or not they agreed with her.

As noted by Secretary Dole, the Department of Transportation weighed the offers made by the fifteen candidates against service variables to shippers and communities throughout the Northeast as well as competitive impacts on other rail systems. Several aspects of the Norfolk Southern offer proved attractive. First, Norfolk Southern was the only candidate willing to pay $1.2 billion in cash out of its own pocket. It also agreed to surrender Conrail's accumulated tax benefits amounting to $2.1 billion in net operating losses and $275 million in investment tax credits.[23]

Additionally, the acquisition was expected to strengthen competition. Norfolk

Southern announced its intention to reopen gateways that Conrail had closed and reestablish joint rates discontinued as a result of Conrail divestitures. Moreover, in rejuvinating these branch lines, Norfolk Southern agreed to comply with a series of constraints outlined by the Justice Department and designed to ensure the viability of smaller railroads in the area served by Conrail. Some of these constraints included maintaining certain operations as they then existed.

Besides promising to enhance competition, the Norfolk Southern officials said they would not strip Conrail of its assets. They agreed not to pay dividends on common stock if those payments reduced Conrail's cash base below $500 million, and they promised not to sell controlling interest of the system for at least five years. Finally, Conrail's minority business opportunity programs would be retained, and the carrier's headquarters would remain in Philadelphia.[24]

Secretary Dole emphasized the advantages of the offer, reminding the Committee of the extreme measures taken just to make Conrail profitable. State transit agencies assumed control over many of Conrail's commuter opperations under the Northeast Rail Services Act (NERSA). Employees made wage concessions, and states sacrificed tax revenues from Conrail totaling $25 million annually.[25]

The public offering was much less attractive. Management would draw $300 million out of the company whatever its financial standing, and management's plan would require the company to issue $600 million in preferred stock. As the secretary of transportation noted, this would be the largest issue of this nature in history. Also the management plan required combined common and preferred stock dividends of $126 million per year, while permitting Conrail to borrow in excess of $400 million over a four-year period. Considering that in private hands Conrail would be required to pay $120 to $130 million more to its workers, make provisions for labor protection in corporate transactions, and pay federal taxes, the adequacy of a public offering toward the future stability of Conrail appeared questionable. Finally, the management proposal could at best raise $1.1 billion for the purchase. With the company earning approxiamately $500 million in 1984, the abilities of management to operate under such constraints was doubtful.[26]

The Transportation Section and Economic Policy Office of the Justice Department's Antitrust Division added insight to the DOT study with its own investigation of Norfolk Southern's proposal. Analyzing the possible acquisition of Conrail as a "merger," the Justice Department identified one-hundred markets in twenty-one states where competition might be eliminated. In those markets Conrail and Norfolk Southern both participated in rail movements involving some $516.1 million in rail revenue in 1983. Upon further investigation, however, the Justice Department found that divestiture of some of Conrail's gateways in Buffalo, Chicago, East St. Louis, and Toledo would guarantee competition in those markets. In other instances, the combination expected to enhance efficiency for shippers and facilitate single-line service.

Senator Ernest F. Hollings of South Carolina agreed with the secretary's choice. Hollings argued that the sale would provide "reasonable return to the Federal Government; a purchase that brings financial strength to the Conrail System; an arrangement that ensures the continuation of high quality service in the Conrail region and as a link to other parts of the country; and a sale which recognizes the sacrifices that rail labor has made and the importance of labor participation to the future of the rail system in the Conrail region."[27]

Despite the arguments of those favoring the proposed sale of Conrail to Norfolk Southern, and compensatory plans to offset adverse effects, many opposed the idea.[28] For example, Senator Arlen Specter of Pennsylvania denounced the offer, concerned about the 15,000 employees and 2,300 shippers who would be affected. He argued that the sale was not in the national interest. He considered $1.2 billion for 85 percent of Conrail stock to be "woefully inadequate." After all, the federal government had already infused $7 billion into the northeastern giant.[29] The book value for Conrail was in the $4 billion range and the scrap value was $3 billion. Specter, like others who opposed the deal, favored selling Conrail, but he preferred to hold out for a better offer.[30]

Others opposed to the Norfolk Southern acquisition shuddered at the unforseeable anticompetive implications of an 18,000-mile Norfolk Southern acquiring a 15,000-mile Conrail. This combination would result in a single-system controlling 60 percent of the rail market in Michigan, 95 percent of the market in northeast Indiana, and 70 percent of the eastbound rail traffic in the New England, New York, and Texas corridors.[31] Norfolk Southern also admitted that at least 2,500 employees would lose their jobs. Among those fearful of such prospects were Conrail's management, Grand Trunk Western, CSX Transportation, and the Eastern Coal Transportation Conference.

To the dismay of Norfolk Southern and its supporters, Congress decided to sell Conrail in a public stock offering. Legislators believed that they could obtain a better deal than what NS offered and, at the the same time, assuage growing concern that an NS-Conrail system might monopolize northeastern freight transportation. Congress's decision was legislated in the Conrail Privatization Act included in the Omnibus Budget Reconciliation Act of 1986.[32]

Conrail was sold on March 26, 1987, in the largest public stock offering in U.S. history. The issue yielded a phenomenal $1.65 billion. Considering that Congress took $300 million back from Conrail before the offering, the federal government netted more than $1.8 billion from the transaction.[33]

Following its transfer to the private sector, Conrail continued with a program of corporate expansion that already began in the late 1970s. In June 1978, the system acquired a leasehold interest in the Lehigh & Susquehanna Railroad from the Lehigh Coal & Navigation Company for approximately $5.2 million. In 1979 and 1980, Conrail purchased two rolling stock companies—SHPX Fourth Corporation and Relco-Pa.[34]

Shortly after 1980, Conrail expanded further. Among its aquisitions were Merchants Dispatch Transportation, Philadelphia Reading & Pottsville Telegraph, Detroit Terminal Railroad, and Pennsylvania Car Leasing Company. Meanwhile, Conrail sold Excelsior Truck Leasing, Illinois Terminal Railroad, Lake Erie Eastern Railroad, and Toledo Railroad.

The company continued to rationalize operations in the late 1980s and early 1990s. In 1985, Conrail sold the Canada Southern Railway and the Detroit River Tunnel. The Pennsylvania Truck Lines was sold in 1990, and the following year an

81-mile portion of the company's line between Shelbyville, Indiana, and Cincinnati was sold to the Central Railroad of Indiana.[35]

Conrail continued to invest in its growth while rationalizing operations. In 1989, the company raised its interest in Trailer Train to 21.8 percent through the purchase of $43 million in common stock. That same year, the company contributed $5 million in a joint venture with OHM Corporation to develop a treatment and disposal facility for hazardous waste.

Two year later, Conrail expanded again, purchasing the remaining two-thirds interest in the Monongahela Railway for $40 million. The combination was important because it increased Conrail's coal-hauling competitiveness. Although the fourth largest hauler of coal in the nation, far behind the Burlington Northern, CSX Transportation, and Norfolk Southern, Conrail generated enormous efficiency through the acquisition of the seventh largest coal hauler. Conrail already exchanged over 80 percent of Monongahela coal traffic. Consolidation of operations was the logical next step in the system's horizontal expansion.

In 1993, Conrail completed two additional major transactions. In April, the company joined with the Norfolk Southern Corporation to form Triple Crown Services. The new company was a domestic retail intermodal venture designed to compete with trucking companies. Major traffic corridors included New York-Chicago, Chicago-Atlanta, and Atlanta-New York.[36] In December, Conrail, Inc. (renamed on July 1, 1993) publicized its repurchase of 50 percent of the stock of the 13-mile Pittsburgh, Chartiers & Youghiogheny Railway (PC&Y) held by P&LE Properties, Inc. Since the company already held 50 percent interest in PC&Y, the transaction made Conrail, Inc., the only remaining stockholder.

By the time it joined with Norfolk Southern Corporation to exploit intermodal markets, Conrail was one of the nation's leading freight haulers. The rail system operated in 14 states and Canada over 12,400 miles of line stretching from Quebec in the north, west to Ohio, and south to Virginia. By 1995 the company maintained 17,715 miles of road, 2,023 locomotives, and 51,404 freight cars. Its 23,500 employees were extremely effective in providing freight transportation to the regions it served.[37]

GRAND TRUNK WESTERN

While Conrail was enjoying its first profitable year and the industry was mesmerized with the freedoms provided by the Staggers Rail Act, Grand Trunk Western (GTW) was completing two major transactions. GTW, a subsidiary of the Canadian National Railway, accomplished its two important combinations of the period when it merged with the Detroit, Toledo & Ironton (DT&I) and the Detroit, Toledo & Shore Line (DTSL).

The Norfolk & Western and the Baltimore & Ohio sparked proceedings when they filed a merger application with the Commission on October 21, 1977. Both carriers sought ICC authority to purchase stock control of DT&I from the Pennsylvania Company.[38] The two buyers offered $23.6 million for stock control and promised to make no change in DT&I operations, thereby eliminating Commission concerns over labor welfare.

The request grew out of concern for the financial stability of DT&I. The system was owned by PennCo, an affiliate of the former Penn Central. After the collapse of Penn Central and the subsequent sale of most of its railroad properties to the Consolidated Rail Corporation, the future of DT&I was uncertain. The Baltimore & Ohio and the Norfolk & Western wanted to make DT&I's future certain to ensure their own access to markets.

The B&O operated 5,411 miles of line in twelve states, while the Norfolk & Western operated 7,659 miles of line in fourteen states.[39] Both had important connections with DT&I, which operated 588 miles in Michigan and Ohio with lines extending from Detroit south to Ironton and west to Cincinnati. As with most unification proposals, the applicants pointed to estimates of increased equipment availability, more efficient coordination, and better service to shippers.

On February 16, 1978, while the application of the NW and the B&O was being considered, the Grand Trunk Western submitted its application for control of DT&I. GTW operated just to the north of DT&I, and its lines extended from Detroit north to Port Huron and Bay City, and from Detroit northwesterly to Pontiac. From Pontiac DT&I lines went to Muskegon and to Chicago. Tied to its application for control of DT&I was GTW's application to acquire the Detroit, Toledo & Shoreline (DTSL), a 50-mile Toledo-Detroit line jointly owned by GTW and NW.

Both applications were part of a plan by GTW's parent company to strengthen its rail network. Canadian National (CN) controlled the Grand Trunk Western, the Central Vermont, and the Denver, Winnipeg & Pacific through a holding company, the Grand Trunk Corporation.[40] Each of the three railroads connected with widely separated lines of the Canadian National. Over time the success of CN's U.S. carriers had varied. The Denver, Winnipeg & Pacific had been financially stable, but the Central Vermont was weak. The GTW, however, had been unprofitable, producing deficits for twenty years prior to 1977. By 1971, CN had subsidized this losing investment to the extent of $300 million.[41] Although the system showed slight improvement after 1972, the Canadian National believed that the GTW would only become profitable by means of a unification with the DT&I and the DTSL. Both lines served the same kinds of traffic through the Michigan-Ohio industrial complex, and the CN expected both lines to provide GTW with the carloads necessary to make it profitable.

Ultimately, the deciding factor leading to GTW's acquisition of DT&I and DTSL was competition. GTW president John H. Burdakin summarized the Commission's attitude toward the transaction. He pointed out that GTW, DT&I, and DTSL were all small systems. However, "through consolidation, there would be a self-sustaining, single-line service stronger and more competitive with the area's other three major railroads, Chessie, NW and Conrail."[42] The combination was expected to produce a system that would "be more efficient, maintain a competitive balance, and produce greater financial return." On the other hand, the Canadian National believed that GTW's financial improvement could not be sustained if DT&I fell under the control of its competitors, the Norfolk & Western and the Baltimore & Ohio.

In 1979, the ICC approved GTW's application to acquire the DT&I and the

DTSL. By June 1980, the company completed its acquisition of 245,329 shares of DT&I stock, and by April 1981, GTW completed its purchase of 1,500 shares of the DTSL stock. The ICC decision meant rejection of the joint application by the B&O and the N&W.[43] According to the Commission, that joint application, if implemented, could have reduced competition and therefore was counter to the public interest.

Aside from the DT&I and the DTSL acquisitions and an Agreement for Voluntary Coordination of Railroad Freight Services with the Burlington Northern in 1985, Grand Trunk Western expanded little in subsequent years. Nevertheless, by the end of the decade it was still among the Class I carriers. In 1990, the company operated 925 miles of road in Michigan, Indiana, Illinois, and Ohio with principal lines extending from Port Huron to Chicago and Detroit and from Detroit to Cincinnati. The company provided important rail service to automotive, chemical, utility, steel, forest product, and food industries in the region it served.

CSX TRANSPORATION

Unlike Grand Trunk Western, CSX Transportation (CSXT) did not exist in name at the beginning of the 1970s. However, the system's predecessor, Seaboard Coast Line, was a thriving railroad operating through more than a dozen southern states and was itself the product of a merger between the Atlantic Coast Line and the Seaboard Air Line in 1967. Aside from its purchase of the Durham & Southern in 1976, Seaboard engaged in little expansion until the transaction which spawned CSXT.

In 1978, the Seaboard Coast Line sought a unification with the Chessie system, a major mid-Atlantic Class I operation and itself the product of a 1967 unification between the Chesapeake & Ohio and the Baltimore & Ohio. This new merger was expected to produce a 27,500-mile super-system stretching from Michigan on the north to Miami on the south.

The Chessie System consisted of 11,464 miles of line in fourteen eastern and midwestern states, the District of Columbia, and Ontario. It consisted of three major carriers: the Chesapeake & Ohio (C&O), the Baltimore & Ohio (B&O), and the Western Maryland (WM). The lines of the C&O ran from Norfolk and Newport News, Virginia, through Richmond, Lynchburg, and Clifton Forge, Virginia; Hinton, Charleston, and Huntington, West Virginia; Ashland, Maysville, and Covington, Kentucky; Cincinnati, Ohio; and Richmond, Muncie, and Peru, Indiana, to Chicago.

The principal lines of the B&O extended from Philadelphia through Baltimore, Maryland, to Washington, DC. From the nation's capital the B&O continued to Cumberland, Maryland, and from Cumberland by separate routes to Chicago and St. Louis. The line to Chicago passed through Pittsburgh, Akron, and Willand, Ohio. The line to St. Louis passed through Parkersburg, West Virginia, and Cincinnati.

The WM was a much less important carrier. It stretched from Baltimore through York and Lurgan, Pennsylvania, and from Baltimore through Hagerstown, Maryland, to Cumberland, Maryland. From Cumberland the system ran by separate routes to Connellsville, Pennsylvania, and to Elkins, Virginia.

Seaboard Coast Line Industries (SCLI), on the other hand, operated 16,638 miles through thirteen southeastern states. The system's principal lines extended from

Richmond, Virginia, to Jacksonville, Orlando, Tampa, and Miami, Florida, through Rocky Mount, North Carolina, Florence and Charleston, South Carolina, and Savannah and Waycross, Georgia. Other lines extended from Richmond, Virginia, to Atlanta, Georgia, and Birmingham, Alabama via Petersburg, Virginia, Raleigh and Hamlet, North Carolina, and Greenwood, South Carolina.

Principal lines connected Atlanta and Birmingham with Florida points through Manchester and Waycross, Georgia, and from Montgomery, Alabama, by way of Thomasville and Waycross, Georgia. Additionally, SCL owned principal lines stretching from Jacksonville to Tallahassee and Chattahoochee, Florida, via Baldwin, Florida. Included were the principal lines of the Louisville & Nashville, an SCLI subsidiary, which served the states of Kentucky, Tennessee, Illinois, and Virginia.

Overall, the end-to-end combination was expected to create the "first major rail system extending from the Northeast industrial centers and many of the industrial centers of the Great Lake region to the Southeast."[44] The transaction was designed to consolidate six subsidiary carriers of the Chessie and nine subsidiaries of SCLI as well as the Richmond, Fredericksburg & Potomac, a carrier 40 percent owned by each company. This new railroad would offer for the first time single-system service over many major interregional corridors including Jacksonville-Philadelphia, Atlanta-Philadelphia, Detroit-Jacksonville, Pittsburgh-Birmingham, Toledo-Atlanta, Detroit-Savannah, and Jacksonville-Baltimore.

Because of these increases in single-system traffic flows, a variety of carriers worried about challenges to their markets. The Southern Railway was particulary nervous, pointing out that as a result of the combination there were only two carriers, Norfolk & Western and Conrail, to compete for its northbound traffic.[45] The transaction would eliminate Chessie's dependence on connections with southern systems like Southern Railway.

The Commission argued, however, that the combination was not seriously threatening to other carriers. It noted that "in no relevant market does the transaction tend to lessen competiti[on] substantially."[46] Consequenty, despite protests from the Boston & Maine, the St. Louis-San Francisco, and the Detroit, Toledo & Ironton, the Commission refused to mandate traffic conditions. Other protestors, including the Southern, Norfolk & Western, Delaware & Hudson, Florida East Coast, Grand Trunk Western, and the Commonwealth of Virginia, all came to agreements with the merger applicants.[47]

Aside from the public advantages of single-system service, the prospective unification, which would consolidate the Chessie System and Seaboard Coast Line Industries under CSX Corporation, had a number of advantages for the applicants. The end-to-end merger was expected to generate $65.9 million a year in savings and revenue gains. A unified system would provide service to twenty-two states, the District of Columbia, and Ontario, and would attract new business, expand piggyback operations, provide more efficient service to isolated regions like the Kentucky coal fields, and save 14.6 million gallons of diesel fuel annually.[48]

A greater flow of north-south traffic was also expected as a result of the transaction. Traditionally, northern carriers were not eager to develop north-south flows because interchanges reduced the share of revenue for each carrier involved in a given traffic movement. Run-throughs and particulary run-through piggyback service were expected to enhance north-south flows and entice an enormous amount of traffic away from motor carriers.

Finally, a variety of shippers supported the transaction. Among the largest were Amoco Chemicals, Bethlehem Steel, Martin Marietta, General Motors, and Coca-Cola USA. They sought the advantages of single-line service and access to new markets, and they believed the combination of the Chessie and SCLI was the key. Ultimately, the Commission concurred.

After the transaction was completed on November 1, 1980, CSXT spent the rest of the decade acquiring new systems or consolidating the ones it already controlled through stock ownership. In 1982, the company acquired three new systems, the Carolina, Clinchfield & Ohio in June; the Georgia Railroad in November; and the Louisville & Nashville in December. The Clinchfield was merged through CSX Corporation, the company's parent, and the Georgia was merged through the Seaboard Coast Line which, following the transaction, changed its name to Seaboard System Railroad.[49]

At the end of the decade, the company began rationalizing operations again. In September 1987, the company merged the Baltimore & Ohio into the Chesapeake & Ohio and then, after four months, fully merged that product into CSXT. A year later, CSXT transferred all its intermodal operations to CSX Intermodal, a newly formed subsidiary of CSX Corporation. Independent supervision of intermodal operations suggested enhanced efficiency. In 1989, CSXT merged many of its subsidiaries in an attempt further to rationalize operations. They included the Baltimore & Ohio Warehouse Company, Baltimore & Philadelphia Railroad, Chesapeake & Curtis Bay Railroad, Chessie Services, Dayton & Union Railroad, Fairmont, Morgantown & Pittsburgh Railroad, Kanawha-Ohio Corporation, Philadelphia Perishable Products Terminal, Railease, Schuylkill Improvement Land Company of Philadelphia, Toledo Lakefront Dock Company, Toledo Terminal Railroad, Western Maryland Railway, and the Western Maryland Warehouse Company.[50]

In 1990, several other railroad companies were merged into CSXT. In June, the Carolina, Clinchfield & Ohio started the process, followed by the Port Huron & Detroit and Savannah River Terminal in August. In October, the Cincinnatti, Indianapolis & Western and the Evansville Connecting Railroad joined the list of mergers followed by the Nashville & Decatur in December.

A year later, CSXT completed one of its last transactions of the period. In October 1991, the CSXT acquired the railroad operations of the Richmond, Fredericksburg & Potomac Corporation (RF&P) in return for 3.8 million nonvoting shares of RF&P stock and for assumption by the company of various RF&P liabilities.

By 1995, CSXT was one of the leading carriers in the East. Exclusive of New England the carrier served twenty states east of the Mississippi River, Ontario, and the District of Columbia with 18,645 miles of first main road, 2,925 miles of second main line, and about 10,000 miles of miscellaneous track. With 2,805 locomotives and 100,218 freight cars (owned and leased) the company provided jobs for more than 29,000 employees.[51]

NORFOLK SOUTHERN

One carrier comparable in size to CSXT by the 1990s was the Norfolk Southern (NS). Like CSXT, moreover, the NS did not exist in its modern form in 1970. In the 1970s, the Southern Railway comprised most of the system that would become Norfolk Southern.

The Southern was already engaged in horizontal expansion and rationalization when the seventies opened. In a corporate simplification effort in 1970, the company merged the Chattanooga Traction Company, the Cincinnati, Burnside & Cumberland River Railway, the Harriman & Northeastern, and the New River Railway into their parent, the Cincinnati, New Orleans & Texas Pacific (CNO&TP). Southern became sole owner of CNO&TP in a stock exchange with minority owners.[52]

In January 1971, the Southern approached the stockholders of the Tennessee, Alabama & Georgia (TAG), offering three-tenths of a share of Southern stock for each of the outstanding shares of TAG capital stock. After receiving ICC approval for this transaction in December 1970, Southern issued 90,319 shares of common stock to consummate the exchange. By January 1971, Southern had 100 percent stock control of the TAG.[53]

In June 1971, the Southern reorganized operations further. It consolidated the Central of Georgia Railway, the Georgia & Florida, Savannah & Atlanta, and the Wrightsville & Tennille into a new Central of Georgia Railroad Company. The consolidation involved 2,251 miles of line largely in Georgia with some Central of Georgia extensions into Alabama and Tennessee. Ultimately, the transaction was designed to "simplify accounting and financial reporting, eliminate the necessity of separate corporate boards of directors and officers, permit various operating and managerial economies, eliminate certain interchanges, and simplify tariff and routing provisions."[54] In December, two wholly owned subsidiaries—Live Oak, Perry & Gulf and South Georgia Railway—were merged into the Live Oak, Perry & South Georgia Railway. Also in December, the Albany Northern and the Georgia, Ashburn, Sylvester & Camilla were merged into the Georgia Northern.

The following year, the Southern started its acquisition of the Tennessee Railroad. In September, principal stock holders of the Tennessee agreed to exchange their company stock for 20,000 shares of Southern stock. The Tennessee, a 57-mile coal hauler in the eastern part of the state, had its only connection with the Cincinnati, New Orleans & Texas Pacific, a subsidiary of Southern. By the time the Southern made the stock offering, however, the Tennessee was undergoing receivership hearings. Nevertheless, on February 20, 1973, after receiving Commission and court sanction, the Southern acquired the assets of the Tennessee and consolidated the new system under a newly formed subsidiary, the Tennessee Railway.[55]

In 1974, the Southern merged old Norfolk & Southern Railway into a company subsidiary, the Carolina & Northwestern. Seven-tenths of a Southern serial preference share was exchanged for each Norfolk Southern (old) common share. In April of that same year, the company acquired 50 percent interest in the Algers, Winslow & Western.

Not until the next decade did the Southern engage in another major railroad transaction. In December 1980, the Norfolk & Western filed an application to combine its operations with the Southern railway under a newly formed holding company. The applicants explained that the recent combination of the Chessie System and the Seaboard Coast Line into the CSX created a 27,500-mile system that served the same territory as did the NW and SR. CSX had an advantage over the NW and the SR with its ability to ship freight from origin to destination on one system. As a necessary and competitive response to the creation of CSX, NW and SR believed their application deserved ICC approval.[56]

The Norfolk & Western's 7,454 miles of line served numerous markets in fifteen states.[57] Its principal lines stretched from Norfolk, Virginia; Hagerstown, Maryland; and Buffalo, New York, westward to Kansas City, Missouri; and Omaha, Nebraska. It served Detroit, Cleveland, Toledo, Akron, Columbus, and Cincinnati, Fort Wayne, Muncie, Indianapolis, Chicago, Decatur, St. Louis, and Pittsburgh. NW also offered north-south movements between Chicago and St. Louis and between the upper Midwest and western Virginia through the Shenandoah Valley.

The Southern was just as extensive, with 10,215 miles of line in thirteen states. Principal lines stretched from Alexandria, Virginia, through Atlanta and Birmingham to New Orleans, and from Cincinnati and East St. Louis, Illinois, through Chattanooga and Atlanta to Jacksonville, Florida. Southern also served Norfolk, Virginia; Charlotte, North Carolina; Columbia and Charleston, South Carolina; Savannah and Macon, Georgia; Mobile, Alabama; and Memphis, Tennessee.[58]

Besides arguing the need to provide competition for CSX, the applicants contended that an NW-SR combination would increase the South's interdistrict market avenues. During the previous forty years, the Southeast had emerged as a "significant economic force" in the nation, having become the largest supplier of textiles, furniture, pulpboard, and paperboard. As these industries grew and others emerged, the applicants argued, the Southeast would require increased capabilities to ship its products outside the South.[59] The applicants noted that the end-to-end merger would combine NW's coverage of the northeastern and midwestern markets with SR's access to most southern markets while diverting no more than $22 million worth of traffic annually from other transportation companies, most of which were motor carriers. The fact that each carrier was already involved in more than 75 percent of its co-applicant's traffic ensured less than dramatic changes following the merger.

Officials of the NW and SR also projected a total annual savings of $95 million with the combination after the third year. These savings would result from the elimination of circuitous routes and fuel savings. Route rationalization would generate a savings of 1.45 billion ton-miles, and fuel savings would amount to 5 million gallons annually.[60]

Managers further argued that the new system would expand the rail transportation network through the creation of five new routes. One route, through Altavista, Virginia, would increase service between points in eastern and central Virginia and North Carolina and points in the Midwest. A new Lynchburg-Knoxville Cutoff Route would shorten the present route between Potomac Yard in Alexandria, Virginia, and points north and east of Roanoke and between southern points in eastern Tennessee and NW stations west of Roanoke. A new Shenandoah Corridor would improve traffic flows to the Northeast, bypassing congestion north of Potomac Yard where carriers like Southern and CSX routed north-south flows. A Mid-South Corridor would connect Norfolk & Western points in the Midwest with Southern-served points in the Southeast. Finally, a merger would allow the NW, the only eastern carrier connecting Kansas City with single-line service to Virginia and North Carolina, to connect other points in the Southeast with single-line service to Kansas City.[61]

In addition to the new routes, new single-system transportation would be created elsewhere. Single-line service would be provided to midwestern and northeastern points like Chicago, Cleveland, Detroit, and Buffalo. Southeastern cities like Atlanta, Birmingham, Chattanooga, and Jacksonville would also reap the benefits of single-system service.[62]

On June 1, 1982, after receiving ICC sanction, the Norfolk & Western and the Southern merged into the newly formed holding company, Norfolk Southern Corporation. Under the agreement, each share of NW common stock was converted into one share of Norfolk Southern common stock, and each share of Southern common stock was converted into 1.9 shares of Norfolk Southern common stock. The result was that Norfolk Southern Corporation attained 100 percent voting control of NW and 93.9 percent voting control of the Southern.[63]

While the Norfolk Western/Southern combination was still being reviewed, the NW closed another transaction. In 1981, NW purchased the Illinois Terminal (IT). The 420-mile Class II carrier served many of the same points as the NW in Illinois and Missouri. However, the IT was struggling financially, having lost more than $4.5 million in operations during the previous two years.[64] The transaction was significant in that it represented the first time that the Commission, acting under the "competitive impact" standard included in the Staggers Rail Act, approved a combination that did not involve two or more Class I carriers. According to the law, the NW-IT union was exempt from Commission review. Such was also the case for Norfolk Southern's acquisition of the Kentucky & Indiana Terminal which came in December of the same year.

The NS continued to expand in this manner in the late 1980s and early 1990s. In 1987, through its subsidiary, Southern Railway, the NS purchased a 200-mile line between Haleyville, Alabama, and Fulton, Kentucky, from the Illinois Central Gulf for $38 million. In June 1988, a subsidiary, Carolina & Northwestern, was fully merged. In September, Norfolk Southern's other major rail subsidiary, Norfolk & Western, rationalized its operations by merging its subsidiary, the Wheeling & Lake Erie Railway (W&LE). W&LE stockholders received $110 in cash for each share of W&LE common stock, bringing the aggregate payment to $4.1 million. As a result, W&LE, formerly leased by its parent, became fully owned by NW.[65]

A year later, Norfolk Southern was still making acquisitions and reorganizing what it already owned. In November 1990, NS acquired the assets of the Ohio River Terminal from Kentucky-Ohio Transportation through its subsidiary, Southern Railway. In December of the same year, the company transferred its common stock of the Norfolk & Western Railway to the Southern Railway, and the name of the latter was changed to Norfolk Southern Railway. As a result, the Southern (now the Norfolk Southern) held 100 percent voting control of the NW.

Further rationalization of the NW came in November 1991. At that time, the Wabash Railroad was fully merged into its parent company, Norfolk & Western. Under the terms of the agreement, Wabash stockholders, with the exception of the NW, received $75 in cash plus $3.90 for each share of Wabash preferred stock and $649.97 in cash for each share of Wabash common stock. The aggregate cost of the transaction was $8.9 million. Prior to the exchange, the Wabash was a leased company. As a result of this transaction, the Wabash became a wholly owned subsidiary of NW.[66]

By 1995, the Norfolk Southern Railway had developed into one of the leading railroads of the Southeast and Midwest, operating 14,500 miles of line through twenty eastern states and with lines extending northward to Ontario, Canada. With its 2,113 locomotives, 96,298 freight cars, and 24,418 employees, the system served most of the large industrial and trading centers of the Southeast and Midwest. Those points included Atlanta, Birmingham, New Orleans, Memphis, St. Louis, Kansas City, Chicago, Detroit, Cincinnati, Buffalo, Norfolk, Charleston, Savannah, and Jacksonville. Norfolk Southern primarily carried raw materials, intermediate products, and finished goods, but the system also reached coal mines in western Virginia, eastern Kentucky, and southern West Virginia.[67]

REPERCUSSIONS

By the 1990s, Class I railroad freight operations in the East had consolidated into five super-systems. Those primarily serving the Northeast included Conrail and Grand Trunk Western. The Norfolk Southern and CSXT were the two giants that connected the northern and southern districts via the South Atlantic states. The Illinois Central served the north-south corridor in the Mississippi Valley. Together, these systems handled over nine-tenths of railroad freight traffic east of the Mississippi River.

The Class I carriers in the East were different from their predecessors of the late 1960s. These new railroads were more aligned with their respective markets, more financially stable, and more diversified than those of the past. For two decades, rail carriers had undergone enormous change. They had adapted themselves to the fluctuations in the marketplace through unifications, abandonments, and internal consolidations. During the 1970s and the 1980s, railroads in the West were undergoing a similar transition.

NOTES

1. *Illinois Central Gulf-Acquisition-Gulf, Mobile & Ohio and Illinois Central, et al.* 338 ICC 805; ICC, *Annual Report, 1972*, 9; *Railway Age* 172 (January 10, 1972), 17.

2. 338 ICC 808; *Railway Age* 173 (August 28, 1972), 60–61.

3. 338 ICC 808.

4. Ibid., 812.

5. Ibid., 813.

6. Ibid., 820; *Railway Age* 173 (August 28, 1972), 61.

7. 338 ICC 821.

8. Ibid., 874.

9. Ibid., 826–827.

10. Ibid., 831.

11. Ibid., 835.

12. Ibid., 835–836.

13. Ibid., 852–853; Richard Saunders, *Railroad Mergers and the Coming of Conrail* (Westport, Conn.: Greenwood Press, 1978), 221.

14. *Moody's Transportation Manual, 1994*, 36.

15. *Moody's Transportation Manual, 1996*, 39 .

16. *Railway Age* 170 (January 25, 1971), 67. See also *Economist* 235 (June 20, 1970), 11.

17. *Railway Age* 169 (July 27, 1970), 11; 170 (March 29, 1971), 28–31; *Business Week*, August 22, 1970, 48.

18. *Business Week*, August 22, 1970, 75; ICC, *Annual Report, 1970*, 30.

19. ICC, *Annual Report, 1970*, 30; *Business Week*, September 28, 1974, 62–64.

20. U.S. Congress, Senate, Committee on Commerce, Science and Transportation, *Sale of Conrail*, 99th Cong., 1st sess., February 27 and 28 and April 4, 1985, 1; *Omnibus Budget Reconciliation Act of 1981*. U.S. Code 95 STAT 643; *Staggers Rail Act of 1980* 94 STAT 1948.

21. U.S. Congress, *Sale of Conrail*, 1–2; *Business Week*, January 23, 1984, 43.

22. *Financial World* 155 (February 19–March 4, 1986), 50–51.

23. U.S. Congress, *Sale of Conrail*, 8; *Business Week*, July 2, 1984, 31–32; *Fortune* 110 (July 23, 1984), 95.

24. U.S. Congress, *Sale of Conrail*, 8.

25. Ibid., 9.

26. Ibid., 10.

27. Ibid., 3.

28. *Industry Week* 224 (March 18, 1985), 18–19; *Fortune* 110 (July 23, 1984), 95.

29. *Fortune* 115 (March 30, 1987), 9.

30. U.S. Congress, *Sale of Conrail*, 103–104.

31. Ibid., 107.

32. *Omnibus Budget Reconciliation Act of 1986*, 100 STAT 4012; *U.S. News & World Report* 101 (November 10, 1986), 64.

33. *Fortune* 115 (May 25, 1987), 91–92. See also *Barron's* 67 (February 23, 1987), 18; 66 (September 8, 1986), 26; *Business Week*, October 27, 1986, 42–43.

34. *Moody's Transportation Manual, 1994*, 416.

35. Ibid.

36. Ibid.

37. *Moody's Transportation Manual, 1996*, 417.

38. Finance Docket No. 28499 (Sub-No. 1), *Norfolk & Western and Baltimore & Ohio-Control-Detroit, Toledo & Ironton,* application, October 21, 1977, 1.

39. Ibid., 39–40; *Railway Age* 181 (June 30, 1980), 42.

40. Finance Docket No. 28676, *Grand Trunk Western-control-Detroit, Toledo & Ironton,* vol. 1, application, February 16, 1978, 14; *Railway Age* 179 (March 13, 1978), 10; 181 (June 30, 1980), 38–39.

41. Finance Docket No. 28676, 15.

42. *Railway Age* 179 (March 13, 1978), 10.

43. Finance Docket No. 28676, 17.

44. *CSX Corporation-Control-Chessie System and Seaboard Coast Line Industries* 363 ICC 533.

45. *Business Week*, December 4, 1978, 28.

46. *CSX Corporation-Control-Chessie System and Seaboard Coast Line Industries* 363 ICC 565.

47. Ibid., 579.

48. Ibid., 554–556.

49. *Moody's Transportation Manual, 1994,* 422.

50. Ibid.

51. *Moody's Transportation Manual, 1996,* 424.

52. Ibid., 86.

53. Ibid.

54. *Central of Georgia, Georgia & Florida, Savannah & Atlanta-Consolidation-Central of Georgia* 338 ICC 358.

55. Ibid.

56. Finance Docket No. 29430 (Sub-No. 1), *NWS Enterprises, Inc.-Control-Norfolk & Western Railway and Southern Railway,* vol. 1, application, December 4, 1980, 7.

57. Ibid., application, vol. 2 and 2A, 18, 20.

58. *Norfolk Southern Corporation-Control-Norfolk & Western Railway and Southern Railway* 366 ICC 179.

59. Finance Docket No. 29430 (Sub-No. 1), *NWS Enterprises, Inc.-Control-Norfolk & Western Railway and Southern Railway,* application, vol. 1, 3.

60. Ibid., 15, 20.

61. *Norfolk Southern Corporation-Control-Norfolk & Western Railway and Southern Railway* 366 ICC 196.

62. Ibid., 195.

63. *Moody's Transportation Manual, 1994,* 73.

64. *Norfolk & Western-Purchase-Illinois Terminal* 363 ICC 884–885.

65. *Moody's Transportation Manual, 1994,* 100–101.

66. Ibid., 73.

67. *Moody's Transportation Manual, 1996,* 90.

7

Mastodons of the West

Between 1970 and 1995, western carriers, like those in the eastern district, consolidated in dramatic fashion. When the 1970s opened, some twenty-seven Class I carriers served the United States west of the Mississippi River. By 1995, after reclassification, bankruptcy, and consolidation, that number had already decreased to eight. In the northern tier of states the carriers that survived included the Burlington Northern, the Chicago & North Western, and the Soo Line. In the central corridor were the Union Pacific and the Denver & Rio Grande Western. The Kansas City Southern ran north to south just west of the Mississippi and Missouri rivers, and the Atchison, Topeka & Santa Fe and the Southern Pacific Transportation dominated the Southwest.

BURLINGTON NORTHERN

Juxtaposed to the collapse of Penn Central in the Northeast was the merger of the Great Northern Railway, the Northern Pacific Railway, and the Chicago, Burlington & Quincy in the West.[1] The Supreme Court's 7-0 decision on February 2, 1970, in favor of the combination represented the end of a campaign that first began almost eighty years earlier. In 1893 the court denied the unification on the grounds that merging two parallel systems, Great Northern and Northern Pacific, would violate a Minnesota statute outlawing the combination of competitive parallel railroads. Two subsequent attempts to merge the lines failed on the same grounds. In 1960, the Northern Lines tried again.

This fourth application for merger was successful, but it took ten years. After the ICC rejected the application in 1966, the applicants resubmitted it in 1967 with stipulations that protected the Chicago, Milwaukee, St. Paul & Pacific Railroad, a system that expected to be affected drastically. Thereupon, the ICC approved the transaction, only to have its decision appealed to a district court by the U.S. Department of Justice and several stockholders groups in early 1967. Those making the appeal claimed that the combination created a monopoly. A subsequent hearing finally brought the case to the Supreme Court.[2]

The operations of the northern lines were extensive. At the time of application, the Great Northern owned 8,277 miles of road. Its main line served ten states and two Canadian provinces and extended from Duluth and St. Paul, Minnesota, westward to Portland, Oregon, and Seattle, Washington. The Northern Pacific, which generally paralleled the Great Northern, operated 6,800 miles of road. Its principal main line, which traversed seven states and the Canadian Province of Manitoba, extended from St. Paul, Minnesota, to Portland, Oregon. The Burlington operated 8,648 miles of road. Its principal lines spanned eleven states, branching out from Chicago to the west and the southwest to form an extensive network in the Middle West. For nearly sixty years, the Great Northern and the Northern Pacific jointly owned the Burlington. All three systems hauled significant amounts of forest, agricultural, and mineral products.[3]

Although the three carriers were financially strong, their spokesmen argued that unification would generate numerous benefits to the companies and to shippers. The combination would facilitate a more efficient utilization of equipment, eliminate duplicate facilities at common points, and provide faster transportation over more direct routes. More expeditious service, along with better loading and unloading privileges, improved claims service, and the consolidation of yards, repair centers, and train services, meant higher quality service at lower rates for shippers. In addition, the applicants estimated that the transaction would allow each carrier to reduce its labor force, thereby saving the companies nearly $32 million annually.[4]

In addition to the benefits to shippers and to the merging carriers, the transaction also promised enormous gains for the Chicago, Milwaukee, Saint Paul & Pacific (Milwaukee). Under previous practices, traffic acquired by the Milwaukee east of the Twin Cities and bound for the West Coast had to be surrendered to the northern lines in Milwaukee or St. Paul. The Milwaukee feared that after merger, the Northern Lines could suspend transfers from the Milwaukee, crippling its east-west traffic flows. Stipulations in the merger agreement, however, protected the Milwaukee and gave it access to eleven western gateways. In addition, the Milwaukee's access to Longview Junction, Oregon, was extended another forty-seven miles to Portland, giving the railroad a connection to the north-south traffic of the Southern Pacific and the Spokane, Portland & Seattle. The extension into Portland also connected the Milwaukee to Canadian roads while providing it with greater transcontinental strength against the Union Pacific.

As the Milwaukee joined in support of the northern lines unification, others warned the Commission of the detriments of a union. The U.S. Department of Justice, the Railway Labor Executives Association, and the U.S. Department of Agriculture, among others, opposed the merger. They were concerned about adequate service to agricultural regions, geographical monopolization, and the 5,172 jobs the ICC examiner claimed would be lost from the transaction.[5]

Despite these concerns, however, the Commission approved the combination in a decision that would later receive the sanction of the Supreme Court. In the 1967 hearing, the ICC found that competition from other modes was more threatening to the railroad industry than was previously thought. Moreover, the Commission began to view the application more in light of the Transportation Act of 1940 which promoted consolidation. The ICC noted that "as a factor in determining the propriety of [railroad mergers] the preservation of competition among carriers, although still a value, is significant chiefly as it aids the attainment of the objective of the national transportation policy."[6] The Commission began to see the northern lines merger as fulfilling the objectives of that policy.

The combination of the northern lines created the largest railroad in the nation, combining the operation of four subsidiary railroads along with the "big three." The subsidiary lines included the Spokane, Portland & Seattle (922 miles), the Fort Worth

& Denver (1,279 miles), the Colorado & Southern (709 miles), and the Pacific Coast Railroad (32 miles). The entire system spanned 27,000 miles from the Mississippi River and the Great Lakes, through the northern tier of states, then south to California. Through affiliates the network extended to the Gulf of Mexico.

After its birth in 1970, the Burlington Northern wasted little time before seeking to expand its operations. On December 28, 1977, the Burlington Northern and the St. Louis-San Francisco (Frisco) filed a joint application with the ICC to join their operations in an end-to-end merger. The Frisco operated 4,530 miles of line through Kansas, Oklahoma, Texas, Arkansas, Missouri, Tennessee, Mississippi, Alabama, and Florida.

According to the BN, the positive effects of the combination included "reduced handling of cars; the handling of more efficiently sized trains, heavier and more efficient utilization of principal routes; [and] elimination of need for interchange between the two carriers at both St. Louis and Kansas City."[7] The BN claimed that the efficiency of single-line service between southern cities like Birmingham and Mobile and western cities like Portland and Seattle would save $32 million annually after the third year of the merger.[8] Additionally, 183,590 cars would be available for the longer hauls, translating into $66 million in added gross revenue.[9] Mileage reductions would also facilitate more rapid service. For example, a shipment originating in North Dakota bound for a point in Oklahoma previously might have been routed by BN through St. Louis. There the shipment would have been transferred to the Frisco for movement to Oklahoma. A merger would allow a direct shipment. Considering that the end-to-end combination meant little employee displacement and few line abandonments, the applicants expected a favorable ICC decision.[10]

They were not disappointed. In 1979, the ICC approved the Burlington-Frisco application. Despite a year of investigation and the request of fourteen different carriers seeking assurances against traffic diversions, the regulatory agency found the combination to be in the public interest.

Shortly after seeking to combine with the Frisco, the BN submitted an application to acquire for $3.4 million the Green Bay & Western , a small Class I system running from Kewaunee, Wisconsin, westward to Winona, Minnesota. The GB&W operated 250 miles of main line and serviced five major paper manufacturing companies in the region.[11] The BN had a strong interest in the GB&W because of its significant shipments to and from industries in central Wisconsin via GB&W lines. The BN also "encouraged use of GB&W as a bridge in connection with movement of transcontinental traffic via Lake Michigan car ferries."[12]

The request to merge the GB&W stemmed from BN's concern that the Wisconsin carrier might not be able to sustain itself in the long term. The BN feared that low traffic levels on ferry routes limited the GB&W's ability to grow with an expanding industry, a circumstance that could lead to the BN's loss of market access via the land routes of the GB&W.

More than a year after the BN submitted its application, three other railroads submitted a joint application to acquire the GB&W. They were the Soo Line, the Milwaukee, and the North Western Transportation Company. These railroads sought ICC authorization to purchase the GB&W for $4 million, an amount significantly greater than that offered by the BN. The new applicants, however, were interested in the GB&W for entirely different reasons. Executive officers of the Soo Line, the Milwaukee, and the North Western Transportation Company readily admitted that the offer was designed specifically "to avoid traffic losses which would occur if Burlington Northern acquired control of the Green Bay & Western."[13] If they received ICC sanction, they intended to eliminate 146 miles of GB&W line and recover some of the purchasing costs by selling the railroad's real estate. Rail officials of the three carriers also promised to promote the "disposition of materials through abandonment of lines,"[14] while they utilized the remaining GB&W operation to help conserve fuel and reduce the operating costs of their own systems. In order to avoid ICC concern over employee displacement, however, the three roads agreed to find jobs for contract employees elsewhere in their systems.

As proceedings dragged through 1977, the ICC considered the requests of the carriers that wanted inclusion in a GB&W settlement. At that point, the BN withdrew its proposal in disgust over what it called "a classic case of regulatory lag." BN's executive vice president, Thomas J. Lamphier, objected to the way the BN was being portrayed in the proceedings. He emphasized that BN-GB&W interchanges accounted for 31 percent and 45 percent of all GB&W land and ferry route traffic, respectively. He added that the large size of BN in comparison to other carriers in the region should not be the determining factor when considering a BN-GB&W union. Instead, he believed focus should be placed on the service improvements that a BN-GB&W merger would afford.[15]

With the BN out of the way, additional companies offered to purchase the GB&W. The Itel Corporation and Brace Corporation, two multifaceted conglomerates, were prospective buyers. However, Brace rescinded its offer in March 1978, and Itel was permitted to pick up the road. The joint application of the Milwaukee, North Western,and Soo Line was denied.

Itel was a huge corporation whose operating revenues amounted to $400 million.[16] Incorporated in 1967, the company specialized in providing financial services to the rail industry. Itel brought together parties whose interest lay in leasing rail equipment to rail carriers. The company focused on leasing freight cars and piggyback trailers.[17] The parent of sixty-eight corporations, two-thirds of which were enterprises outside the United States, Itel had some knowledge of rail operation. It owned three short lines—Hartford & Slocomb, the McCloud, and the Ahnapee & Western. With no plans to alter the Green Bay & Western after the combination, Itel viewed the merger with the Wisconsin-based system as an opportunity to solicit additional customers desiring to lease freight cars. Itel believed its leasing business would directly benefit the GB&W, which would obtain large sums of capital and equipment from Itel. The ICC agreed.

Despite its loss of the GB&W to Itel, Burlington Northern was still among the largest carriers in the West. By 1995, the system maintained 30,600 employees and used 2,574 locomotives and 67,421 freight cars to transport freight across 24,400 miles of line. This railroad giant connected points from Vancouver and Seattle in the Northwest to Pensacola, Florida, in the Southeast.[18]

CHICAGO & NORTH WESTERN

About the same time the BN was forming from the combination of the northern lines, the Chicago & North Western was transforming into a different system. The Chicago & North Western Transportation Company was incorporated in 1970 as the North Western Employees' Transportation Company (NETCO). It was established to begin the purchase of the assets of the Chicago & North Western Railway. At that time, Larry S. Provo, president of the C&NW, led 14,000 of the carrier's employees in purchasing the system from its parent, Northwest Industries. The holding company wanted to pull out of the railroad business, but the company's employees wanted to maintain operations and preserve their jobs.

Although the C&NW was a relatively large Class I system, it was in poor financial condition. The carrier operated 11,300 miles of roadway through eleven midwestern states and served such major industrial centers as Chicago, the Twin Cities, Milwaukee, Omaha, Kansas City, and St. Louis. Unfortunately, the system was not profitable. In 1969 alone, it lost nearly $15 million, adding to the belief of Northwest Industries that the C&NW was a poor investment.

One of the biggest problems of the rail carrier was that it was overextended. The company had undertaken an extensive program of line abandonment in an attempt to eliminate unprofitable line segments, but strong opposition had delayed these efforts. In an effort to preserve jobs and service to individual shippers, the Commission often forced the company to maintain operations over unprofitable or marginal routes. Nevertheless, after the North West Employees' Transportation Company assumed control of the system, its officials continued to send abandonment applications to the ICC. As Provo pointed out, "There's no way this industry can reach its full potential if it's required to always be innovative and creative and come up with new services, new equipment, and so on, while at the same time its got to hang on to the obsolete and then pay for the obsolete with the benefits gained from the new."

Ultimately, the employees paid a large sum for the railroad. According to the purchase agreement, NETCO was required to pay $19 million in cash over a twenty-year span to Northwest Industries. In addition, it had to assume the system's publicly held debt of $401 million.

As the details of the NETCO purchase were being worked out, the transaction put an end to another long-pending proposal of the Chicago & North Western Railroad, the purchase of the Chicago, Rock Island & Pacific. The C&NW, lacking a parent company, no longer had the resources to purchase the other midwestern system.

The Rock Island (RI) was a large railroad. Its 7,000 miles of line ran through fourteen states and reached Chicago and the Mississippi River, the Rocky Mountains, the Texas Gulf Coast in the South, and Minnesota in the North.[19] The system had important connections with the Southern Pacific and operated other lines connected with the Fort Worth & Denver. Having reported an operating loss for every year since 1967 and a net loss for every year since 1965, the Rock Island was in poor financial and physical shape. The Rock Island "had been forced to defer maintenance, had difficulties in acquiring adequate modern equipment, and its service had accordingly deteriorated."[20]

During the 1960s, two sets of partners, the Chicago & North Western and the Atchison, Topeka & Santa Fe on one side and the Union Pacific and the Southern Pacific on the other, vied for a piece of the Rock Island. In July 1963, the Chicago & North Western sought control of the Rock Island by purchasing its capital stock. By obtaining the Rock Island, the C&NW could increase its traffic base in the hopes of becoming profitable.

While the Chicago & North Western's application was under review, the Santa Fe submitted an application in December 1965 in an effort to preclude negative repercussions from a possible C&NW-RI union. The Santa Fe asked that, if C&NW's requests were granted, it be permitted to purchase all of the Rock Island's lines south of Salina and Herington, Kansas, and Rock Island's interest in a dozen bridge and terminal companies. The Santa Fe also wanted to gain limited operating rights with the Rock Island Motor Transit Company and to hold trackage rights on the Rock Island line between Kansas City and St. Louis, Missouri.

The Santa Fe, one of the four largest western systems, extended into twelve midwestern states with 12,000 miles of track. Although it provided single-line service betweeen major Texas points and western cities, it lacked direct access to Mississippi gateways like St. Louis, Memphis, and New Orleans.[21]

In 1964, a year after the C&NW's proposal, the Union Pacific submitted its application to acquire the Rock Island. The Union Pacific operated over 9,000 miles of track in thirteen states and was considered the primary carrier in the territory between Chicago, St. Louis, and San Francisco known as the central corridor. Despite its centrality to the region, UP still depended on bridge carriers to move goods from western terminals to destinations outside its serving area. The UP sought to eliminate this dependence.

In April 1965, Southern Pacific submitted an application asking that if the UP-RI merger went through, it be allowed to buy from UP most of the Rock Island's lines south of Kansas City, Missouri, for $120 million.[22] Southern Pacific, with over 12,000 miles of track, provided single-line service from Mississippi River gateways to destinations in New Mexico, Arizona, and California. Nevertheless, the needs of Southern Pacific customers and competition with the Santa Fe required extension into additional markets.

Like the Southern Pacific, the Denver & Rio Grande Western also had a request provided the UP-RI unification was approved. In November 1973, the Rio Grande submitted its application to purchase from the Union Pacific all Rock Island lines between Denver and Colorado Springs on the west and between Omaha, Nebraska, and Kansas City, Missouri, on the east. The Denver & Rio Grande Western was a financially healthy carrier operating 1,800 miles of line in Colorado and Utah, the only carrier competing successfully with the Union Pacific in the central corridor. The Rio Grande also provided Union Pacific with transcontinental connections from eastern points to Salt Lake City gateways.[23] The system's managers worried, however, that if applications of the UP, SP, or SF were approved, those carriers might practice wage or route discrimination against DRGW. Officials of the DRGW wanted the ICC to safeguard their traffic.

Essentially, all the carriers involved were concerned with market access. Among those carriers already mentioned, the Burlington Northern, the Milwaukee, the Western Pacific, and the Kansas City Southern also wanted conditions to protect their markets. The interests of these carriers were like those of the C&NW, which worried that concessions to other systems, including relief to the Kansas City Southern, would cost C&NW important bridge traffic.

In 1972, the Chicago & North Western's hopes to obtain control of the Rock Island were smashed when Northwest Industries, parent of C&NW, relinquished financial and operational control of the railroad. The carrier suffered financial losses from 1965 to 1970 averaging $11.2 million per year, a drain on its parent. Northwest Industries wanted the responsibility no longer. The ICC did not object, for Commission administrators believed that a C&NW operating independently might be better than one operated by a disinterested and diversified giant whose "sole interests are admittedly toward making more attractive investments."[24] This transaction ruined the C&NW's chances to obtain the Rock Island.

Meanwhile, in order to close the Rock Island case, the ICC's administrative law judge, Nathan Klitenic, reasoned that all western carriers must be consolidated.[25] Rock Island's interaction with so many systems was too complex to unravel in a judicious manner, so he drew up a plan that did not attempt such an impossible task. According to Klitenic, the West should be served by four systems—Burlington Northern, Santa Fe, Union Pacific, and Southern Pacific. Each of these systems would serve two midwestern gateways, including St. Louis, Chicago, Memphis, and New Orleans. The northern, central, and southern corridors each would have two competitors.

Unfortunately, the plan did not gain the enthusiasm of the industry.[26] All parties found some fault with the judge's idea. Reminiscent of those who formulated proposals in the 1920s and 1930s, Klitenic failed to recall an important lesson of the past—the railroads would not be forcibly consolidated.

Meanwhile, the remaining application for acquisition of the Rock Island was recalled. The Union Pacific, wearied by the whole affair, withdrew its application, thereby making moot the applications of the Southern Pacific and the Denver & Rio Grande. By March 17, 1975, the Rock Island, still independent, slipped into bankruptcy.

Ultimately, the Rock Island failed because the ICC prevented the carrier's officials from acquiring access to capital or markets. For more than a decade Rock Island officials sought a remedy for the system's financial problems through a combination with another major railroad. For all that time the Commission prevented such a merger. Meanwhile, the federal government was unwilling to capitalize the system or permit substantial trimming of unprofitable segments necessary for continued operation. The Rock Island's fate was sealed.

While the Rock Island faced a certain end, the Chicago & North Western struggled to maintain its own solvency. Without a powerful holding company to ensure access to capital and unable to expand its markets through the acquisition of the Rock Island, the C&NW remained a marginal agricultural carrier over the next decade with after-tax earnings below $50 million per year.

In 1984, however, the C&NW's president, Jim Wolfe, completed a $300 million coal project. Originally started in 1976, the project was a joint venture with

Burlington Northern for the construction of a 103-mile rail line into the Powder River Basin, the nation's largest low-sulfur coal reserve, in eastern Wyoming. Although C&NW quit the project in 1979 because of a cash shortage, the company won a 1983 court battle with Burlington Northern and reaquired half interest in the coal line for $76 milllion.[27]

In order to help finance this project, C&NW secured an agreement with Union Pacific Corporation. In return for financial support, the C&NW agreed to allow the Union Pacific Railroad to participate in east-west shipments of coal through Nebraska.

As a result of its access to the Powder River Basin, the C&NW was able to exploit a market of enormous potential. A year before the line was completed, Jim Wolfe had already sealed an eleven-million-ton-per-year contract with Arkansas Power & Light. In 1984, C&NW's president was negotiating contracts for another eighteen million tons per year. By 1988, the C&NW was moving about thirty-five million tons of coal annually.[28]

The Powder River Basin line along with growing movements of intermodal traffic helped change the prospects of C&NW. Instead of remaining a marginal agricultural carrier, the railroad became a more diversified system with the potential to grow. In the meantime, C&NW officials focused their efforts on rationalizing the system they already operated.

The Chicago & North Western did not expand its operations over the next decade through the acquisition of other companies. On May 22, 1986, the company acquired a snowplow manufacturer at a cost of $53.7 million, only to sell it two years later to Park-Kenilworth Industries, Inc., for $100 million. In July 1992, the C&NW sold its 98-mile rail line between Superior and Cameron, Wisconsin, to Wisconsin Central Limited for $5.8 million. Aside from these two transactions, the C&NW remained inactive.

Nevertheless, by the early 1990s the Chicago & North Western was a prospering midwestern Class I freight carrier operating 5,388 miles of railroad through nine states. Although the system owed its prosperity to its access to coal reserves in Wyoming and Nebraska, C&NW's east-west span between Chicago and Omaha continued to provide an important bridge between the Union Pacific railroad and lines of major northeastern carriers.[29]

SOO LINE

The Soo Line was another rail carrier that survived the merger craze that consolidated Class I railroads. Like the C&NW, moreover, the Soo endured while engaging in little horizontal expansion. Originally incorporated in 1949 as the Duluth, South Shore & Atlantic, the Soo was controlled by a foreign system, the Canadian Pacific, one of the largest carriers in North America.

In February 1985, the Soo made its single most important acquisition. The midwestern line acquired the assets of the Milwaukee, St. Paul & Pacific (Milwaukee) through the parent company, Soo Line Corporation.[30] Aside from its acquisition of the Minneapolis, Northfield & Southern in June 1982, the acquisition of the Milwaukee represented its most important transaction since 1970. Considering that the

Milwaukee operated over 10,000 miles of road through the Midwest and the northern tier of states, the transaction also represented the Soo's largest acquisition.

The Soo Line's control of the Milwaukee was the result of a complex turn of events stemming back to the late 1970s. On December 19, 1977, the Chicago, Milwaukee, St. Paul & Pacific (Milwaukee) filed a reorganization petition pursuant to Section 77 of the Bankruptcy Act. Subsequently, a trustee took charge, and several parties made proposals to the Commission as to how best to deal with the weakened carrier.[31] In 1979, the trustee proposed reorganization of the railroad around a 3,900-mile core, selling the remainder to pay off the system's debt. Meanwhile, a coalition of Milwaukee employees and shippers, known as the New Milwaukee Lines, submitted a reorganization plan of their own that did not reduce the Milwaukee so drastically. The Chicago Milwaukee Corporation, the holding company which owned the Milwaukee, filed a third plan that proposed liquidating the railroad entirely.

Initially, the ICC rejected all three proposals. The Commission argued that the trustee plan and the suggestion made by the employees and shippers coalition would not create a viable railroad and give fair and equitable treatment to the Milwaukee estate.[32] Moreover, the Commission rejected the Chicago Milwaukee Corporation's call for liquidation claiming that the move "would blindly dismantle the Milwaukee system with no more than passing consideration for continued service."[33]

Shortly thereafter, however, the Commission approved a modified plan of the trustee to begin disposing of Milwaukee lines outside a core system. Pursuant to the stipulations outlined in the Milwaukee Road Restructuring Act of 1979, officials abandoned nearly 7,000 miles of lines. Concomitantly, the trustee maintained operation of the 3,900 miles of the core system.

Meanwhile, in October 1981, negotiations opened between Grand Trunk Corporation (GTC) and the Milwaukee. The GTC was a holding company of the Canadian National designed to oversee operations of CN's three railroad systems in the United States—Grand Trunk Western; Duluth, Winnipeg & Pacific; and the Central of Vermont. Both the GTC and Milwaukee signed a letter of intent to have the former purchase stock control of the latter, and both parties signed a Voluntary Coordination Agreement to begin adjusting operations. The Milwaukee's plan to consumate this action was filed on March 31, 1983.

Shortly thereafter, however, three alternative proposals came before the Commission. Once again, the Soo Line and the Chicago & North Western submitted applications. Both wanted to acquire the Milwaukee. The Chicago Milwaukee Corporation submitted a third application. Although it previously proposed liquidating the Milwaukee, the Chicago Milwaukee Corporation's new plan called for the reorganization of the carrier as an independent system.

At the time applications were submitted to the Commission, the Milwaukee was a 3,100 mile system operating through the states of South Dakota, Minnesota, Iowa, Wisconsin, Michigan, Illinois, Indiana, Kentucky, Missouri, and Kansas. Its principal routes extended from Chicago and Milwaukee throughout northern Michigan, Chicago and Milwaukee to Minneapolis-St. Paul, Chicago to Omaha and Kansas City, and from Minneapolis-St. Paul to Washington and Oregon. The system carried mainly food products, pulp and paper goods, and coal.[34]

The railroads seeking to acquire the Milwaukee varied in size. The Grand Trunk Corporation (GTC) was a huge holding company earning more than $354 million in 1983. The corporation owned the 1,514-mile Grand Trunk Western and the 170-mile Duluth, Winnipeg & Pacific. The C&NW owned more rail, however, with 7,900 miles through some eleven midwestern states; and the Soo Line operated 4,438 miles through seven states.

The Commission ultimately rejected the proposals of the GTC and the C&NW. The GTC failed to make an adequate offering for the Milwaukee's core assets. Although the GTC agreed to assume $160 million in current liabilities and $250 million in long-term liabilities, the company would offer no more than $80 million for the Milwaukee's core assets. As far as the Commission was concerned, that amount was insufficient.

The C&NW proposal, on the other hand, was considered to be destructive of competition. The C&NW and the Milwaukee were largely parallel systems serving seventy-eight common points and competing in eight major corridors in a five-state area. A C&NW-Milwaukee combination expected to give the new system more than 70 percent of the total rail tonnage running in four corridors—Chicago-Milwaukee, Chicago-Green Bay, Duluth/Superior-Kansas City, and Twin Cities-Kansas City.[35] The Commission believed such control was excessive.

The Soo Line offer, however, won ICC favor. The system offered $150.2 million for the Milwaukee's core assets, a bid far exceeding the offer made by C&NW. Second, new single-line service would give Soo shippers direct access to Kansas City and Louisville gateways. The combination would also create a direct link between Kansas City and international gateways at Portal, North Dakota; Noyes, Minnesota; and Sault Ste. Marie, Michigan, thereby benefiting Canadian shippers and creating competition with the gateway at Duluth. In addition, the Soo expected to provide extended hauling capabilities for grain shippers in North Dakota and Minnesota. The Commission estimated that benefits to the system as a result of the combination would amount to $800,000.[36] Because of such advantages the ICC approved the Soo Line offer on September 12, 1984.

After the Milwaukee acquisition, the Soo Line did not expand much more. Most of its subsequent transactions were sales to other systems. In April 1987, it sold its Lake States Division to the Wisconsin Central. The transaction consisted of 1,800 miles of line in Wisconsin, northern Michigan, northern Illinois, and eastern Minnesota which sold for a price of $133 million. In December 1991, the Soo Line sold a 102-mile segment extending from Superior to Ladysmith, Wisconsin, to the Wisconsin Central for $15.8 million, and in July 1992, the company sold 145 miles of line connecting Hopkins and Appleton, Minnesota, and joining those points to the Twin cities. In the latter transaction, the Western Railroad bought the line for $10.4 million.[37]

By 1995, the Soo Line continued to be an important carrier in the Midwest. The system operated more than 5,062 miles of line through eleven states between eastern Montana and Detroit, Michigan, and south to Louisville, Kentucky, and Kansas City, Missouri.[38]

UNION PACIFIC

Unlike the Soo Line or the C&NW, the Union Pacific engaged in extensive horizontal expansion between 1970 and 1994. By the end of the period, the Union Pacific was a drastically different system. In 1969, the railroad formed a parent company, the Union Pacific Corporation. A year later, the system acquired the Champlin Petroleum Company and Pontiac Refining Company in Fort Worth, Texas, for $240 million, and in 1978 UP, in a joint transaction with the Southern Pacific, purchased the assets of the Pacific Fruit Express Company. In 1980 the company expanded its rail network by purchasing approximately 100 miles of line in Washington and Idaho from the Chicago, Milwaukee, St. Paul & Pacific for $19 million. Finally, in 1982, the UP, through its parent, made its single largest railroad transaction. At that time, the UP acquired the Missouri Pacific Corporation and its wholly owned railroad subsidiary.[39]

The Missouri Pacific (Mopac) operated a large network throughout the Midwest and was itself engaging in a variety of transactions before combining with the Union Pacific. The first was a corporate simplification rather than a merger. In a joint application filed on November 1, 1974, the Texas & Pacific and the Chicago & Eastern Illinois asked to be merged into their parent, the Missouri Pacific. The administrative law judge argued the transaction "would permit further simplification of the corporate structure and the accounting and reporting requirements of applicant railroads, it would improve transportation and related service to communities and shippers served by them, and it would produce a more economical and efficient utilization of plant and equipment."[40]

Despite Rock Island's objections that the merger would divert $4 million in traffic from other carriers, the Commission noted that "since applicants are presently part of a coordinated system, common ownership will have no material adverse effect on other railroads." Savings from the transactions would come "from the elimination of separate financial and administrative records and the reduction in the number of reports required by various federal and state agencies."[41] The saving to accounting departments alone was projected to exceed $440,000 annually.

In April 1975, the Missouri Pacific made headlines with the announcement that it was considering a combination with the Southern Railway. Talks began between the carriers' executives but they filed no application with the Commission. Rumors that the combination was imminent generated enormous industry activity. A number of concerned railroads expecting a Mopac-Southern union began unification talks of their own in the hopes of preempting the anticompetitive effects that a Mopac-Southern combination might engender. The Atchison, Topeka & Santa Fe was one carrier that feared these consequences. Threatened by Mopac-Southern Pacific merger talks, the Santa Fe considered a combination with the St. Louis-San Francisco and with the Seaboard Coast Line. News of the Santa Fe's intentions boosted Frisco and Seaboard stock by 25 percent between April and July.

The concern of the Santa Fe proved to be unfounded. By September, Mopac and the Southern Pacific had still not reached an agreement nor did they submit an application to the Commission. Enthusiasm for the combination disappeared late in the year, and an agreement was never reached. With each railroad being among "the best managed, best maintained and most consistently profitable in the industry," it was unlikely from the beginning that the two largely parallel systems would make the concessions necessary for such a combination.[42]

On September 15, 1980, the Union Pacific and the Missouri Pacific submitted an application to the Commission. At the time the Union Pacific Railroad, a subsidiary of Union Pacific Corporation, operated 9,315 miles of line in a dozen western states stretching from Pacific Coast ports and terminals in Seattle, Portland, and Los Angeles to such Missouri River gateways as Kansas City.[43] The Missouri Pacific Railroad, a subsidiary of the Missouri Pacific Corporation, operated 11,500 miles of line in twelve midwestern and southwestern states connecting major midwestern gateways like Chicago, Omaha, St. Louis, Memphis, and Kansas City with ports and terminals in New Orleans, Lake Charles, Galveston, Houston, Corpus Christi, Brownsville, and Laredo.[44]

According to the unification application, the Union Pacific Corporation, a diversified company with interests in real estate, energy, and natural resources development, sought to gain control of the Missouri Pacific Corporation, a conglomerate with assets of its own in natural gas and cement, and the Western Pacific Railroad. By the application, the existing railroads and their respective holding companies would retain separate corporate identities but would fall under the control of Union Pacific Corporation and its newly formed subsidiary, the Pacific Rail System.

Ultimately, the Union Pacific designed the proposal to create a three-way rail system that provided single-system service between the Pacific Northwest, the growing Southwest, and important Gulf ports like New Orleans, Houston, and Galveston. This double merger would generate economic benefits totaling $106 million.[45] Net traffic increases would generate an additional $193 million in revenue. Arguing the positive aspects of such combinations, including more efficient system services, improved terminal operation, and increased traffic, the applicants also took the necessary steps to placate labor for any losses. Spokesmen for the UP and MP emphasized that the unification would not result in the abandonment of lines or service to shippers. They also explained that the combination would have no environmental impact and would actually help the carriers involved save 10.3 million gallons of fuel annually.[46]

The ICC ultimately approved the merger with conditions that guaranteed affected carriers' access to various markets. The details involved in these guarantees were extensive. The docket dealing with the merger and its conditions fills more than 40 volumes and 25,000 pages of transcript.

Not until 1986 did the UP engage in another major unification. At that time, the Union Pacific Corporation and its two rail carrier subsidiaries, Union Pacific and Missouri Pacific, sought to purchase stock control of the Missouri-Kansas-Texas Railroad (Katy), a small Class I carrier that ran from St. Louis, Kansas City, and Omaha, to the Gulf of Mexico.[47]

Approval of the application would ensure numerous advantages for the merging parties. The projected benefits included $48 million in annual operational savings and another $12.7 million in administrative savings.[48] Additionally, new single-line service would emerge between Union Pacific and Katy points to Mexican gateways as well as to points in the Southwest and on the West Coast. Finally, the union would save the Katy as an operational system. The railroad had been in a financially weak condition, experiencing pressure from a declining traffic base, a market shift to less-income-producing bulk commodities, and competition from other railroad and trucking companies. In addition to administrative and operational savings following union, the new system would earn $18 million in additional annual revenues from diverted traffic.[49] These estimates were important in convincing the Commission to approve UP's $98 million offer for the 3,100-mile railroad.

By 1995, the Union Pacific was among the largest carriers of the West. The system's 28,800 employees utilized 4,138 locomotives and 65,447 freight cars to transport freight over 18,000 miles of line. The carrier extended from Seattle and San Francisco on the West Coast to Chicago and to New Orleans and Galveston.[50]

DENVER & RIO GRANDE WESTERN

The Denver & Rio Grande Western (DRGW) operated a medium-sized railway network. Lines extended from Ogden, Utah, southeasterly to Grand Junction, Colorado, and east to Pueblo. From Pueblo, separate lines extended north to Denver and southwesterly to Antonito, Colorado. A wholly owned subsidiary of Rio Grande Industries, the Denver & Rio Grande Western operated 3,411 miles of line through Utah and Colorado with principal yards in Denver, Pueblo, and Grand Junction, Colorado, and Salt Lake City, Utah.

DRGW officials waited until the late 1980s to expand operations. When it finally acted, Rio Grande Industries (RGI) completed its single largest rail acquisition of the period. On December 30, 1987, the Santa Fe Southern Pacific Corporation, a newly formed holding company, agreed to sell Southern Pacific Transportation for $1.02 billion to SPT Holding, Inc., a subsidiary of Rio Grande Industries (itself a subsidiary of the Anschutz Corporation). The ICC sanctioned the proposal on August 25, 1988.[51] As a result, RGI acquired an 11,699-mile railroad that spanned fourteen states. The newly acquired system served end-to-end with RGI's subsidiary, Denver & Rio Grande Western.

The combination was expected to enhance DRGW's ability to compete in the central corridor against the Union Pacific-Missouri Pacific system and to augment SPT's competitive position in the southern corridor against the Atchison, Topeka & Santa Fe. Applicants sought financial savings largely through efficiency gains. Together the carriers offered single-line service between points in the Pacific Northwest, central and northern California, and the Midwest gateways of Kansas City, East St. Louis, and Memphis. This service combined with the single-line operation over the southern corridor formed an extensive transportation network.

By 1995, the Denver & Rio Grande Western's growth had come to an end, but it remained an important rail carrier in the western portion of the central corridor. With 241 locomotives and 9,060 freight cars as of 1993, the system served alongside the Southern Pacific to provide shippers with an important source of rail transportation.[52]

KANSAS CITY SOUTHERN

The Kansas City Southern Railway (KCSR) also survived the consolidation in the West while engaging in even less rail expansion than did the DRGW. The system, originally incorporated at the turn of the century, in 1995 operated about 2,385 miles of road in Missouri, Kansas, Arkansas, Oklahoma, Louisiana, and Texas. Through trackage rights arrangements with the Union Pacific, the carrier also served points in Nebraska and Iowa.

The lines of the KCSR provided service to a variety of cities. Between Kansas City and the Gulf of Mexico, the system served the ports of Beaumont and Port Arthur, Texas; and New Orleans, Baton Rouge, Reserve, and West Lake Charles, Louisana. Through trackage rights arrangements the railroad also served Houston and Galveston, Texas.

The Kansas City Southern continued to ship a variety of commodities. These included coal, grain, farm products, petroleum, chemicals, paper, and forest products. Since the 1970s, coal was the most important source of revenue for the carrier. Coal mined from the Powder River Basin in Wyoming moved via the Burlington Northern and the Union Pacific to Kansas City where it picked up Kansas City Southern for shipment south. KCSR transported the coal to six electric generating plants in Amsterdam, Missouri; Flint Creek, Arkansas; Welsh, Texas; Mossville, Louisiana; Kansas City, Missouri; and Pittsburg, Kansas. Serving the petroleum and chemical industries through refineries in Texas and Louisiana, the KCSR moved petroleum to the Southeast and Northeast through interchanges with other carriers.

Although the railroad did not expand its network through mergers between 1970 and 1993, it did make several acquisitions. In July 1988, the KCSR entered an agreement with the Union Pacific wherein the UP gave KCSR haulage rights for all commodities between Omaha and Lincoln, Nebraska, and for movements of grain to Beaumont, Houston, and Galveston, Texas. In May 1992, the KCSR signed an agreement with the Santa Fe Railway to purchase a 90-mile portion of its track and an 88-acre piggyback intermodal facility in the Dallas, Texas, vicinity. The transaction gave KCSR access to the Dallas area for the first time in the company's history.

In 1993, the Kansas City Southern made its largest purchase of the period. On May 27, the ICC approved the system's acquisition of the MidSouth Corporation through its parent company, Kansas City Southern Industries. The combination created a 2,800-mile system connecting the north-south Kansas City Southern with the east-west operations of MidSouth through their primary connection at Shreveport, Louisiana.

Even before the combination, MidSouth already had extensive operations of its own. The carrier operated 1,100 miles of line in Mississippi, Louisiana, western Alabama, and southern Tennessee through four subsidiaries: MidSouth Rail Corporation, MidLouisiana Rail Corporation, Southrail Corporation, and Tennrail Corporation. Lines extended from Shreveport east to Birmingham, northeast to Counce, Tennessee, and southeast to Gulfport, Mississippi. MidSouth complemented Kansas City Southern's system running from Omaha, Nebraska, south through Shreveport, Louisiana, to Houston and New Orleans.

The unification offered several benefits to KCSR. First, the merger, consummated in June, provided for the first-time single-line service between Birmingham, Alabama, and Dallas, Texas. The combination also permitted KCSR to "aggressively compete in the rapidly-growing transcontinental intermodal market, as well as [to] gain access to the thriving farm products, poultry-processing, and pulp and paper industries throughout the South."[53] The union, in addition, reduced KCSR's dependence on coal traffic, cutting it from 30 percent of the system's total revenue to 25 percent.

Purchase of MidSouth did not come cheap. Kansas City Southern Industries, which already owned 40 percent of MidSouth stock, paid $213.5 million for the remaining shares. The original 40 percent was acquired for $18.50 per share, while the rest cost $20.50 per share.[54]

While the cost of expansion was high, the results may have been worth it. Despite the rise of super-systems, like the BN and Conrail, the medium-size KCSR was still among the Class I carriers by 1995. With some 422 locomotives and 15,402 freight cars, the system continued to dominate routes between the northwest and southern cities.[55]

ATCHISON, TOPEKA & SANTA FE

One of two major Class I railroads dominating the Southwest throughout the period was the Atchison, Topeka & Santa Fe (ATSF). Although the 12,300-mile system engaged in little expansion during the 1970s, the carrier did simplify the corporate structure of two of its subsidiaries. The company absorbed the Illinois Northern in 1975 and the New Mexico Central in 1977.

Not until the 1980s did the Santa Fe expand through acquisitions. In 1981, the carrier effected a transaction with the Toledo, Peoria & Western (TP&W).[56] The ATSF already owned 50 percent of the Class II, 325-mile railroad. The Santa Fe paid the other 50 percent shareholder, PennCo (a former subsidiary of Penn Central), $3 million for its 45,000 shares of TP&W stock. The TP&W, a bridge carrier between eastern and western roads which operated in Illinois, Indiana, and Iowa, expected to earn $2.7 million in traffic as a result of the new arrangement while providing ATSF with important interchanges in Indiana.[57]

Two years after its subsidiary combined with the TP&W, Santa Fe Industries merged with Southern Pacific Company, the holding company of Southern Pacific Railroad, to form the Santa Fe Southern Pacific Corporation. Officers of Santa Fe Industries and the Southern Pacific Company first met in January 1980 to discuss the possibility of merger. At the time, the Union Pacific had announced its desire to acquire the Missouri Pacific and the Western Pacific, a combination that would facilitate service for the UP-MP-WP to all principal ports at western traffic centers as well as all principal midcontinent gateways. Simultaneously, the proposed Burlington-Frisco combination threatened to create a 29,000-mile system with direct routes between the Midwest and the Gulf of Mexico, access to most midcontinent gateways, and connections to southeastern ports like Mobile and Pensacola.[58] The UP and BN cases threatened the traffic of both the Santa Fe and the Southern Pacific. The two southwestern systems concluded that a combination of their respective operations would limit potential losses resulting from either of the other two unifications.

Both the Southern Pacific and the Santa Fe were formidable systems. The former was a 13,600-mile carrier that served midwestern gateways at Kansas City and St. Louis, reached Gulf ports like New Orleans and Galveston, and extended westward to San Fransisco, Los Angeles, and Portland. The ATSF was nearly as large, with 12,950 miles of line, serving much of the same territories over different routes.[59] A union of the two railroads would create a 25,500-mile operation that extended from the West Coast to all important midcontinent gateways and all principal Gulf Coast ports in Texas and Louisiana.

Both carriers expected several benefits from the merger.[60] The unification would allow the individual carriers to avoid investment in more than one hundred capital projects, thereby saving the two systems an estimated $521 million in outlays. Moreover, train- and car-mile reductions were projected to produce an annual savings of $60 million. The Santa Fe and Southern Pacific also intended to gain from diversion from other carriers. They expected to divert $90 million worth of traffic from the UP, $42 million from the BN, and another $90 million from other transport companies. Moreover, although the combination would displace more than 1,000 employees, the Santa Fe Pacific planned to provide compensation.

Considering the Commission's inclination to approve combinations in the mid-1980s, along with the particulars of the case, railroad observers expected the Commission to sanction the merger. The holding companies of each carrier had already merged in December 1983, hoping to integrate their railroads shortly thereafter. Until the ICC decision was issued, however, those subsidiaries were placed in a voting trust, a situation that continued for more than two years. In the meantime, the Santa Fe Pacific Corporation began preparing itself for the enormous restructuring task that newly merged systems required.

However, in 1986, the Commission made a surprising announcement. By a four to one vote, the board rejected the merger proposal on grounds that it would reduce competition.[61] Members believed that the merger would eventually eliminate competition for traffic moving across the Southwest between California and the Gulf and southeastern points. The Commission predicted that a rail monopoly would arise at points like Phoenix, Arizona, where shippers were served exclusively by the Santa Fe and the Southern Pacific. Moreover, the merger would injure the Denver & Rio Grande Western, one of three major transcontinental carriers serving the central corridor.

The decision came as a shock to the Santa Fe Southern Pacific Corporation (SFSP) which countered the verdict with a modified proposal. But the Commission rejected the alternative also. Moreover, it required the SFSP to submit a divestiture plan relinquishing one of its railroads. After coming to terms with the ICC decision, the SFSP divested itself of Southern Pacific Transportation. SFSP sold SPT to SPT Holding, a subsidiary of Rio Grande Industries (a subsidiary of the Anshutz Corporation), parent of the Denver & Rio Grand Western.

In the years following the Commission's rejection of the Santa Fe-Southern Pacific combination, the Santa Fe remained relatively inactive. Aside from its acquisition of a 50 percent interest in the Oklahoma City Junction Railway, the Santa Fe completed no other major acquisitions through 1995. Nevertheless, the 15,075 mile system, stretching from Chicago and the Gulf of Mexico to points on the West Coast, employed 15,323 people and maintained 1,766 locomotives and more than 30,000 freight cars. These impressive statistics ranked the Santa Fe among the leading railroads in the nation.[62]

SOUTHERN PACIFIC

Southern Pacific lost its craving for expansion following the Commission's 1986 decision against the Sante Fe Pacific Corporation. Moreover, like the Santa Fe, the Southern Pacific had a small appetite from the start, expanding little after 1970. In August 1973, a company subsidiary, the St. Louis Southwestern, completed the purchase of 50 percent of the Alton & Southern Railway from the Chicago & North Western for $8 million. The Alton & Southern was a switching and terminal company connecting thirteen trunk lines and three switching lines in East St. Louis. About a year later, the company sold its 50 percent interest in the Oregon, California & Eastern.

Although SP's operations changed little in the subsequent decade, ownership of the railroad did. After the ICC's rejection of the SF-SP combination in July 1986, the federal agency required that the Santa Fe Pacific Corporation divest itself of one of the two railroad subsidiaries remaining in voting trust. Executives of the holding company decided to relinquish the SPT. In December 1987, SFSP reached an agreement with Rio Grande Industries, and in October of the following year, the Rio Grande purchased the SP for $1.02 billion.

The SPT was operated as an independent Class I carrier in subsequent years, as a wholly owned subsidiary of another company. By 1995, the rail carrier's 19,089 employees operated some 2,427 locomotives and 46,224 freight cars along more than 22,000 miles of line, stretching from St. Louis and New Orleans westward through El Paso, Texas, and on to points on the Pacific Coast.[63]

ASSESSMENT

By the early 1990s, Class I railroad freight service west of the Mississippi River was in the care of eight major systems. In the Northwest, the Burlington Northern, Chicago & North Western, and the Soo Line controlled the primary rail movements. In the central corridor, the Union Pacific and the Denver & Rio Grande Western directed east-west shipments. The western counterpart of the Illinois Central, serving north-south movements, was the Kansas City Southern. Dominating the Southwest were the Santa Fe and the Southern Pacific.

As in the East, many of these Class I systems were very different from those existing in 1970. The BN, UP, Soo Line and SP-DRGW systems had grown significantly. Federal restriction, exemplified by the Northern Securities case at the turn of the century, had prevented the growth of such super-systems in the past. By the 1990s, however, the regulatory environment was less restrictive, and rail networks of twenty thousand miles were no longer objectionable.

While several of these western giants changed considerably, several others did so less dramatically. The Chicago & North Western, Kansas City Southern, and Santa Fe had expanded their respective rail systems little between the 1970s and the 1990s. Because of the great distances between industrial centers, little market shift, and a lessened threat from alternate modes of transportation, such carriers maintained their viability at the Class I level despite extensive overhauls or expansions by other railroads.

Regardless of the lack of rail growth by some systems, the carriers that dominated United States Class I rail traffic west of the Mississippi were the strongest systems in the regions they served. They hauled more freight than ever before, and they were more fitted to their respective markets. Like their cousins in the eastern district, the western Class I's had evolved in dramatic fashion.

NOTES

1. *Railway Age* 168 (February 2/9, 1970), 38–39; *Financial World* 133 (February 25, 1970), 6–7.

2. Great Northern Pacific-Merger-Chicago, Burlington & Quincy-Merger-Great Northern Railway Company 328 ICC 463; 331 ICC 228.

3. 328 ICC 468.

4. *Fortune* 86 (August 1972), 128–133.

5. 328 ICC 477–478.

6. 331 ICC 269.

7. Finance Docket No. 28583, *Burlington Northern-Merger-St. Louis San Fransisco*, application, December 28, 1977, 2.

8. Ibid., 56.

9. Ibid., 52–53.

10. *Forbes* 119 (May 15, 1977), 81–82. See also *Railway Age* 179 (February 27, 1978), 19–20.

11. *Soo Line and Chicago, Milwaukee, St. Paul & Pacific-Control-Green Bay & Western* 354 ICC 451, 459; Finance Docket No. 27770 *Burlington Northern Inc.-Control Through Acquisition of Securities of-Green Bay & Western Railroad Company*, decided July 15, 1977.

12. 354 ICC 474.

13. Finance Docket No. 28143, *Soo Line and Chicago, Milwaukee, St. Paul & Pacific-Control-Green Bay & Western*, vol. 1, application, March 16, 1976, 35–36.

14. Ibid., 63.

15. Ibid., vol. 1, exhibit #23, correspondence, October 7, 1976.

16. Finance Docket No. 28654 (Sub-No. 1), *Itel Corporation-Acquisition-Green Bay & Western*, application, March 22, 1978, 2.

17. Ibid., 18.

18. *Moody's Transportation Manual*, 1996, 1.

19. *Chicago & Northwestern-Control-Chicago, Rock Island & Pacific* 347 ICC 684; ICC, *Annual Report, 1975*, 17–18.

20. 347 ICC 565.

21. Ibid., 568.

22. Ibid., 563–564; ICC, *Annual Report, 1970*, 29.

23. 347 ICC 568.

24. *Northwestern Employees Transportation-Purchase-Chicago & Northwestern* 342

25. *Forbes* 110 (October 15, 1972), 33.

26. Richard Saunders, *Railroad Mergers and the Coming of Conrail* (Westport, Conn.: Greenwood Press, 1978), 239.

27. *Forbes* 134 (September 24, 1984), 50–51.

28. Ibid.; *Railway Age* 189 (April 1988), 38.

29. *Moody's Transportation Manual,* 1994, 412.

30. *Forbes* 137 (February 10, 1986), 56–57; *Railway Age* 186 (August 1985), 34–35.

31. *Chicago, Milwaukee, St. Paul & Pacific Railroad Company-Reorganization-Acquisition-Grand Trunk Corporation* 2 ICC 2d 169.

32. Ibid.

33. *Railway Age* 181 (April 14, 1980), 26.

34. 2 ICC 2d 173.

35. Ibid., 224.

36. Ibid., 216.

37. *Moody's Transportation Manual,* 1994, 234.

38. *Moody's Transportation Manual,* 1996, 216.

39. *Forbes* 131 (January 31, 1983), 90–91.

40. *Missouri Pacific-Merger-Texas & Pacific and Chicago & Eastern Illinois* 348 ICC 415.

41. Ibid., 419.

42. *Business Week,* May 24, 1976, 56.

43. Finance Docket No. 30000 *Union Pacific Corporation, Pacific Rail System, Inc., and Union Pacific Railroad Company-Control-Missouri Pacific Corporation and Missouri Pacific Railroad Company,* vol. 1, application: vol. 1, September 15, 1980, 37–38. See also *Railway Age* 182 (April 27, 1981), 20–26.

44. Finance Docket No. 30000, 38.

45. Ibid., 9–10.

46. Ibid., 27.

47. *Union Pacific Corporation, Union Pacific Railroad and Missouri Pacific Railroad-Control-Missouri-Kansas-Texas* 4 ICC 2d 420. See also *Railway Age* 186 (June 1985), 23; *Traffic Management* 26 (January 1987), 13–14.

48. 4 ICC 2d 429.

49. Ibid., 555.

50. *Moody's Transportation Manual, 1996,* 132–133.

51. *Rio Grande Industries, Inc., SPTC Holding, Inc., and the Denver & Rio Grande Western Railroad Company-Control-Southern Pacific Transportation Company*4 ICC 2d 834. See also *Railway Age* 189(October 1988), 28–29; 189(September 1988), 24–25; *Forbes* 135(20 May 1985), 106–107; *Traffic Management* 27(October 1988), 16.

52. *Moody's Transportation Manual, 1996,* 249.

53. *Railway Age* 194(July 1993), 44.

54. Ibid.

55. *Moody's Transportation Manual,* 1996, 68–70.

56. *Atchison, Topeka & Santa Fe-Control-Toledo, Peoria & Western* 363 ICC 715–716.

57. Ibid., 718.

58. Finance Docket No. 30400 *Santa Fe Southern Pacific Corporation-Control-Southern Pacific Transportation-Merger-Atchison, Topeka & Santa Fe and Southern Pacific Transportation,* vol. 3, application: vol. 1A, March 23, 1984, 3.

59. Ibid.

60. *Business Week*, June 2, 1980, 29–30; *Railway Age* 181 (May 26, 1980), 13–14; *Business Week*, October 10, 1983, 32–33.

61. *Economist* 300 (August 2, 1986), 51–52; *Traffic Management* 25 (September 1986), 13–14.

62. *Moody's Transportation Manual*, 1996, 403–404.

63. Ibid., 282–283.

8

Railroad Holding Companies:
Keys to Diversification

While railroads utilized combinations with other carriers to expand their operations between 1970 and the 1990s, they also used holding companies to alter their corporate structures. The latter facilitated smoother horizontal expansion of railway systems and made possible diversification into business activities outside of railroading with less intereference from the federal government. The old constraints of right-of-way and regulation could at long last be circumvented.

The Interstate Commerce Commission remained concerned with the implications of railroad transactions being conducted without regulation.[1] Congress considered various bills in 1971, 1973, and 1975 to permit ICC regulation of the new activities, but the efforts failed. To alleviate concern with this issue, however, Congress ordered an ICC investigation of holding companies in 1976.

More than a decade after that investigation, legislators again addressed the issue of conglomerates in the railroad industry. Some members of Congress remained concerned with the practices of these relatively independent corporate structures. They claimed that rail systems faced new issues as the conglomerates that controlled them grew. To assuage these concerns the Senate Committee on Commerce, Science, and Transportation held hearings in 1989 and again discussed the possibility of regulating the activities of railroad holding companies.

COMMISSION INVESTIGATION

During the 1960s, corporate expansion through the use of holding companies became extremely popular on Wall Street. As the nation's economy grew in the wake of the World War II, businesses sought to increase their per share earnings on investments, and thus attracted investors through the acquisition of other companies. Even the purchase of low-revenue producing companies generated increased per-share earnings for stockholders of conglomerates, as the assets of the target companies could be leveraged for further acquisitions. The result was the emergence of enormous corporations.

Railroads, like other businesses, sought to expand through corporate acquisitions, and as they grew, the federal government sought to identify the potential impact of conglomerates on the industry. In Section 903 of the Railroad Revitalization and Regulatory Reform Act of 1976, Congress authorized the ICC to investigate railroad holding companies. On February 5, 1977, the Commission submitted its findings.

The Commission explained that before the emergence of holding companies, all railroad income, whether obtained as a result of rail operations or through nonrail related holdings, was at the disposal of the carrier. According to the ICC, this setup was not that beneficial to the railroad or to the companies they owned. The railroads tended to use the assets of subsidiaries to overcome their own financial difficulties, but since those companies were nonexpansive, they provided a limited degree of support. Conversely, the subsidiaries were unable to expand as they could not acquire from struggling railroads the capital necessary for growth.

Rail executives, however, were inventive. If railroading continued to be so unprofitable, corporate officers might expand their nonrail holdings and funnel their assets into those ventures. They believed that diversification could provide financial stability by spreading investment risks over a broader spectrum of business. Diversification could also produce tax advantages, reduce fluctuations in earnings from seasonal downturns, permit the development of expensive research and development programs, and lead to a reduction in costs per unit of output.[2] The only way such goals could be reached, however, would be through the creation of a parent company that could separate the corporate accounts of the rail systems from those of their affiliates.

In addition to allowing railroads to diversify their assets, holding companies permitted carriers to avoid federal regulation of noncarrier operations. Section 20a(2) of the Interstate Commerce Act mandated that a railroad obtain ICC authority before "issuing capital stock, bonds, or other securities, or assuming obligations or liabilities as lessor, lessee, guarantor, endorser, surety, or otherwise."[3] That mandate meant that if a railroad wished to finance an acquisition of nonrail holdings through the issuance of securities, it would need to obtain ICC approval. If the rail carrier did not own those other holdings, however, the Commission could not regulate them.

Prior to the 1960s, the ICC permitted relatively little diversification by railroads. The intent was to limit railroads to the business of railroading. In 1960, however, the Bangor & Aroostook, a small Class I system, formed the first modern conglomerate holding company in the industry, the Bangor Punta Corporation.[4] When the ICC declared that it lacked jurisdiction over the new company, other railroads copied the New England system by forming parent corporations of their own. By 1974, nearly 70 percent of Class I railroads were subsidiaries of holding companies.

Ultimately, the Commission found that these corporate structures achieved two things for carriers: railroads relinquished their nonrail holdings to their parent corporations, and those nonrail holdings were no longer subject to Section 20a of the Interstate Commerce Act.[5] Control changed little as the leading officials of the railroads filled the executive management positions of the newly formed parent holding companies.

According to the Commission, this new corporate strategy could prove detrimental to the railroads. While the separation of rail and nonrail assets insulated carriers from the high risks associated with diversified investment, that segregation also prevented carriers from enjoying the profits of successful nonrail holdings.

In addition, the potential existed for newly formed holding companies to tire of the capital intensive nature of the railroad business and to dispose of their rail operations. Northwest Industries, former owner of the Chicago & North Western, and

Bangor Punta, holder of the Bangor & Aroostook, were prime examples. Both conglomerates disposed of their subsidiary rail carriers, denouncing them as unprofitable ventures and drains on aggregrate operations.[6]

Aside from these larger concerns, the Commission found that holding companies and their railroad subsidiaries often created a conflict of interest. This first manifested itself when rail management formed the parent company. Established with minimum capitalization, the holding company might offer to exchange its shares for the railroad's stock. Acceptance of such an offer gave the holding corporation control of the railroad through stock ownership, a transaction which generated problems with minority interests who refused to accept the offer and often threatened legal action.

Directors of new parent companies, however, found a strategy to outmanuever the minority stockholders. First, managers of a given holding company created a third corporation which they controlled through 100 percent stock ownership. Then they merged the third corporation and the railroad. As part of the merger agreement, the holding company required minority stockholders to exchange their railroad stock for that of the holding company or accept payment for their stock at a price set by the managers of the holding corporation. This manuever "eliminated the minority shareholders and the threat of minority derivative suits which could arise from the transfer of railroad assets to the holding company at less than fair market value."[7] The Commission identified several railroads which holding companies absorbed through this process. They included the Union Pacific; Atchison, Topeka & Santa Fe; Penn Central; Seaboard Coast Line; Southern Pacific Transportation; Denver & Rio Grande Western; and Western Pacific.

The Commission also worried about tax manipulations. Holding companies filed consolidated income tax returns that incorporated tax losses and investment tax credits generated by subsidiary companies. The subsidiary companies would each pay a quarterly tax liability to the holding company. The parent company would then pay the consolidated income tax liability to the Internal Revenue Service. This amount was nearly always smaller than the aggregate of the income taxes collected from the subsidiaries separately because of the elimination of intercompany dividends and a broader use of company losses and tax credits. For example, the Commission noted that for the years 1963 through 1974 subsidiaries of Illinois Central Industries (ICI) would have paid $104 million in taxes had they filed separate returns.[8] Under consolidated income tax procedures, ICI paid only $43 million.

These consolidated income-tax advantages came at the expense of the Illinois Central Gulf and the Chicago & Illinois Western, two rail subsidiaries. The transfer of the tax responsibilities of these carriers to the parent company eliminated deductions that these carriers might have otherwise made. The same situation applied to the Kansas City Southern Railway. It paid more than $2 million toward income taxes between 1962 and 1976 to its parent, Kansas City Southern Industries. This money would have been deductible had the railroad filed its taxes independently; instead, KCSI reaped the benefit.[9]

While tax advantages were transferred from the rail subsidiaries to their respective holding companies, so too were cash advances in the form of loans and unsecured notes. For example, in January 1970, Union Pacific Railroad advanced a loan of $120 million to one of its subsidiaries, Union Pacific Development Corporation. The latter needed the capital to purchase two other companies, Champlin Petroleum and Pontiac Refining. Shortly after this transaction, control of Union Pacific Development Corporation was transferred to Union Pacific Corporation, parent of Union Pacific Railroad, along with the newly acquired subsidiaries which the railroad purchased. In addition, the railroad's board of directors, which also served on the board for the holding company, repositioned all of the Union Pacific Railroad's nonrail holdings under Union Pacific Development Corporation. Several subsidiaries were thereby transferred to Union Pacific Corporation along with nearly $255 million in advances made by the railroad to these companies.

Railroads generally had to pay for the administrative costs of their respective holding companies. As investment corporations, holding companies depended on their respective subsidiaries to meet expenses. The executives of those holding companies, however, could secure loans from banks by using the assets of rail carriers as collateral. Considering that executives could use those funds for transactions outside railroading, the potential existed for stripping railroads of their financial base.

Another potential problem existed with regard to dividend practices. Often the directors of the holding companies, who also served as directors of the railroads, had to decide which had priority, the railroads or the stockholders of the holding companies. A situation with Western Pacific Railroad in 1974 and 1975 exemplified this conflict.[10] The chairman of the board of the holding company, Western Pacific Industries, proposed paying WPI stockholders a special dividend of $1 million obtained from the railroad. One of the directors serving on the boards of both companies opposed paying the dividend and questioned the propriety of individuals serving as directors of both the holding company and the railroad. Ultimately, leading directors dismissed the dissident from both boards, and over the protests of those directors who served only on the railroad board, they sanctioned the dividend.

Two other financial concerns of the Commission involved protection of holding company management and the use of subsidiary credit. The Commission cited a case involving the Kansas City Southern Industries and Lee National Corporation, an investment company, in 1969 and 1970 to illustrate its first concern.[11] In that case, Lee National Corporation purchased 21.4 percent of KCSI stock in an effort to gain management control of KCSI. The railroad's management attempted to thwart this hostile action by amending the company's corporate charter, a step which led to a legal battle. In a settlement, KCSI agreed to transfer certain assets of several subsidiaries to Lee National, including those of the Kansas City Southern Railway. In exchange, Lee National turned over KCSI stock that it held. The assets that KCSI transferred, however, were appraised at $9 million more than the value of the stock that it obtained from Lee National. As the Commission pointed out, this transaction showed how holding company directors might unnecessarily threaten the assets of a railroad in an attempt to protect their own interests.

Holding companies also used railroads to obtain loans at low interest rates.[12] For example, Bangor Punta paid its railroad subsidiary a mere 3 percent on cash balances in excess of $1.3 million. The Kansas City Southern Industries used the Louisiana &

Arkansas Railway to guarantee loans for another KCSI subsidiary that leased equipment to the railroad. In another case, the C&O guaranteed a loan for a subsidiary, Western Pocahontas Corporation. When the Chessie System emerged as the parent company of the C&O, Western Pocahontas spun off the C&O and became a direct subsidiary of the new company. The C&O, nevertheless, was still responsible for the outstanding loan if Western Pocohantas defaulted.

Rail carriers suffered other disadvantages as a result of the creation of holding companies. The Commission noted that most railroads purchased supplies and materials from former subsidiary companies that spun off to newly formed parent corporations.[13] For example, Standard Office Building, a former subsidiary of the Atchison, Topeka & Santa Fe, leased office space to the ATSF for $2.4 million from 1973 to 1975. Considering that the ATSF never paid for space when the building company was its subsidiary, the amount was signficant. In a comparable situation over the same span of time, the Union Pacific Railroad paid $21.8 million to Champlin Petroleum, a former subsidiary, for fuel and lubricants.

Aside from the concerns that railroad holding companies generated, the Commission's 1976 study found that carriers that were part of such corporate structures fared better financially than they had in the past. The rail subsidiaries of Union Pacific Corporation, Santa Fe Industries, Missouri Pacific Corporation, and Rio Grande Industries recorded increased traffic levels, earnings, and operating efficiency.[14] Although the Commission could not determine definitively whether these gains were due to the existence of holding companies, the ICC discounted the notion that the existence of parent corporations was a threat to the operation of subsidiary railroads.

The Commission contended that many of the difficulties that rail carriers encountered should not be attributed to railroad holding companies. The rail subsidiaries of Seaboard Coast Line Industries, Western Pacific Industries, Southern Pacific Company, and the Chicago Milwaukee Corporation showed deficits in some years, but they nevertheless realized net traffic increases between 1965 and 1975. There was no evidence, moreover, to suggest that the respective holding companies pursued policies that produced deficits or proved detrimental to rail operations. Additionally, although such holding companies as Illinois Central Industries, Katy Industries, Chessie System, Kansas City Southern Industries, Bomaine, and Amoskeag owned rail subsidiaries that were financially strained to varying degrees, the Commission could only identify Illinois Central Industries and Kansas City Southern Industries as the possible cause of the problems of their respective subsidiaries. The culpability of holding companies thus remained amorphous.[15]

THE CORPORATE PARENTS

Even as the Commission was attempting to understand the nature of conglomerates and predict their effect on the industry, their numbers grew. In the East, four of the five Class I systems still in existence in 1990 were subsidiaries of larger and more diversified corporations. CSX, Norfolk Southern, Illinois Central, and Grand Trunk Western were those rail systems with parents whose investments extended beyond railroading. Only Conrail remained unaffiliated with a corporate parent.

The Illinois Central entered the 1970s with a holding company already in place. Illinois Central Industries had been the parent of the Illinois Central since its incorporation in 1962. When the Illinois Central Gulf was formed in 1971 to merge the Illinois Central and the Gulf, Mobile & Ohio railroads, the new carrier fell under the control of IC Industries.

The Grand Trunk Western was already a subsidiary when the 1970s opened. Its parent was the Canadian National, a multifaceted government-owned corporation operating Canada's largest transcontinental railroad, a system that spanned more than 28,100 miles by the 1990s. In September 1970, Grand Trunk Industries was formed as a holding company to consolidate CN's Class I rail operations in the United States, including those of the Grand Trunk Western; Duluth, Winnipeg & Pacific; and the Central of Vermont.

Unlike the Canadian National or Illinois Central Industries, Norfolk Southern Corporation and CSX Corporation did not exist prior to 1970. Norfolk Southern Corporation was formed in July 1980 to combine the Norfolk & Western Railway Company and the Southern Railway Company. CSX Corporation appeared in November of the same year to unite the Chessie System and the Seaboard Coast Line Industries, themselves holding companies of Class I railroad systems.

Like other conglomerate holding companies, CN, ICI, CSX, and NS diversified their investments widely. When the 1970s opened, Canadian National was already a diversified company with investments in real estate, oil exploration, transportation equipment manufacturing, and telecommunications.[16] It continued to expand between 1970 and the early 1990s. In 1970, it acquired Husband International Transport and Canadian National Hotels. The following year, the company purchased three trucking companies, Swan River, The Pas Transfer, and Royal Transportation. In August, CN consolidated its three U.S. rail subsidiaries under the Grand Trunk Corporation and established Canac Consultants, a transportation consulting service, in September. By the end of the year, Autoport Limited, jointly owned by CN and another firm, was incorporated to deliver automobiles by auto-carrying vessels. The following August, Husband Transportation joined CN operations, and Canalog Logistics, a consulting service in the logistics field, was added in December.[17]

CN's investment in transportation, real estate, and communications continued in the late 1970s. The company purchased all the stock of the Gulf Terminal Railway and nearly half the interest in the Compagnie de Gestion de Matane. In November 1975, it acquired an 18 percent interest in Intercast S.A. of Switzerland and Eurocanadian Shipholding, a container shipping company, and later it acquired Cronin Transport. On June 26, 1976, the world's tallest free standing structure, designed for communications, opened under the newly formed corporation, CN Tower Limited (transferred to the Canadian government in 1995). In 1979, the company added CN Marine and Coastal Transport to its list of subsidiaries.

During the 1980s and early 1990s, the Canadian National continued to secure interests in transportation, communications, and real estate. Among its acquisitions were interests in Northern Alberta Railway; Lakespane Marine Incorporated; EID

Electronic Identifications Systems; OCRA Communications; Detroit, Toledo & Ironton Railroad; Railroad Association Insurance; and Dome Consortium Investments.[18]

By 1995 the CN looked to rationalize its operations in such a way as to promote earnings growth and increased shareholder value. This agenda was particularly important to CN directors after November of that year, when, pursuant to the stipulations of the CN Commercialization Act, the government of Canada completed the sale of all its shares of Canadian National in a public offering. Thereafter, CN handled its affairs as any other Canadian corporation.

Illinois Central Industries was just as active as CN with investments in such diverse ventures as specialty food products, soft drinks, and automotive services. The holding corporation had acquired several companies after 1962 and continued the process in the 1970s and 1980s. During the 1970s alone, IC Industries acquired or merged Pepsi Cola General Bottlers; H.F. Phillipsborne, a Chicago mortgage banking and real estate firm; Perfect Plus Hosiery, a manufacturer and distributor of women's hosiery; Signal-Stat Division of Lehigh Valley Industries; Dad's Root Beer Company; Hunter Moss & Company; Midas International; Lincoln Financial Company; Illinois Central Railroad and Gulf, Mobile & Ohio Railroad; Bubble Up Corporation; Midwest Life Insurance Company; Consolidated Acceptance Corporation; A.L. Hansen Manufacturing; Stanray Corporation; Waukeeska Foundry; Security Investment Company; Pet Incorporated; Pepsi Cola Bottling of Kenosha & Racine; Pepsi Cola Kantor Bottling; and Applied Air Systems.[19]

During the 1980s, IC Industries and its subsidiaries acquired other firms. These included Blanchard-Ness Ltee and Wm. Underwood Company, both acquired early in the decade. In 1982, the company purchased 2,149,319 shares of its own stock for $72 million that was previously held by the Union Pacific Corporation. The following year, IC Industries acquired the Havana Pepsi Cola Bottling Company and in 1984 Turner Refrigeration; Refrigeration Contracts; Pepsi Cola Bottling Company of Springfield and of Flat River, Missouri; Infrisa, a joint Mexican venture; 1,2,3 AutoService, a German joint venture; Riordan Holdings; and Midas U.K. Limited, a United Kingdom joint venture. By 1985, Pet Incorporated, a subsidiary, acquired E. B. Evans Company; and IC Industries directly acquired BIH Food Services and Bastian-Blessing Food Service Equipment Company for $77.3 million.

This kind of growth continued in the late 1980s. In 1986, IC Industries acquired Le Silanciaux, a Midas joint venture in France; Pepsi Cola Bottling Companies of Sedalia and Columbia, Missouri; Primo Foods of Canada; Hussman Corporation; and Ogden Food Products. The latter cost the company $320 million. In 1987, IC Industries acquired Facchin Foods; Country Queen's Foods products facility; Oronoque, Incorporated; Equi Tech Incorporated; Miloni Foods; CBM Kaltetechnik Reicherstorfer; CBM Contracting; Southbend Escan Corporation; and Canparts Automotive International. RKO Bottlers and Gallagher Company of St. Louis joined the company the following year.[20]

The late 1980s brought dramatic change. In September 1987, the board of directors of IC Industries approved a management plan to spin off Illinois Central Gulf. Subsequently, IC Industries changed its name to Whitman Corporation in the hopes of gaining a higher price/earnings ratio as a food company than as a rail-based conglomerate.[21] The change left the railroad as an independant company lacking the financial stability that a parent company provided and without the assets retained by the holding corporation. In March 1989, however, financier Louis Marx and the Prospect Group purchased Illinois Central Gulf Railroad in a leveraged buyout that cost Prospect $435 million.[22] This arrangement did not last long. In July, Rail Acquisitions, a subsidiary of Railway Holdings (subsequently Illinois Central Corporation), purchased the assets of the carrier, making Illinois Central Railroad a wholly owned subsidiary and only material asset of Railway Holdings.

A few years later, this new holding company expanded again. On April 30, 1996, the Surface Transportation Board of the Department of Transportation announced it vote in favor of allowing Illinois Central Corporation to purchase CCP Holdings, Incorporated with funds from its line of credit and with proceeds of public debt issued by the Illinois Central Railroad. The transaction cost $125 million in cash along with another $31 million in net debt and capital lease obligations.

When CSX Corporation formed, it expanded in much the same way as IC Industries before the latter disposed of its railroad. One of its newly acquired subsidiaries, Chessie System, had already begun the process of diversification. Besides operating more than 11,000 miles of rail line, the Chessie System owned interests in such businesses as coal production, land development and sales, hotel operation, forest lands, and oil exploration.

CSX continued its diversification in the 1980s and 1990s, emphasizing transportation: rail, container shipping, intermodal, barging, trucking, contract logistics, and related services.[23] Among the interests acquired were the Carolina, Clinchfield & Ohio Railway; Louisville & Nashville Railroad; Western Maryland Railway; Texas Gas Resources Corporation; American Commercial Lines, a trucking company; Port Huron & Detroit; Rockresorts, a premier resort management firm; Sea Land Corporation, a container shipping company; Yukon Pacific, a corporation promoting the construction of a Trans-Alaska Gas System to export natural gas to countries on the Pacific rim; SCNO Barge Lines; Richmond, Fredericksburg & Potomac Railway; barge terminal facilities of TTI Systems, the coal transportation subsidiary of Transasco Energy Company; a railway yard in Little Ferry, New Jersey, which it acquired from the New York, Susquehanna & Western; the Valley Line Company, a barge unit of the Sequa Corporation; and Customized Transportation, Incorporated. In 1992, the company joined with the AMR Corporation and PTT Telecom Netherlands to establish Encompass Europe NV, a company designed to create logistics information management systems.

Although less diversified than CSX, the Norfolk Southern also expanded operations both in railroading and in other kinds of enterprises.[24] NS started the process in 1982, when it acquired the Norfolk & Western and the Southern railways. It expanded its transportation interests dramatically in 1985, acquiring control of North American Van Lines, a diversified motor-carrier operation. In 1987, the company bought a 200-mile line extending from Haleyville, Alabama, to Fulton, Kentucky, from the Illinois Central for $38 million, and three years later NS acquired the assets of the Ohio River Terminal Railway. In April 1993, it engaged in a joint venture with Consolidated Rail Corporation to create Triple Crown Services, a domestic retail intermodal operation to compete for truckload service. A couple of months later, a subsidiary of NS, Pocohontas Land Corporation, joined with the International Lumber Company to build a saw mill for the production of crossties in Gilbert, West Virginia.

Meanwhile, all the rail carriers in the Western district became subsidiaries of holding companies. The Burlington Northern, Kansas City Southern, Chicago & North Western, Santa Fe, Southern Pacific, Denver & Rio Grande Western, Soo Line, and Union Pacific were integrated into larger, diversified, conglomerates.

Before forming a holding company in 1981, the Burlington Northern was already engaged in businesses outside railroading, including the sale of timber, manufacture and sale of forest products, exploitation of petroleum resources, motor carrier operations, and real estate development.[25]

After Burlington Northern Incorporated (BNI) took over the railroad, the new conglomerate continued to expand. In 1983, BNI acquired the El Paso Company for $962 million in cash and 7,031,018 in shares of stock. In December 1985, BNI expanded again with the purchase of Southland Royalty Company for $730 million, and in 1988 the company formed Burlington Resources to consolidate the system's investments in natural resources utilization.[26] The BNI completed its most important transaction in September 1995 when it merged with the Sante Fe Pacific Corporation.

Kansas City Southern Industries, formed in 1962 to assume control of the Kansas City Southern Railroad, was nearly as diversified as the BNI. Already heavily invested in television and radio companies, the KCS continued its expansion. In 1970, the company acquired an 83 percent interest in DST Systems, and in 1979 it paid $34.1 million for Pioneer Western Corporation. Three years later, KCS aquired the remaining shares of the KCS Railroad and a 12.5 percent interest in LDX, Incorporated. In 1984, Pioneer Western Corporation acquired a 60 percent interest in the Derby Oil & Gas Corporation; a 60 percent interest in Derby Petroleum Incorporated; and 100 percent interest in D&H Well Service and Twin Hills Supply. The company also paid $10.9 million for a 67 percent interest in Janus Capital, increasing its interest to 80 percent by 1985. Two years later, the LDX Group, an 85.6 percent subsidiary, combined certain of its operations with William Telecommunications to form the William Telecommunications Group of which LDX Group owned 16.3 percent. The LDX Group sold that interest for $100 million two years later.[27]

In the 1990s, Kansas City Southern Industries expanded further.[28] In 1990, it obtained complete control of DST Systems and a 43 percent interest in Policy Holder Service Corporation (PSC), increasing DST's total interest in PSC to 87 percent. Two years later, KCSI bought the Graysonia, Nashville & Ashdown Railroad, and in 1993, it purchased MidSouth Corporation, a railroad holding company.[29] By 1994, the company expected to increase from 20 to 80 percent its interest in Berger Associates, a mutual fund manager, and in August it announced that its subsidiary, DST Systems, and Kemper Financial Services had signed a letter of intent to acquire the Investors Fiduciary Trust Company in a stock exchange valued at $225 million. Kansas City Southern Industries also signed a letter of intent to sell the assets of the Kansas City

Southern Railway to the Illinois Central Corporation.[30] In November 1995, KCSI purchased a 49 percent interest in Mexrail, Incorporated and its subsidiary Texas-Mexican Railway in order to participate in the north/south flow of traffic between Mexico and the United States. A month later, the company announced that it had concluded an agreement with Transportacion Maritima Mexicana to form a joint venture that will compete for the operation and traffic of portions of Mexico's soon-to-be-privatized railway network.

Further north and pursuant to a plan of merger and reorganization sanctioned by stockholders, the CNW Corporation emerged in 1985 to assume control of the Chicago & North Western Transportation Company, the employee-controlled rail company. Aside from operating the ninth largest rail carrier in the country, the holding company also had investments in trucking and computer software. In 1985, 400 Freight Systems was formed as a subsidiary to provide motor carrier service, and in 1986 the company invested $53.7 million in Douglas Dynamics, a snowplow manufacturer, which it sold in 1988 to Park-Kenilworth Industries for $100 million. Although not as large as other holding companies of Class I rail systems, CNW Corporation was, nevertheless, committed to growth and diversity.[31]

As a result of this committment, CNW became an attractive target to corporate raiders. In 1989, CNW Corporation expended an enormous effort to defend itself against a hostile takeover bid by Japonica Partnership, an investment firm. The CNW, however, was not successful against Blackstone Capital Partners which, during that same year, acquired control of CNW Corporation for $1.6 billion.

Railroad holding companies also recognized the worth of CNW. In April 1995, CNW was purchased in a stock buyout by Union Pacific Corporation for $35 per share. The latter was seeking to expand the network of its subsidiary, Union Pacific Railroad.

Like the CNW Corporation, Santa Fe Industries and the Southern Pacific Company were two expanding conglomerates committed to growth and diversity, a commitment that ultimately led to the combination of their operations. Santa Fe industries, incorporated in 1967, began its expansion in 1973 with the acquisition of all the outstanding stock of Robert E. McKee, a general construction contractor, and of The Zia Company, which provided maintenance support and other services. That same year the company acquired Security Guard Services and the Walker-Kurth Lumber Company. In 1976, Security Guard Services purchased the assets of Global Security, and the following year Santa Fe Resources, a company subsidiary, paid $68.8 million for Westates Petroleum. The company organized Gallow Wash Coal, Hospah Coal, and Pintada Coal in 1977, and Santa Fe Industries acquired the business and assets of Gross-Yowell of Killeen, Texas. In 1979, the company purchased 22,000 acres of timberland from the International Paper Company and formed Santa Fe Energy Products to buy and resell crude oil.[32]

Southern Pacific Company was less active than Santa Fe Industries but it had investments in trucking, pipelines, natural resources, communications, and real estate. In 1979, the company acquired Ticor, the largest title insurance company, a leading mortgage insurer, and the second largest financial printing company in the country. A year later, it expanded its natural resources investments with the purchase of a 50 percent interest in GeoProducts, an engineering firm that designed systems to convert waste products into ethyl alcohol and that sought to harness California's abundant geothermal energy resource. Aside from the Southern Pacific Railway, the company also controlled Seaboard Coast Line Industries. That control, however, ended in August 1980 when the Southern Pacific Company sold its interests in Seaboard Coast Line Industries for $60.2 million. Shortly thereafter, the Seaboard joined with the Chessie System under the CSX Corporation.[33]

As discussed previously, in September 1983, another holding company, the Santa Fe Pacific Corporation, was formed to combine Santa Fe Industries and the Southern Pacific Company. In 1987, the new holding company acquired California oil and gas properties from Petro-Lewis, American Royalty Trust, and others for $140 million. A year later, the company purchased Western Rock through a subsidiary, Santa Fe Mineral Corporation, for $14 million.

After 1988, the Santa Fe Pacific Corporation focused its business activities in three main areas: rail service, gold mining, and pipeline service.[34] The latter consisted of 3,300 miles of pipeline and fourteen truck-loading terminals used in the transportation of petroleum. Its rail operations principally consisted of the Atchison, Topeka & Santa Fe with more than 8,000 miles of line in twelve midwestern, western, and southwestern states. In 1988, Southern Pacific Corporation sold its rail subsidiary, Southern Pacific Transportation, to Rio Grande Industries for $1.02 billion. An ICC ruling against the combination of the Atchison, Topeka & Santa Fe Railway and the Southern Pacific Company's rail operations forced the sale.

By 1994, Santa Fe Pacific Corporation was at the center of bidding war between Burlington Northern and Union Pacific for the purchase of the former's stock. The imbroglio ended in September 1995 with the merger of Santa Fe Pacific and Burlington Northern into the Burlington Northern Sante Fe Corporation.

Rio Grande Industries had been the corporate parent of the DRGW since the holding company emerged in 1968. Ninety-nine percent of its interests remained in the DRGW. In 1970, the company formed a subsidiary, Leavell Development, to acquire Texas Homes Incorporated, but it soon sold that property and discontinued real estate development operations.

Expansion came to the company and its rail subsidiary in 1984 when the Anschutz Corporation acquired Rio Grande Industries through Rio Grande Holding.[35] In 1988, Anschutz formed a new company, Rio Grande Industries, to assume control of Rio Grande Holding and SPTC Holding, a company created to manage the acquisition of the Southern Pacific Transportation from the Santa Fe Pacific Corporation.[36] This reorganization permitted more efficient functioning of Anschutz's transportation operations, the Denver & Rio Grande Western and Southern Pacific Transportation Company.

Like the DRGW and SPTC, the Soo Line was controlled by a megacorporation, Canadian Pacific Limited (CPL). CPL engaged in rail freight and container shipping; motor-carrier operations; exploration and production of oil, natural gas, coal and other minerals; real estate and hotel operations; telecommunication services; and environmental management.[37]

CP waited until the late 1980s to expand its operations, reorganizing the businesses it already had in the 1970s and early 1980s.[38] In April 1988, the company purchased CN Hotels for C$265.5 million through its subsidiary Canadian Pacific Hotels Corporation, and in July CP acquired 22 million shares of Laidlaw Incorporated for C$499.3 million. In December, CP bought Canadian National's share of net assets in CNCP Telecommunications and Telecommunications Terminal Systems for C$235 million. Laidlaw, a CP subsidiary, made several acquisitions in 1989, including a 34.2 percent interest in Attwoods (U.K.) for $197.2 million; a 28.8 percent interest in ADT Limited (Bermuda) for $700 million; and control of Tricil for C$240 million. CP also increased its ownership of Soo Line Corporation, the holding company of Soo Line Railway formed in 1984, from 55.8 percent to 100 percent for C$108.2 million.

During the early 1990s, CP's operations continued to grow. At the opening of the decade, CP purchased 80 percent interest in Doubletree Hotels for $62.6 million, and in 1991 the company acquired the Delaware & Hudson Railway for $26 million. It then reorganized its rail operations—CP Rail, Soo Line, and Delaware & Hudson—under a newly formed CP Rail System. A year later, Unitel Dominion Industries Limited, a subsidiary, acquired the door and architectural and industrial wall systems and floor decking businesses of the Robertson-CECO Corporation and the stock of Bredel Exploitatie B.V. for C$180.7 million. Furthermore, in 1993, the company augmented its control of Canada Maritime Limited from 67 percent to 100 percent.

Like Canadian Pacific, Union Pacific Corporation was another rail holding company that found strength in diversification. Incorporated in 1969, the company completed acquisition of the Union Pacific Railroad and siphoned the carrier's investments in oil and gas, mining, and real estate subsidiaries. In 1982, it purchased Missouri Pacific Corporation and its subsidiaries for approximately $1 billion. The Union Pacific Corporation expanded its other transportation operations in 1986 with the acquisition of Overnite Transportation, a major motor-carrier operation, for $1.2 billion. Moreover, in 1988, the company acquired United States Pollution Control, Incorporated, a hazardous waste management company, and the Missouri-Kansas-Texas Railroad, the latter at a cost of $117 million. Union Pacific Resources Company purchased more than $91 million worth of interests in various oil and gas properties in 1990, and three years later the Union Pacific Corporation acquired Skyway Freight Systems, augmenting Union Pacific's commitment to alternate modes of transportation. In March 1994, Union Pacific Resources Company signed an agreement to acquire AMAX Oil & Gas for $725 million. A year later, Union Pacific Corporation acquired 100 percent interest in the Chicago & North Western Transportation Company, and in 1996 the company merged with Southern Pacific Corporation.   That same year Union Pacific formed South Jersey Resources Group in a joint venture with South Jersey Fuel, Incorporated to provide natural gas storage for customers in Delaware, Maryland, New Jersey, New York, and Pennsylvania.[39]

While Congress sought to revitalize the railroad industry in the 1970s through subsidization and regulatory relief, railroads sought avenues to financial resources. The most common way to acquire these resources was through the creation of, or affiliation with, conglomerate holding companies that maintained diverse investments and controlled huge sources of capital.

REEMERGING CONCERN

Despite the Commission's inaction against holding companies in 1976, Congress continued to have reservations about the activities of these corporations throughout the 1980s. On June 22, 1989, the Subcommittee on Surface Transportation of the Senate Committee on Commerce, Science and Transportation held a hearing to discuss one activity in particular, the possible need for ICC regulation of non-railroad company acquisitions of railroads.

Congress was especially concerned with leveraged buyouts (LBOs), that is, one company's acquisition of another through heavy borrowing. The major problem with such transactions was that the purchasing company paid off the debt incurred with funds from the newly acquired company, perhaps using cash reserves or liquidating assets. In 1979 in what was the nation's first major LBO, Kohlberg, Kravis and Roberts, an investment banking firm, acquired Houdaille, a Florida-based conglomerate with heavy investments in building machine tools, for $343 million.[40] Following that transaction, the nation experienced a flurry of LBO's in numerous industries, including railroad freight transportation.

The impetus for the congressional hearing in June 1989 was Japonica Partnership's proposed takeover of the CNW Corporation, parent of the Chicago & North Western Railroad, a month earlier. As part of the transaction, the CNW would find itself $650 million in new debt.[41] The ICC was very concerned about that debt, especially considering the history of railroad financial ills. In a letter to members of the Commerce Committee, however, Commission officials explained that the extent of its jurisdiction over such a transaction was unclear even though such a circumstance could mean grave consequences for the nation's railroads.

Although the offer dissolved after CNW directors came to a merger agreement with another investment group, Blackstone Capital Partners, the issue attracted the attention of legislators. Senator Tom Harkin of Iowa proposed a bill, S. 1005, amending Section 11343 of Title 49 in the U.S. Code to give the Interstate Commerce Commission jurisdiction over "acquisition of control of a Class I railroad carrier by a non-carrier, the result of which may produce a significant diminution or deterioration of service to be provided by the carrier, or which may increase the debt of the acquired carrier and adversely affect the ability of the carrier to provide an adquate level of service consistent with the public interest."[42]

Under existing law, the Commission only had jurisdiction to authorize the control or unification of two or more Class I rail carriers and to regulate the issuance of securities by a railroad. Leveraged buyouts were often constructed to circumvent this regulation, a national transportation problem to Senator Harkin and some of his colleagues.

According to Senator Harkin, leveraged buyouts could threaten railroad viability by generating enormous debt-to-capitalization ratios. Harkin noted that although such transactions had posed few problems prior to 1980, conditions had changed after that date. Between 1983 and 1988, U.S. corporations doubled their debt, causing their net worth to fall by $300 billion in 1988.[43] The leveraged buyout of RJR Nabisco by Kohlberg, Kravis & Roberts for $25 billion in 1988 exemplified the increasing use and scope of such transactions. Harkin believed that huge debt could devastate the capital intensive operations of railroads.

Supporting Senator Harkin in his call for legislation was Darrel Rensink of the Iowa Department of Transportation, who believed that leveraged buyouts threatened rail carriers as "going concerns," that is, businesses that are expected to be maintained because they provide an essential public service.[44] He suggested further that LBOs represented short-term thinking on the part of finance directors who desired to increase stock values dramatically with a single transaction.[45] Considering that going concerns generally required long-term perspectives, LBOs were unfavorable mechanisms for the raising of capital. Such devices could potentially affect shippers' access to markets, shipping rates, and quality of service.

Citing Robert C. Higgins, Professor of Finance at the University of Washington business school, Rensink also pointed out that acquiring a cheap source of capital through debt leveraging was often misconstrued.[46] In his book, *Analysis for Financial Management*, Higgins explained that although debt-leveraging appeared to reduce the cost of capital for financing, leveraging actually increased the risk borne by shareholders. Since they were bearing a greater risk, shareholders tended to demand a greater return on their investment.[47] The supposed savings were thereby lost.

Rensink also raised the issues of increases in cost of capital and in debt-to-capitalization ratios. The wave of LBOs sweeping the nation in the 1980s could have raised the 9.7 percent average cost of railroad bonded debt, through the issuance of junk bonds, to interest rates in the 16–17 percent range. Moreover, the railroad industry's average 31 percent debt-to-capitalization ratio could, as a result of LBOs, rise to a 70–85 percent level.[48]

The result of this increased debt could vary. The Commission might be forced to allow railroad rate increases to offset increased debt, thereby transferring the burden to shippers. In extreme circumstances, railroads might be pressured to abandon branch lines not meeting higher revenue standards. In other instances, carriers might be forced to sell portions of a line, rolling stock, or other equipment. In the worst cases, rail systems would be prone to liquidation during cyclical downturns in the economy. According to Rensink, the federal government would ultimately foot the bill for such a catastrophe. Like the bailout of the industry in the Northeast during the 1970s, the public would pay for the failures resulting from leverage buyouts.

Rensink cited cases involving the Santa Fe Pacific Corporation, Burlington Northern, Incorporated, and CNW Corporation to demonstrate some of the more obvious problems generated by LBOs. In 1987, the Henley Group attempted a hostile takeover of the Santa Fe Pacific Corporation. Although SFP successfully fended off the threat, it cost the company $4.68 billion, of which $3.66 billion was borrowed.[49]

In 1988, Burlington Northern, Incorporated, spun off its natural resources holdings to a new corporation, Burlington Resources. When this company spun off, it left BNI with a debt of $2.5 billion, much of which was incurred as a result of operations dealing with natural resources.[50] The railroad, the only remaining subsidiary of BNI, was left with the debt. This meant that the railroad was less vulnerable to a corporate takeover financed through debt leveraging, but it also strained the system financially.

The CNW Corporation was particulary vunerable to the potential disadvantages of leveraged buyouts. Since CNW was less diversified than other holding companies, the railroad subsidiaries would absorb nearly all the debt incurred as a result of an LBO or even an attempted LBO. In 1987, CNW Management and Gibbons, Green van Amerongen, Limited, sought to buy out CNW in a transaction that would have generated $473 million in debt.[51] Although the buyers argued that the debt could be paid off through line sales, midwestern states and institutional shareholders objected.

The subsequent offer by Japonica Partners would have added $615 million in debt. That kind of burden would have required $112 million per year in principal and interest payments. Considering that CNW's 1988 available cash flow was $95 million, the new debt would have been unusually burdensome. Even the Commission noted that such a buyout could result in the elimination of CNW rail service "in the event of any combination of recession, grain market decline, or logjam in the formation (divestiture) of short-line operations."[52] Japonica ultimately withdrew its offer.

But Japonica's withdrawal left the door open for Blackstone Capital Partners which was expected to add $678 million in new debt to the CNW. When the transaction was ultimately sanctioned, the same concerns that existed in the CNW Management and Japonica offers remained. Blackstone, however, did not withdraw.

Heather Gradison, chair of the ICC, explained the attractiveness of railroad systems like CNW as targets of leverage buyouts. She pointed out that in a comparison with more than two dozen industries, rail companies had the lowest percentage of debt-to-total capitalization. Deregulation of the industry in 1980 allowed railroads to adjust their operations to prevailing economic conditions, while investment tax credits assisted carriers in meeting their maintenance costs.[53] The combination enabled railroads to control debt, a circumstance that made them attractive targets for corporate takeovers.

Conrail presented an example of the dangers of leveraged buyouts. The federal government aided that system with more than $7 billion, making it virtually debt free. In the private sector, the railroad could become the object of a leveraged buyout, a prospect which could harm the carrier in one of two ways. The assailant would pay for a successful takeover by borrowing against Conrail's assets, thereby generating enormous debt. Alternatively, an unsuccessful takeover could leave the carrier weak and debt-ridden as a result of financing a defense against the corporate assailant.

Despite these concerns, Gradison noted that leveraged buyouts also had a positive side. First, she pointed out that additional debt on rail balance sheets was not necessarily detrimental. Debt leveraging was more feasible than some other means of acquiring capital. She suggested that inhibiting access to capital through this means might be unsound policy. Moreover, leveraged buyouts could serve as a check on the power of incumbent managers of rail systems. Corporate directors sometimes produced "excessive costs and slow innovation" when their power base was secure.[54]

As Gradison pointed to the advantages that leveraged buyouts could afford the railroad industry, she also noted that attempting to regulate such activity would be futile under legislation then under consideration. Citing S. 1005, Gradison explained that although the bill would require ICC investigation of leveraged buyouts of the Class I carriers, it "would not give the Commission meaningful direction to determine which buyouts are acceptable."[55] In transactions other than those involving mergers or control of at least two Class I railroads, Section 11344 of the bill noted that the Commission could not approve an application that was likely to lessen competition or produce anticompetitive effects detrimental to the public interest. Stipulations in S.1005 were thus expected to have little effect on leveraged buyouts which did not violate Section 11344. Since the Commission failed to outline a procedure for dealing with such matters, the chairperson saw little value in the bill.

As Gradison noted, these same problems surfaced in an Amtrak bill in the House of Representatives on June 6, 1989, that included a stipulation to place noncarrier acquisitions under Commission control. According to H.R. 2364, the ICC would consider the effect of a given transaction "on the adequacy of transportation, resulting fixed charges, and interest of carrier employees."[56] Gradison pointed out that despite the listing of criteria to be used when evaluating transactions, there was no explanation of how the Commission was to proceed in weighing these factors.

Overall, Gradison considered existing regulations sufficient in the new era of leveraged buyouts. She explained that the Commission already had the power to inquire into the intentions of leveraged transactions, despite its lack of direct authority. Such inquiry could provide the ICC with knowledge of an intended breakup of a rail system. A simple announcement by the Commission that such a dismemberment would be unfavorable to the public would likely "dry up the transactional investment monies that are needed to proceed."[57] The chairperson worried that new legislation would permit the ICC to "second guess" transactions made by corporate directors who, in the long run, were intending to improve service. Considering that past financial problems were largely attributable to excessive regulation, Gradison believed that new legislation was undesirable.

Along with Gradison, W. John Swartz, vice chairman of the $3.1 billion Santa Fe Pacific Corporation, expressed his opposition to new legislation regulating nonrailroad acquisitions of Class I carriers.[58] He argued that such regulation would increase a railroad's cost of equity. Santa Fe Railway had capital expenditures in 1988 alone amounting to $857 million. Financing such expenditures required the efforts of huge corporations that had the capabilities to meet such costs. Swartz noted that corporations with such ability would be discouraged from acquiring rail systems if new regulation drew out proceedings over long periods and required expensive labor protective conditions, considerations some legislators wanted to include in regulation discussions.

Swartz also argued that it was improper for the railroad industry to be targeted for regulation. Railroading was the most thoroughly regulated of American industries, he said, a circumstance that had contributed to poor performance of rail carriers and to the collapse of numerous rail systems by the 1970s. Only after the Staggers Act of 1980 did railroads begin to strengthen themselves significantly. If the benefits generated by that legislation were to remain, noted Swartz, then railroad companies and their corporate parents had to be allowed to participate on an equal footing with other enterprises. To single out the railroad industry for restrictive legislation would be to revert to the conditions of the past.

Echoing the warnings of John Swartz were James M. Voytko, Director of Research and Transportation Analyst for Paine Webber, and James A. Runde, Managing Director of Morgan Stanley & Company, Incorporated. Voytko argued that considering the history of railroading, Congress "should be ecstatic that *anyone* is willing to risk capital by purchasing rail assets."[59] Runde noted that the Interstate Commerce Commission did not have the personnel or expertise to make judgments on holding company financial structures to the degree that some members of Congress wanted. The processing delays alone, recognized to have been a contributing factor to the poor health of combining systems in the 1960s and 1970s, would likely limit the attractiveness of railroads to holding companies. This unattractiveness would exert "downward pressure on railroad stocks and, hence, increase the cost of capital for all railroads and railroad holding companies."[60]

Despite the concerns raised in the 1989 hearing, Congress did not pass legislation extending ICC jurisdiction over leveraged buyouts. Legislators understood the enormous gains that the deregulatory provisions of the Staggers Act generated, and few wanted to risk losing those benefits. Officials in Washington had weakened the industry in the past through excessive regulation. They did not wish to make the same mistake again.

NOTES

1. Phillip D. Locklin, *Economics of Transportation*, 7th ed. (Homewood, Ill.: Irwin, 1972, 577; James M. Daley, "Holding Companies, Common Carriers, and Public Policy," *Transportation Journal* 19 (Winter 1979), 71.

2. U.S. Interstate Commerce Commission, *Railroad Conglomerates and Other Corporate Structures: A Report to Congress as Directed by Section 903 of the Railroad Revitalization and Regulatory Reform Act of 1976* (Washington, D.C.: GPO, 1977), 2. For more discussion of these advantages, see also Howard L. Feinsand, "The Diversifying Corporation: Section 7 Darwinism and the Elusive but Essential Test of the Marketplace," *St. John's Law Review* 44 (April 1970), 677–757; Michael Gort and Thomas F. Hogarty, "New Evidence on Mergers," *Journal of Law & Economics* 13 (April 1970), 317–327; *Railway Age* 173 (August 28, 1972), 18.

3. ICC, *Railroad Conglomerates and other Corporate Structures*, 9.

4. Edward L. Sattler, "Diversified Holding Companies and their Impact on the Railroad Industry," *Transportation Journal* 20 (Fall 1980), 65.

5. ICC, *Railroad Conglomerates and Other Corporate Structures*, 10. See also Manley R. Irwin and Kenneth B. Stanley, "Regulatory Circumvention and the Holding Company," *Journal of Economic Issues* 8 (June 1974), 398–400.

6. ICC, *Railroad Conglomerates and Other Corporate Structures*, 26–27. For further discussion of the negative results, see L. L. Waters (moderator), "Panel Discussion: Pros and Cons of Conglomerates as They Affect Transportation," *ICC Practitioner's Journal* 37 (September-October 1970), 971. John Narver explains how resources will be shifted to that part of the conglomerate where profit opportunity is greatest in *Conglomerate Mergers and Market Competition* (Berkeley: University of California Press, 1967), 137.

7. ICC, *Railroad Conglomerates and Other Corporate Structures*, 11.

8. Ibid., 13.

9. Ibid., 14.

10. Ibid., 21.

11. Ibid., 22–23.

12. Ibid., 25–26. See also *Railway Age*, 176 (October 27, 1975), 16.

13. ICC, *Railroad Conglomerates and Other Corporate Structures*, 29.

14. Ibid., 46–47; James Kock, *Industrial Organization and Prices* (Englewood Cliffs, N.J.: Prentice-Hall, 1974), 208; Daley, "Holding Companies, Common Carriers, and Public Policy," 69.

15. For two attempts to measure the impact of holding companies, see Kenneth R. Graham, "Rail-Based Holding Companies: A View of Some Indicators of Strategy, Management Change and Financial Performance," *Transportation Journal* 19 (Summer 1980), 73–77; Sattler, "Diversified Holding Companies and Their Impact on the Railroad Industry," 65–74. Also see the analysis by economist Lemont Richardson, who argues that limits on diversification would not put more money into the pockets of the railroads. *Railway Age* 178 (June 27, 1977), 32–33.

16. *Moody's Transportation Manual*, 1994, 203–205.

17. For discussion of multimodal operations of the Canadian National and Canadian Pacific, see Trevor D. Heaver, "Multi-Modal Ownership—The Canadian Experience," *Transportation Journal* 11 (Fall 1971), 14–28.

18. *Moody's Transportation Manual,*1994, 204; *Railway Age* 186 (June 1985), 60–61.

19. *Moody's Transportation Manual*, 1994, 19; *Barron's* 51 (November 8, 1971), 3.

20. *Moody's Transportation Manual*, 1994, 19.

21. *Forbes* 142 (December 12, 1988), 36.

22. *Forbes* 143 (April 17, 1989), 94–96.

23. *Moody's Transportation Manual*, 1994, 419–420. For discussion of investment in some of these business, see *Forbes* 140 (November 30, 1987), 54; *Business Week*, February 16, 1987, 36; *Forbes* 141 (May 16, 1988), 60; *Business Week*, October 17, 1988, 60; April 30, 1990, 26–27; *Money* 20 (July 1991), 60–61.

24. *Moody's Transportation Manual*, 1994, 73; *U.S. News & World Report* 116 (March 21, 1994), 46–47; *Business Week*, February 9, 1987, 37; *Forbes* 151 (March 15, 1993), 166.

25. *Railway Age* 181 (February 25, 1980), 44–45.

26. *Moody's Transportation Manual*, 1994, 1. See also *Oil & Gas Journal* 83 (October 28, 1985), 58; *Business Week*, January 10, 1983, 32; *Fortune* 119 (January 2, 1989), 28; *Forbes* 149 (March 30, 1992), 45–46.

27. Ibid., 46. See also *Forbes* 122 (July 24, 1978), 66–68.

28. *Forbes* 145 (June 25, 1990), 298.

29. Ibid., 151 (June 7, 1993), 100–101.

30. Ibid.

31. *Moody's Transportation Manual*, 1988, 25.

32. *Moody's Transportation Manual,*, 1983, 177.

33. Ibid., 205–206.

34. *Moody's Transportation Manual*, 1987, 749.

35. *Forbes* 135 (May 20, 1985), 106–107.

36. *Forbes* 142 (October 31, 1988), 51.

37. Heaver, "Multi-Modal Ownership—the Canadian Experience," 14–28; *Forbes* 122 (October 16, 1978), 127–128.

38. *Moody's Transportation Manual*, 1994, 211–212.

39. Ibid., 107.

40. U.S. Congress, Senate, Committee on Commerce, Science, and Transportation, *Acquisition of Certain Railroads: Hearing Before the Subcommittee on Surface Transportation of the Committee on Science, Commerce, and Transportation*, 101st Cong., 1st sess., June 22, 1989, 77.

41. Ibid., 14; *Business Week*, April 10, 1989, 79.

42. U.S. Congress, *Acquisition of Certain Railroads*, 3–4.

43. Ibid., 6; For an overview of LBOs in the 1980s, see *Fortune* 124 (August 26, 1991), 58–70.

44. Fortune 124 (August 26, 1991), 67.

45. Various corporate executives reflected this sentiment in a survey outlined in Fortune 124 (August 26, 1991), 73–74. See also Fortune 117 (February 29, 1988), 45; *Forbes* 141 (June 13, 1988), 66.

46. U.S. Congress, *Acquisition of Certain Railroads*, 70; Robert C. Higgins, *Analysis for Financial Management* (Homewood, Ill.: Dow Jones-Irwin, 1983), 144.

47. *Fortune* 115 (January 19, 1987), 98–100.

48. U.S. Congress, *Acquisition of Certain Railroads*, 70. See also *Business Week*, September 10, 1990, 77; November 7, 1988, 140–142; *Newsweek* 110 (August 24, 1987), 30–31.

49. U.S. Congress, *Acquisition of Certain Railroads*, 80.

50. Ibid., 18.

51. Ibid., 83. See also *Forbes* 141 (May 2, 1988), 96.

52. U.S. Congress, *Acquisition of Certain Railroads*, 84; *Business Week*, April 10, 1989, 79.

53. U.S. Congress, *Acquisition of Certain Railroads*, 18.

54. Ibid., 19. See also *Fortune* 119 (March 13, 1989), 91–92.

55. U.S. Congress, *Acquisition of Certain Railroads*, 22.

56. Ibid., 28.

57. Ibid., 40.

58. Ibid., 108.

59. Ibid., 120.

60. Ibid., 143.

9

Intermodal Mania

From 1970 to the early 1990s, railroad companies expanded enormously though the historic method of horizontal integration. Railroads unified with other rail systems and their respective subsidiaries to form megacarriers that spanned upwards of 20,000 miles, reaching every major corridor and industrial center throughout the nation. By the 1980s and early 1990s, moreover, such horizontal expansion included combinations with other modes of transportation. The alliance of rail companies with water and motor carriers resulted in the emergence of diversified super-systems capable of delivering freight "door-to-door" from and to points within the United States and to ports around the world.

RAIL-TRUCK COORDINATION

In the decade before 1914, few Americans could have imagined that motorized trucks would someday challenge railroads for control of freight transportation in the United States, and even fewer could have predicted the rise of large-scale cooperation between the two modes.[1] It was only in 1892 that Charles and Frank Duryea produced the first gas-powered automobile, and not until 1908 did Henry Ford introduce the Model T to the public. In addition, no interstate highway system existed to provide right-of-way.

During World War I, after officials in Washington learned of the usefulness and versatility that trucks provided overseas, authorities made plans to exploit this new mode of transportation domestically. In 1916, Congress passed the Federal-Aid Road Act. The new legislation encouraged states to construct sections of a national highway system for which Congress would underwrite half the costs.

The new highway system would serve two purposes. First, as military leaders like General John J. Pershing pointed out, it would aid in any future national war mobilization. Trucks could transport troops and supplies to the nation's ports as the railroads did. Second, a national highway system would be good for the growing automobile industry. By 1915, Henry Ford had already sold his millionth Model T.

By the end of the war, a primitive interstate right-of-way was available to motor vehicle operators. At that time, Lt. Colonel Dwight D. Eisenhower was able to lead a military convoy across the nation in sixty-two days. That was important considering the explosion in motorized transportation that was taking place. By 1917, 4,840,132 motor vehicles were registered in the United States, and of that number 435,000 were trucks.[2]

Over the next seventy years a motor carrier industry developed and expanded rapidly. When the "roaring twenties" arrived, so too did a national system of improved roadways. Meanwhile transportation-related businesses emerged like the Fruehauf Company which began the first manufacture of semitrailers. World War II contributed to industry growth as truck revenue ton miles increased 190 percent between 1940 and 1950. In 1956, President Dwight D. Eisenhower further augmented the growth of trucking when he signed the Federal-Aid Highway Act that financed a modern interstate highway system of more than 41,000 miles.[3] With additional funding, highways grew in subsequent decades, and by the mid-1980s, the nation had a 40,000-mile network that linked 90 percent of the nation's cities with populations in excess of 50,000.[4]

In the 1920s and 1930s, while the trucking industry was still in the early stages of growth, motor carriers increasingly dominated short-haul markets. Motor carrier officials found that door-to-door service by trucks was more popular with customers needing transportation between points that were separated by relatively short distances. Soon motor carrier officials discovered that a short-haul market also existed between rail stations and businesses wishing to send freight long distances by railroad. As a result, a relationship began to develop between the two modes. In the late 1920s, freight handlers sought to exploit that relationship by improving freight transfers between railroads and motor carriers. Freight handlers began to use containers regularly to facilitate smooth transfers of less-than-carload (LCL) freight between the two modes. They also discovered that highway trailers could serve as freight containers for all kinds of freight and be shipped "piggy-back" by railroad flatcars.[5] At destination points freight handlers offloaded the trailers, attached them to trucks, and drove them away. In 1926, the Chicago, North Shore & Milwaukee Railroad made history with the first recorded carriage of freight by this method of transport. Thereafter, piggyback service grew.[6]

Ironically, while containerization and piggyback service eventually augmented intermodal operations in the 1970s and 1980s, railroad use of LCL containers and participation in piggyback service waned in the post-World War II era. There were at least two reasons for this development. First, freight forwarders, the middlemen in the transfer of freight, became more efficient. They combined LCL shipments to create full carloads, thus negating the need for LCL containers. Furthermore, motor carriers evolved into long-haul operators so they had less interest in using the railroads. Consequently, the motor-rail cooperation that had emerged in the late 1920s and 1930s, when trucks were primarily short haulers, disappeared. Greater competitive friction developed between the two modes, and instead of being complementary, they became adversarial.

Intertwined with these early impediments to intermodalism were regulatory restraints. In 1931, the Interstate Commerce Commission decided that it would not permit LCL containers to be transported at less than the carload rates or more than "one class lower than the any-quantity basis applicable to the commodities in question."[7] Multiple rates on shipments ranging from 4,000 to 10,000 pounds were prohibited. Adding to the Commission's policy was a resolution that the newly established Association of American Railroads adopted in 1935. The Association vigorously opposed Commission sanction of motor-rail alliances, such as joint-rates or through routes, that encroached on the markets of competing railroads.[8]

Despite the impediments to rail-motor cooperation, intermodalism was not dead. Some railroads continued offering intermodal movements as a standard service to the public. In 1936, for example, the Chicago Great Western published an open piggyback rate and a joint motor-rail-motor rate. A year later, the New York, New Haven and Hartford Railroad published an open piggyback rate of its own.

In 1953, the New Haven Railroad asked the Commission to evaluate the legal status of railroads providing piggyback service. The ICC determined that piggyback service was a positive development for the national transportation system, the primary concern of the ICC as outlined by the Transportation Act of 1940. The Commission also found that the establishment of through routes and joint rates between rail- and motor-carriers was legal, and it delineated the role of the parties involved in such rate agreements. The courts later affirmed these rulings.

While the Commission and the courts were providing the legal framework for piggyback service, individual companies instituted intermodal operations. During the 1950s and the 1960s, three companies led the way—Flexi-Van, Railway Express, and Trailer Train.[9] Flexi-Van started piggyback operations in April 1958 and moved more than 23,000 vans over the New York Central in its first year alone. In 1964, Railway Express started an Express Unit Haul System whereby it shipped uniquely designed freight vans on specially constructed rail cars between New York, Chicago, and San Fransisco. Trailer Train started operation in 1956. Ten years later, it owned 29,000 flat cars for piggyback service.

Piggyback traffic continued to grow in the 1960s and 1970s but not at the rate expected. The primary constraint on growth continued to be the regulatory structure, the inflexibility of which limited the usefulness of piggyback service. In addition, many railroad officers continued to view intermodal operation as an adjunct to traditional rail operations. They failed to see the potential of offering it to the public as a distinct service.[10] Consequently, railroad executives failed to explore the full range of possibilities.

At the end of the 1970s, however, new policies generated enthusiasm for intermodalism. In May 1979, the ICC deregulated rail rates on the shipment of fresh fruits and vegetables. This step was important for the cause of intermodalism since most of these commodities moved by piggyback. The most comprehensive change came in March 1981, however, when in Ex Parte 230 the ICC virtually freed piggyback traffic from regulation. Rail executives, having become increasingly aware of the potential of intermodal traffic, sought to exploit this freedom. Thereafter, piggyback traffic grew at an unprecedented rate. Between 1978 and 1987 the movement of trailers and containers grew from 8 percent to over 16 percent of total railroad carloadings.[11]

The method of piggyback operations varied in accordance with the specific designs of different railroads, the needs of shippers, and the regulation that remained. By the late 1980s, there were fourteen different classifications for legally conducting piggyback service. This versatility attracted other railroads and other motor carriers to piggyback operations.

By the 1980s rail-truck intermodal movements spread so rapidly that carriers began to consolidate movements into hub-and-spoke networks to organize traffic flow.

Motor-carrier operations would radiate from a given rail-piggyback terminal. Hub-and-spoke networks helped consolidate large volumes of traffic into concentrated areas for more efficient interchange. Among those carriers consolidating intermodal terminals were the Santa Fe, Canadian National, Chicago & North Western, and CSX Corporation.[12]

Contributing to an increased volume of traffic were technological innovations for rail-truck transfers. Among those were car-less movements, that is., the use of trailers that could ride the rails as well as the road without specialized piggyback rail cars, larger trailers, and increased weight capacities. The Surface Transportation Assistance Act of 1982 permitted the use of trailers forty-eight feet long with 102-inch widths and with maximum gross weight capacities of 80,000 pounds. Later, the industry considered extending the length of containers to fifty-three feet.[13]

The most important advantage that cooperation with motor carriers provided railroads was access to new markets. At the outset, the inability of railroads to reach off-line points was what gave the trucking industry its opportunity to expand. From the 1920s through the 1970s, trucking companies took advantage of that opportunity. Only when the railroad industry learned to cooperate with its rival did it escape its traditional limitations. Rail-truck intermodal operations allowed railroads to share in those markets that required "door-to-door" service and that had eluded railroads for decades.

RAIL-WATER COOPERATION

Historically, railroads maintained close relationships with water carriers in the transportation of containerized freight. As early as 1839, when the Pennsylvania Canal opened between Philadelphia and Pittsburgh, railroads interchanged containerized freight with barge operators. Between 1847 and 1896, the New York, New Haven & Hartford Railroad and the Fall River Steamship Line regularly coordinated operations and interchanged standardized containers in cargo movements.[14]

Unfortunately, the use of containers during the nineteenth and early twentieth century did not advance the cause of intermodalism. Such containers were strictly an instrument to protect goods in transit rather than to facilitate rapid and efficient transfers between railroads and barge operators. With the decline of the "canal era" by the mid-nineteenth century, railroads focused even less on the efficiency of remaining interchanges. Instead, transportation operators concentrated their efforts on station-to-station rail service, making the shippers of less than carload lots responsible for pickups and deliveries at the stations. Meanwhile, freight handlers restricted the use of containers to the transportation of less-than-carload shipments.

The lack of interest in containerized shipments continued until the 1950s. Previously, transportation operators concentrated their efforts on achieving single-mode efficiency. Nationalization of the railroad industry during World War I provided a prime example of this thinking. In attempting to find solutions to the bottlenecks at eastern ports, federal officials focused their efforts entirely on coordinating the allocation of boxcars. Because the goal was to expedite the traffic flow of a single mode of transportation, federal authorities were not interested in rationalizing cargo transfers to ocean carriers.

The proliferation of unit trains, especially during the 1950s, further discouraged containerization. Railroads instituted specialized operations for the long-distance transportation of such bulk commodities as grain, coal, and other ores. Railroads found that they could link from 75 to 100 hopper cars together, each hauling 100 tons, and move commodities from origin to final destination at a slow but steady pace.[15] Such operations eliminated any possible need for cumbersome intermodal transfers to barges or steamships operating on inland waterways.[16]

Nevertheless, prior to the 1950s, there was some growth of intermodal operations between water carriers and railroads. In 1929, Seatrain Lines, an ocean carrier, placed rail tracks on the decks of several ships to service better its U.S.-Cuban operations. Rail cars serving as containers rolled on and off the ships. In 1953, the Alaska Steamship Company was regularly hauling cargo vans between the cities of Seattle and Seward; and later in the decade, the Bowling Green Storage and Van Company of New York shipped loaded vans across the Atlantic. Despite such experiments, however, transfers of freight between railroads and ships remained a small part of railroad activities.[17]

It was a trucking executive of the Atlantic Steamship Company who in 1956 conducted an experiment that changed markedly the nature of rail-water cooperation.[18] In April, Malcom McLean used two converted tankers, the *Ideal X* and the *Alema*, to transport cargo "containerized" in 58 twenty-foot steel boxes from Newark, New Jersey, to Houston, Texas. The experiment demonstrated the enormous advantages of containerization. The following year, the company had in service ten specially designed ships with mounted cranes and a capacity of 226 thirty-five foot containers. In 1958, the prospering company, with McLean as chairman, became Sea-Land Services. Sea-Land served only New York and Puerto Rico, but the firm later became a world famous containership operation.[19]

Soon other carriers joined Sea-Land in the use of containers. Matson Navigation Company served a mainland-to- Hawaii run, and in 1960 Grace Line offered the first container service to points in Central and South America. In 1966, Sea-Land introduced container service to the transatlantic market when it inaugurated operations from Port Newark to Rotterdam, Netherlands; Bremerhaven, Germany; and Grangemouth, Scotland. Subsequently, foreign carriers entered the business with the Atlantic Coast Line, a transatlantic container operation run by a consortium of six European carriers and CAST, a Canadian-European firm. In 1973, containerships dominated transatlantic cargo shipping, and by the mid-1980s shipping lines handled more than 60 percent of all ocean cargo traffic in that manner.[20]

As the container revolution swept the shipping industry, container interchanges between rail and water carriers also began to develop but at a slower pace. Initially, several factors inhibited the growth of intermodal transfers between rail and water carriers, including investment costs, skepticism, research deficiencies, and pricing practices.[21] The initial investment in containers and other needed equipment was substantial. Significant savings in turnaround time, moreover, could only be realized when entire shipping operations were containerized. Partial containerized operations were unfeasible. Skepticism in the Defense Department, Military Sea Transport, and other organizations ensured that container operations would not receive subsidies from the federal government. Labor unions, fearing that such operations might eliminate the need for large numbers of longshoremen, added to the opposition. Furthermore, where containerized operations did exist, the advantages were sometimes lost. Uninformed operators were not initially aware that stopping at too many ports of call eliminated the quick turnaround advantages generated by container movements. Finally, since container operations involved pricing by the container, commodity pricing was to be eliminated. This concerned many shippers which did not want to change their methods.

Nevertheless, both shipping and rail companies benefited from the container revolution. Railroads gained by acting as "land-bridges" for water carriers. Bridge operations, first introduced in 1972, had two characteristics: the same container was used at every step in the movement of the cargo, and a single all-inclusive bill of lading covered the shipment from origin to final destination.[22] After the Shipping Act of 1984 deregulated pricing, carriers began charging a single rate for all legs of a shipment. For example, a customer wanting goods shipped from a European port to St. Louis, Missouri, would pay a single rate which covered the transatlantic shipment by ocean carrier, the transfer of the cargo to rail or truck in New York or New Orleans, and the delivery to the destination in St. Louis. Meanwhile, the cargo was safe because it was not removed from its container.

This service was so appealing to customers that it attracted new business to the firms providing it. That benefitted the railroads which often provided the overland portion of a shipment. Estimates revealing how lucrative such operations were to railroads showed that about 50 percent of all freight tonnage moving from points in East Asia to the North American East Coast in the late 1980s moved, at some point, on trains consisting of double-stacked containers on flat cars. In the 1980s, the use of double-stacked container trains had grown rapidly. In April 1984, for example, American Presidential Lines was the only operator providing weekly double-stacked service and only between Los Angeles and Chicago. About a year later, eight operators offered double-stacked coast-to-coast service, including Maersk, Burlington Northern Railroad, and the pioneer Sea-Land. By 1988, seventy-six trains a week hauled double-stack container shipments between twenty pairs of cities. Traffic of this kind grew from 10 percent of all rail intermodal movements in 1985 to 40 percent by 1988. Several Class I railroads added this service to their operations during those years. Included were CSX, Grand Trunk, and Santa Fe.[23]

There was little sign that this growth would slow by the mid-1990s. Newly emerging container operators had not yet fully exploited the freedoms generated by deregulatory measures in the 1980s. Greater efficiencies in container movements by railroads attracted shippers dependent on on-time deliveries. Innovations started to make possible the containerization of such bulk commodities as petroleum, grains, and ores; and highly advanced computerized data systems facilitated the interchange of technology and coordination of movements with governments, transportation operators, and customers.[24]

Containerization contributed to the rise of several related industries: container manufacturers and leasing companies, intermodal facilities contractors, and intermodal computer systems manufacturers.[25] In addition, rail-car manufacturers invested in the production of double-stack cars, skeleton flatcars, and spine cars. At the same time, rail carriers invested huge sums in rebuilding underpasses and throughways to accommodate these new cars.

CONVERGENCE: MULTIMODAL ALLIANCES

As railroads cooperated more closely with water carriers and motor carriers, they became more sensitive to the needs of those modes of transportation. Various modes operating in unison began to resemble single multimodal systems. The next logical step in that relationship was to merge various modes within a single corporation. The various modes could then ensure future cooperation, rationalize administrative functions, and diversify investments.[26] For the rail carriers the idea had enormous potential.

Unfortunately for the railroad industry, however, federal regulation restricted such corporate consolidation either between railroads and water carriers or railroads and motor carriers. Traditionally, Congress prohibited rail carriers from acquiring ownership of companies operating other modes of transportation. As early as 1912, the Panama Canal Act restricted railroad ownership of water carriers. As the trucking industry grew in strength, the Motor Carrier Act of 1935 prohibited rail ownership of trucking companies. Only in cases where extenuating circumstances existed, public interest was promoted, and competition was unthreatened did the Commission grant special permission for such combinations.[27] Federal officials even limited combinations with air carriers to operations in which a given air carrier served in an auxiliary capacity to surface transportation.

Government restrictions on combinations between different modes of transportation endured until the 1980s as a result of two assumptions. First, the Commission believed that allowing such unions would inevitably lead to a lessening of competition in freight markets and endanger the public's access to relatively convenient and low-cost transportation. The ICC also argued that the water, motor, and air transportation industries would develop more rapidly as independent modes. The Commission contended that rail carriers might dominate or even suppress the healthy growth of the newer modes.[28] This attitude stifled extensive intermodal development and quelled notions of multimodal enterprises. Despite the Commission's recalcitrance, however, intermodalism expanded in the 1970s and culminated in a change in policy in the 1980s.

By 1973, after more than a year of investigation and proceedings, the Interstate Commerce Commission approved two intermodal combinations.[29] In the first instance, the Commission sanctioned Southern Railway's acquisition of the Southern Regional Coal Transport, a coal-carrying barge line. The Panama Canal Act prevented railroads from purchasing a water carrier if the two carriers were competitive, but in this case the ICC determined that no such competition existed. In a similar combination, Katy Industries, parent company of the Missouri-Kansas-Texas Railroad, acquired Cenac Towing, a water carrier. The ICC determined that the two carriers did not compete and that Cenac Towing was exempt from ICC jurisdiction because it did not qualify as a carrier under the Panama Canal Act.

In 1975, the Commission again revealed its inclination to advance the cause of intermodalism. In *AAA Transfer, Inc., Ext.-Cargo Containers*, the Commission granted new operating authority to various transportation carriers. Many companies had realized that containerization permitted the efficient transfer of freight from carrier to carrier and from mode to mode, and the ICC wanted to allow carriers to exploit those opportunities.[30]

By 1978, the Commission seemed wholly committed to promoting intermodalism, although it had not yet revamped restrictions on intermodal combinations. The ICC began seeking means "to erase institutional barriers which prevent[ed] coordination among various modes of transportation while assuring a proper mix of regulation and healthy competition."[31] With that goal in mind, regulators began to identify those regulations which appeared to limit the flow of intermodal traffic. By eliminating some of those restrictions, the Commission hoped to expand shipper opportunities in the movement of freight.

In another order in 1978, the Commission approved the request of a motor carrier to substitute water-carrier service over a given route.[32] ICC approval of the substitution facilitated the emergence of a motor-water service from points in the continental United States to Alaska. The service produced substantial fuel and cost savings, thus giving support to those who wanted to promote diversified transportation systems.

Meanwhile, the Commission had become more liberal in its interpretation of the Panama Canal Act, thereby permitting railroads to acquire water carriers with more frequency. In fact, by the late 1970s railroad ownership of one or more motor carriers was common. In 1979, sixteen U.S. railroads owned at least one Class I or Class II motor carrier. Eight of those motor carriers had operating revenues in excess of $10 million.[33]

By the 1980s, the ICC altered its policy concerning intermodal combinations. In a 1981 decision, it exempted from various regulations rail and truck operations engaged in Trailer-on-Flat Car (TOFC) and Container-on-Flat Car (COFC) service.[34] This innovation manifested itself in TOFC and COFC traffic increases during the first eighteen months after the decision. Greater traffic, in turn, led to increased coordination between trucking and rail companies as the two modes sought to accomodate new shipments.

Like the 1981 ruling regarding TOFC/COFC exemption, a 1982 decision by the Commission strengthened the relationships between various transportation modes. That year the ICC granted rail and motor carriers the authority to establish international joint rates and through routes with "water common carriers."[35] With this authority, rail carriers could establish relationships with other modes much as they had with other railroads.

In 1982, the Commission eliminated the "special circumstances" provision for rail carrier/motor carrier combinations established in the Motor Carrier Act of 1935. Railroads were allowed to purchase trucking operations even if the acquisitions did not involve extenuating circumstances and despite the fact that many of those motor carriers operated in a capacity beyond auxiliary service.[36]

The Motor Carrier Act of 1980 and the Staggers Rail Act of 1980 were designed to ease the regulation of freight transportation. The Motor Carrier Act facilitated the establishment of new motor-carriers by reducing licensing restrictions,[37] while the Staggers Act emphasized "public convenience and necessity" tests as the criteria for deciding whether or not to approve mergers. Looser rules governing intermodal acquisitions seemed to conform to that policy.

After the removal of restrictions barring intermodal combinations, railroads took the opportunity to combine with trucking and shipping companies. During the 1980s and early 1990s, numerous applications for intermodal combinations came before the Commission. The most important involved the CSX Corporation, Norfolk Southern, Burlington Northern, Union Pacific, and Canadian Pacific.

In 1983, the CSX Corporation moved to acquire a water carrier. The company, which owned two railroads, the Chessie system and the Seaboard system, and one motor carrier, CMX, submitted its application for the acquisition of American Commercial Lines (ACL) and its subsidiary, American Commercial Barge Lines (ACBL). Railroads seeking interests in water carriers were still subject to the Commission by the Panama Canal Act. CSX already had acquired ACL's corporate parent, Texas Gas Resources Corporation, but ACL stock remained in an independent voting trust.[38] Under the new transaction, that voting trust would dissolve and ACL would become a direct subsidiary of CSX.

The operations of CSX and ACL were extensive. The railroad subsidiaries of CSX operated 27,000 miles of line in twenty-one states. The company maintained thirty-seven intermodal facilities in thirty-five cities throughout its system, and it provided inland transportation for numerous ocean-going carriers including Sea-Land Services, United States Lines, American President Lines, Evergreen Marine Corporation, and more than thirty others. ACBL, which operated its barges over 4,500 miles of waterways, served many of the same points as did the railroad along the Mississippi, Ohio, Illinois, Tennessee, Cumberland, Warrior, Alabama, and Missouri rivers and the Intercoastal Canal. The consolidated companies hoped to offer single-system integrated service to points in twenty-nine states.[39]

The combination would provide the individual applicants access to new markets. The merger would facilitate extension of the market from eastern Kentucky coal fields to Texas and to upper Midwest utility customers. Seaboard Coast Line Railroad could carry coal from Kentucky to Louisville and other terminals on the Ohio River. From those points, the ACBL would transport the freight through Cairo, Illinois, or New Orleans, to Houston and Corpus Christi or to northern destinations in Minnesota and Wisconsin.[40]

The merger of the two companies would also permit the intermodal shipment of grain. CSX could offer grain producers in Iowa, Indiana, and Ohio acccess to the Gulf export markets. The unification would also permit more efficient movement of grain to the Southeast for utilization by that section's growing poultry and livestock industries.

New service would also become available for the movement of phosphates, potash, and chemicals. ACBL explored the possiblity of shipping phosphate rock from Bone Valley in Florida to fertilizer producers on the Gulf Coast. Potash, traditionally shipped by rail from Canada to the Southeast, would be transferred to intermodal operations, and the movement of chemicals from points on the Texas-Louisiana Gulf Coast, traditionally shipped by water carrier, would be transported by multiple modes.[41]

While the merger of the two firms received general support from shippers, state and local governments, and the Department of Transportation, the ICC expressed concern that a railroad like CSX might weaken the water-carrier industry. Two important facts lessened these worries. Railroads handled only 36 percent of intercity freight traffic while barge lines handled about 13 percent of intercity freight traffic, a huge increase from 1 percent in 1912.[42] Rail carriers did not threaten the water-carrier market. In the end, the Commission determined that no measurable reduction in competition would result, so it approved the merger.

CSX Corporation soon sought control of another water carrier. In an application filed July 14, 1986, CSX sought ICC approval of its acquisition of the Sea-Land Corporation, the owner of the water carrier Sea-Land Service, and two motor carriers, Sea-Land Freight Service (SLFS) and Intermoda Systems Incorporated (ISI). Sea-Land Corporation hauled container traffic throughout the contiguous forty-eight states, as well as to points in Alaska, Puerto Rico, and foreign countries. The water-carrier subsidiary owned a fleet of fifty-seven ocean-going container vessels.[43] Between 1975 and 1980, Sea-Land was the world's largest container operator, but by 1985 it ranked third, behind Evergreen (Taiwan) and U.S. Lines.

The Commission decided that the CSX/Sea-Land combination did not fall under the constraints of the Panama Canal Act. Although the applicants technically broke the 1912 law in that they served two common points, they did not violate the intent of the legislation, which prevented rail carriers from engaging in predatory practices. Generally, the two companies had an end-to-end relationship. Moreover, the immensely competitive nature of the ocean-carrier trade precluded the possibility of either CSX or Sea-Land monopolizing the shipment of international cargo. The top twenty ocean carriers in the world collectively accounted for only 35 percent of all ocean shipments.

CSX was permitted to expand its intermodal system again in 1988. In August of that year, the company and its subsidiary, American Commercial Lines, filed an application to acquire SCNO Barge Lines, arguing that SCNO Barge Lines would provide market access to Missouri River points.[44] Despite ownership of rail, motor and water carriers of its own, CSX remained outside this important inland market. The barge line's services would complement the rail services of CSX Transportation and the water services of American Commercial Barge Lines which already serviced half of the nation's 15,000 miles of waterway. In light of the benefits, the ICC approved the acquisition by exempting the transaction from the Panama Canal Act. The Commission found that the combination was not designed to drive competing water carriers out of business.[45]

After 1988, CSX combined with several other transportation companies, and in 1992, it purchased another water carrier, Hines Incorporated. Once again, the ICC did not believe the transaction would prove detrimental to water-carrier competition, and later that same year the Commission came to the same conclusion in two other cases. CSX and its subsidiary, American Commercial Lines, acquired the Sequa Corporation's Valley Line Company and Valley Transportation. CSX also obtained control of Customized Transportation, a transportation logistics and management company with motor-carrier authority. The acquisition of this company was expected to augment CSX's transportation logistics expertise.

As CSX expanded intermodally, a Canadian carrier that served U.S. points wanted to engage in intermodal expansion. In September 1986, Canadian Pacific Limited asked the ICC to determine whether its ownership of controlling stock in Incan Ships would violate the Panama Canal Act. CPL controlled the Soo Line Corporation and Canadian Pacific Rail, giving CPL a 15,000 mile rail transportation system.[46] Incan ships provided seasonal rail car ferry service over a 195-mile route between Thunder Bay, Ontario, and Superior, Wisconsin. The merger of Incan Ships would be highly beneficial to CPL, providing the latter with more direct service from Thunder Bay to points in the midwestern United States.

The Commission approved the transaction. No other carrier served the same route as Incan Ships, so there was no fear of reducing competition in the region. Moreover, CPL already owned 38 percent of the stock in Incan Ships in a relationship that had existed since 1973.[47] The ICC did not believe the acquisition would interfere with competition or violate the Panama Canal Act.

Another rail corporation interested in expanding into other modes in the 1980s was Norfolk Southern. In August 1984 the corporation filed an application to acquire North American Van Lines (NAVL), a motor carrier. According to the application, NS would purchase NAVL from its corporate parent, Pepsico Company, for $315 million.[48] As the parent of rail subsidiaries operating 18,000 miles of line in twenty states, NS, like the CSX Corporation, was interested in offering shippers a "total" transportation service.

Before approving the acquistion, the ICC had to address the objections of various groups. For example, the Teamster's Union worried that the combination would be unfair to competing motor carriers that lacked the advantage of a railroad affiliate.[49] In rebuttal, the Commission recalled that other rail carriers, including Conrail and CSX, already had poured large investments into motor-carrier operations of their own. The ICC believed that Norfolk Southern's acquisition of NAVL was no different. The Commission concluded that the transaction "will not result in a substantial lessening of competition, creation of a monopoly, or restraint of trade in freight surface transportation in any region of the United States."[50]

Like the railroads in the Northeast and South, western carriers were diversifying their operations. In 1986, the Burlington Northern received ICC exemption to acquire three Class I motor carriers, including Victory Freight Systems, Monkem Incorporated, and Burlington Northern Motor Carriers. According to the Commission, the acquisitions were limited in scope and would not result in a material reduction in competition.

Shortly thereafter, the BN received exemption in the acquisition of three additional motor carriers, Stoops Express, Wingate Trucking, and Taylor-Maid Transportation,[51] all of which had rapidly growing operations. Stoops' revenues rose from $30.6 million in 1983 to $45 million in 1984, Wingate climbed from $9.9 million to $12 million, and Taylor-Maid increased from $7.5 million to $13.8 million.[52] BN argued that although the transaction would allow its subsidiary BNMC to control six motor carriers, the combined business of these firms amounted to only a tiny portion of the general freight market. After making the traditional arguments about efficiency, BN added that the combination would generate jobs rather than cut employment. Such assurances helped ensure ICC exemption.[53]

Meanwhile, another major western carrier was diversifying its operations. In an application filed December 18, 1986, Union Pacific sought to acquire Overnite Express, the largest nonunion motor carrier in the country. Three days earlier, Overnite merged with a subsidiary of UPC, BTMC, and became an independent subsidiary of UPC.[54] With this new application, UPC would purchase the motor carrier for $1.2 billion and dissolve BTMC, thereby making Overnite a direct subsidiary of UPC. However, until the Commission sanctioned the transaction, Overnite's stock was put in trust, insulating it from UPC manipulation.

Both companies ran extensive operations. UPC, which controlled several subsidiaries, engaged in the extraction of natural resources and in real estate development. It also ran the Union Pacific and the Missouri Pacific railroads. Together, UPRR and MoPac operated the third largest rail system in the country with a work force that numbered 32,000. Overnite Express operated in thirty-four states primarily, east of the Mississippi River, and employed 8,800 people.[55]

The two companies, which generally did not compete for the same traffic, expected a number of gains from the combination. These included coordinated pick-ups, in-transit storage, and single-system service. The combination would generate $101 million in operating revenue, save $2.5 million annually on the transportation of empty equipment, and reduce annual fuel costs by $4 to $6 million.[56] The Commission found that the unification was in the public interest, and Union Pacific became a nationwide intermodal operation.

Union Pacific continued to expand its operation in 1992. In July of that year, UPC acquired the multimodal transportation and logistics company, Skyway Freight Systems. The latter shipped manufactured goods by truck, rail, and air, and it provided information to help shippers coordinate transportation operations. UPC believed that by purchasing Skyway for $7.5 million, it would be able to improve its own logistical expertise as it expanded its multimodal services.[57] With operations in forty-eight states, Skyway complemented Union Pacific's 20,000 miles of rail in western states and its motor-carrier operations in forty-three states.

TOTAL TRANSPORTATION

The combination of rail, motor, and water carriers in the years following enactment of the Staggers Act contributed to the growth of intermodal traffic. In 1980, for example, more than three million trailers and containers moved across the nation's rail network. By 1992, railroads handled more than 6.7 million trailers and containers, results that made that year the twelfth consecutive period in which intermodal traffic experienced growth.[58] Two years later, railroads moved 8.04 million trailers and containers.[59] In a transportation industry survey, Mercer Management Consulting placed the intermodal traffic share at 18 percent.[60]

The railroad industry had essentially been given access to a larger market, and carriers exploited this opportunity to the fullest. Rail systems constructed high-tech intermodal truck, barge, and port facilities to maximize operating efficiency. They rebuilt bridges, tunnels, and overpasses that restricted the movement of double-stacked container traffic, and they continued to seek ICC sanction for the purchase of additional motor and water carriers.

Recognizing the importance of this new form of traffic, Congress passed the Intermodal Surface Transportation Efficiency Act in 1991. Although the legislation was designed as a subsidy bill for the nation's highways, it represented the commitment of the federal government to the cause of new forms of cooperative transportation. The legislation stated that the policy of the United States was "to develop a National Intermodal Transportation System that is economically efficient and environmentally sound, provides the foundation for the Nation to compete in the global economy, and will move people and goods in an energy efficient manner."[61]

Intermodal combinations made rail transportation a global enterprise by providing railroads the avenue to overcome geographical constraints. Although holding companies tended to maintain separate operations for each subsidiary mode, these conglomerates more readily coordinated modal services. Consequently, oceans became incidental to railroads attempting to reach freight traffic in far-away cities like London, Bremerhaven, or Tokyo. Huge ocean-going vessels provided the avenue to this international macroscopic expansion. At the same time, right-of-way no longer blocked railroads from "door-to-door" markets. Their motor-carrier affiliates facilitated access to points within the nation that were distant from railroad terminals. Intermodal combinations gave the railroad industry the opportunity to grow.[62] Rail officials knew from experience what happened when the railroad industry's market share failed to grow in an expanding economy, and they wished never to be in that position again.

NOTES

1. John H. Mahoney, *Intermodal Freight Transportation* (Westport, Conn.: ENO Foundation for Transportation, 1985), 6.

2. Gorton Carruth, *What Happened When: A Chronology of Life and Events in America* (New York: Harper and Row, 1989), 656.

3. Donald V. Harper, *Transportation in America: Users, Carriers, Government*, 2nd ed. (Englewood Cliffs, N.J.: Prentice-Hall, 1978), 368.

4. Mahoney, *Intermodal Freight Transportation*, 7.

5. These piggyback operations allowed railroads to retain a greater share of less-than-carload shipments. Marvin L. Fair and Ernest N. Williams, Jr., *Transportation and Logistics*, 2nd ed. (Dallas: Business Publications Incorporated, 1981), 455–456; Donald V. Harper, *Transportation In America: Users, Carriers, Government*, 2nd Edition (Englewood Cliffs, N.J.: Prentice-Hall), 601.

6. Robert C. Lieb, *Transportation: The Domestic System* (Reston, Va.: Reston Publishing Co., 1978), 144; Josephine Ayre, *History and Regulation of Trailer on Flatcar Movement* (Washington, D.C.: Department of Commerce, 1966), 3–4, 144.

7. Mahoney, *Intermodal Freight Transportation*, 8.

8. Through routes were arrangements between connecting carriers for the continuous movement of freight from origin to destination. Joint rates were all-inclusive charges to customers for the costs of a shipment through all phases and across all modes. See Robert C. Lieb, *Freight Transportation: A Study of Federal Intermodal Ownership Policy* (New York: Praeger, 1972), 19.

9. Mahoney, *Intermodal Freight Transportation*, 9.

10. This problem continued into the 1990s. Timothy L. Rhein, head of American President Lines Transport Services, expressed this ongoing concern at the 1991 annual meeting of the Intermodal Marketing Association and Intermodal Transportation Association. See *American Shipper* 33 (December 1991), 65.

11. Roy J. Sampson, Martin T. Farris, and David L. Schrock, Domestic Transportation: Practice, Theory, and Policy (Boston: Houghton Mifflin, 1990), 92.

12. Gerhardt Muller, *Intermodal Freight Transportation*, 2nd ed. (Westport, Conn.: ENO Foundation for Transportation, 1988), 46–48.

13. Ibid., 183. The public grew increasingly concerned that expanding container lengths might prove awkward on the nation's highways and threaten public safety. See *Railway Age* 192 (May 1991), 24.

14. Mahoney, *Intermodal Freight Transportation*, 5.

15. Ibid., 6.

16. Even as late as the late 1970s, carriers that could ship freight over a single mode hesitated to engage in unnecessary intermodal operations. Harper, *Transportation in America*, 600; John J. Coyle and Edward Bardi, *The Management of Business Logistics*, 2nd ed. (St. Paul, Minn.: West Publishing Compnay, 1980), 221.

17. Mahoney, *Intermodal Freight Transportation*, 15.

18. Ibid, 14; J.R. Whittaker, *Containerization*, 2nd ed. (NY: John Wiley & Sons, 1975), 3.

19. Mahoney, *Intermodal Freight Transportation*, 13–14; *Traffic World* 189 (April 12, 1982), 48.

20. Mahoney, *Intermodal Freight Transportation*, 22; Whittaker, *Containerization*, 3.

21. Mahoney, *Intermodal Freight Transportation*, 16–17.

22. Ibid., 63–65.

23. Muller, *Intermodal Freight Transportation*, 79.

24. Modern electronic data interchange systems enable carriers to track shipments and create electronic bills of lading that accompany shipments throughout their entire journey. *Transportation & Distribution* 34 (April 1993), 46. Intermodal terminals also have begun using small hand-held computers to record and transmit equipment-inspection results, thereby decreasing the amount of time spent on inspection, *Journal of Commerce* 397 (July 12, 1993), 3B.

25. For an example of how intermodal growth encouraged investment in new facilities for CN North America, an intermodal subsidiary of the Canadian National, see *Journal of Commerce* 400 (April 19, 1994), S3. In another venture, GATX Corporation and Envirolease Incorporated joined forces to provide specialized containers and cars to transport wastes and recyclables. See *Railway Age* 195 (May 1994), 28.

26. Lieb, *Transportation*, 335. For other opinions in favor of early intermodal ownership, see *Railway Age* 163 (October 30, 1967), 32; Gayton E. Germaine, N. A. Glaskowsky, and J. L. Hoskett, *Highway Transportation Management* (New York: McGraw-Hill, 1963), 404; Association of American Railroads, *Magna Carta for Transportation* (Washington, D.C.: Association of American Railroads, 1961), 43.

27. Two cases in the 1930s set the precedent for railroad controlled truck service in an auxilliary capacity. See *Pennsylvania Truck Lines Incorporated-Control-Barker Motor Freight* 1 MCC 101; 5 MCC 9; 5 MCC 49; and *Kansas City Southern Transport Company Incorporated, Common Carrier Application* 10 MCC 221; 28 MCC 5.

28. Frederick G. Pfrommer (moderator), "Panel Discussion: The Effect of Diversification into Other Modes of Transportation," *ICC Practitioner's Journal* 36 (September-October 1969), 2004. The fear of monopolistic conditions was the ultimate concern; see Dudley F. Pegrum, *Transportation: Economics and Public Policy* (Homewood, Ill.: Richard D. Irwin, 1963), 250.

29. *Southern Railway Company, Section 5(15) Application*, 342 ICC 416; Katy Industries, Incorporated.-Control-Cenac Towing Company, Incorporated 342 ICC 666.

30. *AAA Transfer, Incorporated, Ext-Cargo Containers* 120 MCC 803.

31. ICC, *Annual Report, 1978*, 61.

32. *Substituted Service-Water-For Motor Service-Alaskan Trade* 361 ICC 359.

33. Harper, *Transportation in America*, 605; Charles A. Taff, *Commercial Motor Transportation*, 6th ed. (Centerville, M.D.: Cornell Maritime Press, 1980), 456.

34. *Improvement of TOFC/COFC Regulation* 364 ICC 391; 364 ICC 731; Ex Parte No. 230 (Sub-No. 6), *Improvement of TOFC/COFC Regulation (Railroad Affiliated Motor Carriers and Other Motor Carriers)*, notice decided February 19, 1981; *Improvement of TOFC/COFC Regulation* 365 ICC 728.

35. ICC, *Annual Report, 1981*, 61; Joint Rates & Through Routes Freight Forwarder & NVO 365 ICC 136.

36. *Acquisition of Motor Carriers by Railroads* 1 ICC 2d 718; ICC, *Annual Report, 1983*, 70.

37. *Motor Carrier Operating Authority-Railroads* 132 MCC 978.

38. *CSX Corporation-Control-American Commercial Lines* 2 ICC 2d 493.

39. Ibid., 496.

40. Ibid., 497.

41. Ibid., 498.

42. Ibid., 506.

43. *Joint Application of CSX Corporation and Sea-Land Corporation Under 49 U.S.C. 11321*. 3 ICC 2d 514.

44. Finance Docket No. 31247, *CSX Corporation and American Commercial Lines Incorporated-Control-SCNO Barge Lines*, vol. 1, application, June 28, 1988, 2.

45. Ibid., a-2, brief summary, 21.

46. Finance Docket No. 31112, *Joint Application of Canadian Pacific Limited and Incan Ships Limited Under 49 U.S.C. 11321*, September 4, 1987, 5.

47. Ibid., 2.

48. *Norfolk Southern Corporation-Control-North American Van Lines* 1 ICC 2d 846.

49. Ibid., 860.

50. Ibid., 874.

51. Motor Carrier Finance Docket 17030, *Burlington Northern Incorporated-Control Exempt-Stoops Express, Wingate Trucking, Taylor-Maid Transpotation*, petition for exemption, January 10, 1986, 4.

52. Ibid.

53. Ibid., 16.

54. *Union Pacific Corporation and BTMC Corporation-Control-Overnite Transportation* 4 ICC 2d 38.

55. Ibid., 39.

56. Ibid., 42.

57. Finance Docket No. 32011, *Union Pacific Corporation-Control-Skyway Freight Systems,* application, July 31, 1992, 5.

58. ICC, *Annual Report, 1993,* 45; Association of American Railroads, *Railroad Facts* (Washington, D.C.: Association of American Railroads, 1993); *Railway Age* 194 (April 1993), 33.

59. *Journal of Commerce* 402 (December 30, 1994), 1A.

60. *Traffic Management* 34 (April 1995), 47. For further discussion of some of intermodal issues facing railroad executives in the mid-1990s, see *Railway Age* 195 (October 1994), 29–47, 88.

61. *Intermodal Surface Transportation Efficiency Act of 1991,* U.S. Code 105 STAT 1914; Department of Transportation Secretary Federico Peña expressed the same idea in August 1994 when he called for the integration of transportation modes "into a seamless system for moving goods and people from coast to coast and within metropolitan communities." *Railway Age* 195 (August 1994), 31.

62. Growth was usually to the advantage of all those involved in the intermodal relationship as noted in *Journal of Commerce* 402 (December 6, 1994), 6A. Generally, analysts have cited lower costs and increasing quality of service as the primary reasons shippers are willing to give their business to intermodal carriers. Technological advances have eliminated many of the problems of limited service, coordination, and equipment. *Traffic Management* 32 (April 1993), 48.

10

The New Railroads: Toward the Twenty-first Century

From the early 1980s to the mid-1990s, the railroad industry underwent enormous change in its financial condition. The low returns on investment, decreasing levels of freight tonnage hauled, and deteriorating equipment and trackage that characterized the industry in the late 1970s no longer applied to the newer systems. Class I carriers that survived the ordeal of that decade evolved during the 1980s into new, highly successful transportation enterprises.

THE 1980s: EVOLUTION

In May 1990, the United States General Accounting Office (GAO) published a report describing the impact of the Staggers Rail Act of 1980 on the railroad industry. That report discussed the industry's financial condition during the 1980s and identified methods by which railroads had tried to raise revenue and cut costs. According to the GAO report, railroads offered tailored rates and services through contracts. Rate contracts were attractive to shippers for a variety of reasons. Not only did rate contracts outline rate levels for the commodities being shipped but they also spelled out damage reports, service standards, and shipping guarantees that tariffs failed to provide. More importantly, however, contracts resulted in lower rates for shippers, a consequence that made railroads a competitive mode of transportation.[1] In March 1984, the Commission reported that ten of eleven railroads it surveyed had attracted additional traffic through rate contracts, and four of those carriers had registered gains of from 5,400 to 65,000 carloads annually. A 1989 survey revealed that Class I railroads handled 60 percent of their traffic under such arrangements, and that the percentage was increasing.[2] Moreover, the Commission believed that the flexibility inherent in contracts would enable carriers to weather downturns in the economy.

While rail carriers utilized rate contracts to generate traffic volumes, lower rail rates in general benefitted shippers. In April 1989, the Commission noted that real rates (measured by revenue per ton-mile and deflated to 1987 dollars) declined by an average of 22 percent between 1980 and 1987. Although declines varied by commodity, they were significant everywhere. For example, rates on agricultural products declined by about 44 percent during that period, and those on coal fell by at least 10 percent.[3]

The use of rate contracts also allowed railroads to exploit more effectively intermodal markets. In particular, rail carriers developed TOFC/COFC traffic as their single most effective means to counter truck competition. Although the Staggers Act exempted TOFC/COFC movements from regulatory constraints, the railroads could only effectively exploit those markets with attractive rate packages. Contract ratemaking provided that attraction, and the TOFC/COFC market exploded. In 1980, the railroads shipped only about 3.1 million containers, but by 1988 that number was up to 5.7 million.[4]

Railroads also benefited from contract rates in another way. A February 1987 study by the ICC found that small- to medium-sized grain shippers could not obtain favorable rate contracts because they lacked the volume required by railroads.[5] This rate discrimination forced smaller shippers out of the market, since farmers preferred to sell to high-volume shippers who, as a result of reduced transportation costs, could pay higher prices for the farmers' commodities. By eliminating services to small shippers, railroads were able to reduce costs while handling the same volume of farm commodities.

While rail officials employed rate contracts to attract business, they continued to cut employment in an effort to reduce operating costs. The average number of employees of the industry declined from about 458,000 in 1980 to about 216,000 in 1990, a 53 percent reduction. Between 1980 and 1988 alone, there was a 48 percent decrease in railroad employment, much sharper than the 16 percent decline the industry had experienced between 1970 and 1979.[6]

According to a 1989 GAO report, the decrease in employment was the result of a variety of factors. The GAO attributed pre-1980 employment declines to the loss of traffic to other modes, but in the 1980s decreases resulted from regulatory reform, recession in the early years of the decade, consolidations, and technological changes.[7]

As a result of employment cuts in the 1980s, rail carriers reduced total labor costs, that is, wages plus benefits, at a rate of 6.1 percent annually. This reduction, however, only marginally affected the percentage of operating expenses that rail labor costs represented. While railroads eliminated jobs, the wages of the remaining employees climbed from an average of $24,700 per year in 1980 to $39,400 in 1988. By 1987, labor costs still amounted to about 50 percent of railroad operating expenses.[8]

According to the Association of American Railroads, as reported by the GAO, another factor keeping labor costs at such high levels was that the railroads had not reorganized their work forces. The AAR estimated that at the end of 1988 there were still some 50,000 unnecessary employees working for the railroads who were retained because of outdated labor agreements and a slow rationalization process. The AAR estimated further that by 2010 the industry's employment level would be reduced to between 71,000 and 185,000.[9]

In addition to employment cuts, railroads abandoned or sold lines in an attempt to reduce costs. The industry (excluding Conrail and certain other exemptions) took full advantage of this cost-cutting measure by requesting ICC approval to abandon 16,000 miles of line between 1981 and March 1989. This represented 6 percent of all railroad miles in 1980. In addition, Conrail was permitted to abandon 3,900 miles of line, or 12 percent of Conrail-owned track in 1980.[10]

While railroads engaged in massive cost-cutting measures, they were also able to increase productivity. According to GAO analysis of AAR statistics, revenue ton-miles per employee hour increased from 148 to 288 between 1980 and 1988 and revenue ton-miles per gallon of fuel increased from 98 to 131.[11] Productivity increases of this sort contributed to railroad financial improvement.

As they improved productivity, railroads allocated more funds for improvement of facilities. Spending on track and other structures increased from $950 million in 1980 to about $3.5 billion in 1985. Although funding fell slightly in subsequent years, it remained higher than during the 1970s. By January 1988, the Department of Defense, commenting on the track necessary to meet national defense purposes, noted that the nation's railroad network "was in its best readiness condition in two decades."[12] The Federal Railroad Administration also agreed that facilities improved, noting that the number of accidents caused by track defects declined almost 50 percent between 1982 and 1987.

As a result of increasing traffic and change in operations, the financial statistics of some railroads began to show improvement by the end of the 1980s. Railroad return on investment, that is, profit earned on assets utilized in transportation service, averaged 4.9 percent during the 1980s compared to a 2.5 percent average during the 1970s.[13] Railroad return on equity, that is, profit earned on stockholder investment, which averaged only 2.3 percent in the 1970s, climbed to 9 percent in the 1980s. Moreover, the ratio of operating expenses to operating revenues declined through the 1980s, exemplifying the industry's ability to cut operating costs. Finally, railroads were able to reduce their debt-to-capitalization ratios from a 41 percent average in the 1970s to about 24 percent in 1988.

Despite these improvements, however, the industry still faced some problems. The ratio of current assets to current liabilities, which showed improvement in the early 1980s, declined by the end of the decade. Prior to 1986, the industry exploited the benefits of the Economic Recovery Tax Act of 1981 which allowed railroads to defer taxes on capitalized track. By 1986 the Tax Reform Act eliminated the investment tax credit, thereby decreasing railroad cash flow.[14]

In addition, cost of capital continued to be greater than return on investment for nearly all Class I railroads. The Commission classified such systems as "revenue inadequate."[15] Although the industry's improved return on investment averaged 4.9 percent during the 1980s, the average cost of capital was 13.9 percent. Moreover, the improved return on investment to cost of capital ratios achieved during this period were largely attributable to lower costs of capital as opposed to greater earnings. Even by 1991, the Commission considered only one Class I railroad, Illinois Central, to be "revenue adequate."[16]

Nevertheless, the economic condition of the railroad industry improved during the 1980s. Railroads had begun improving operations on a massive scale only after 1980, yet that improvement helped to stem the decline in their share of intercity freight shipments. While market share for intercity freight transported by rail declined by 75 percent from 1929 to 1980, railroad market share dropped only slightly in subsequent years from 37.3 percent between 1970 and 1979 to 36.7 percent between 1980 and 1988.[17] In addition, the amount of tonnage shipped by railroads continued to climb. Finally, the effects of combinations with other railroads and other modes of transportation would not be realized until operations were integrated. Improved financial conditions seemed only a matter of time.

TIDYING UP: THE SHORTLINE AND REGIONAL INDUSTRIES

While the nation's Class I railroads were busy improving their financial standings through combinations with other systems and abandonments of less profitable lines, there was an explosion in the shortline industry. From the enactment of the Staggers Rail Act in October 1980 to 1986, approximately 160 new shortlines commenced operations, a significant growth considering that the number of shortlines had declined from 1009 in 1916 to 238 in 1970.[18] Shortlines filled in the service gaps that Class I abandonments generated. As the larger carriers dominated the high volume markets, the shortlines served small- to medium-sized markets in a way that the Class I systems could not.

These new carriers, operating in thirty-four states, varied in size. With a total of 6,932 miles of line (or 4.8 percent of total railroad mileage in 1985), these carriers ranged in from 0.5 miles in length to 169 miles. Forty-six percent were 25 miles or less in length. The longest was 169 miles, and the shortest 0.5 miles.[19] Hauling predominantly bulk commodities, shortlines handled approximately 575,000 carloads per year.

Shortlines, in general, had little difficulty in working with the larger systems. In various surveys, shortlines reported a very cooperative relationship as feeders or distribution systems for Class I carriers. Many were able to establish their own rates for their particular segment of a shipment, while others charged switching fees to the larger carrier with which they were interchanging traffic with little complaint from the larger system. The cordial relationship that existed between shortlines and the larger railroads stemmed from the fact that the smaller carriers negotiated terms of operations before assuming control of a given line. Shortlines reduced their financial risk and friction with their Class I partners by entering only favorable agreements.[20]

This relationship was also typical of that between the larger regional railroads and Class I carriers.[21] Regional railroads identified attractive locations, advanced marketing strategies, tailored rates and service, and favorable labor relations as benefits generated by their cooperation with Class I systems.

Favorable labor relations was a critical factor in such promising performance by the shortlines. Productivity improvements resulted from lower pay scales and more flexible work rules. On the shortlines, many workers were not union members and frequently were part time or were employees who doubled as managers or sales representatives.[22] Among regionals, employment was more standardized and even unionized in many instances. Still, the structures differed significantly from the Class I standard.

One important difference between the operation of other railroads and Class I carriers was an ICC policy against imposition of labor protective provisions in the formation of shortlines or regional systems. Since these carriers provided a service to the public and to labor by assuming the operation of abandoned lines, the Commission believed that labor protection would be an undue burden, one that could retard the growth of this expanding industry.[23]

Recognizing the importance of shortlines to the industry, the Commission took steps to facilitate their emergence.[24] By removing regulatory obstacles, the agency hoped to attract interest in the shortline business. For example, in January 1986 the ICC adopted new procedures for those wishing to begin such an operation. Under the expedited provisions, a shortline owner could begin operations over a newly acquired line only seven days after filing notice with the Federal Register. The ICC recognized the need to allow shortlines to consummate agreements quickly in order to maintain uninterrupted service and to ensure favorable financing.[25]

The Commission adopted several other policies that streamlined regulation of these smaller systems. For example, the Commission did not require shortlines to obtain approval for the issue of company securities associated with a transaction. The ICC also adopted special procedures mandating investigation of Class I joint-rate cancellations that adversely affected the shortlines.[26]

During the late 1980s and the early 1990s, the shortline and regional railroad industries continued to grow. Between 1987 and 1992, more than 140 new shortlines emerged with aggregate trackage of 16,035 miles.[27] By 1993, Class II and Class III systems employed 11 percent of all railroad labor and accounted for nearly 25 percent of the nation's 174,000-mile rail system.[28] As long as consolidating Class I carriers abandoned marginally profitable segments and superfluous routes, shortlines would grow or new carriers would emerge.

By 1995, abandonment projections among the nation's Class I railroads indicated future potential growth for the shortline industry.[29] Conrail revealed that it was considering the abandonment of 4,000 miles of track, and a new Burlington Northern-Santa Fe system was expected to trim its lines. Union Pacific would contribute to the shortline industry with cuts of its own in the attempt to merge its operations with those of the newly acquired Chicago & North Western.

In the main, these Class I systems were expected to sell lines that carried less than 5 million gross tons of freight per year. Consideration of a 4,000-mile line cut was part of a total 11,700 miles that Conrail reviewed for abandonment. With a 9.8 percent return on investment and 11 percent cost of capital, Conrail could not afford to maintain all of the 45 percent of its trackage the of which the traffic fell below the 5 million-ton threshold. The case was similar for the Burlington Northern, which was considering the elimination of 168 line segments totaling 6,000 miles.[30]

THE 1990s: BEARING FRUIT

By the mid-1990s, the finances and operations of the nation's Class I railroads improved dramatically. Attractive financial statistics, traffic increases, and greater capital expenditures for track and equipment development demonstrated progress. As a result, the quality of service that railroads provided stimulated the interest of shippers.

Increased returns on investment, higher returns on equity, and lower debt-to-equity ratios reflected financial improvement. In 1994, Class I railroads had a return on net investment of 8.5 percent, an increase from 6.6 percent in 1993 and a significant rise from the 4.9 percent average for most of the previous decade.[31] Return on equity rose from 6.0 percent in 1989 to 9.1 percent in 1993.[32] Over that same period, railroad operating ratios fell from 89.6 percent to 85.1 percent, and the debt-to-equity ratio declined slightly from 26.4 percent to 25.1 percent.[33]

As their financial statistics improved, Class I carriers posted improved traffic figures during the early 1990s. Total carload freight, excluding intermodal traffic, amounted to 17.8 million in 1994, a 6.1 percent increase from 1993 and the highest level since 1988 when the Commission adopted the modern carload reporting system. Moreover, total traffic increased 8.7 percent from 1993 to 1,202.7 billion ton-miles, representing the eighth consecutive record year for Class I railroads.[34]

The record for intermodal traffic was even more impressive. In 1994, the nation's Class I's moved a record 8.2 million trailers and containers, representing a 14 percent increase from 1993 and the thirteenth consecutive record year for intermodal freight movements. Because intermodal traffic continued to grow so rapidly, it came to repesent a reliable standard by which to measure railroad health. Systems that could attract intermodal traffic were deemed promising, while those that could not might expect troubled times in the future.[35]

With financial growth and traffic increases came improvement in railroad car fleets. In 1994, railroads placed in service 48,819 new rail cars, the most since 1980 when 85,465 cars went into use. While many of the additions represented replacements for older cars, the fleet still grew by 20,000 units. By January 1, 1995, there were 1,192,412 cars in service. In addition, 679 new locomotives supplemented the nation's rail carriers, representing a 26.4 percent increase since 1993 and the most added since 1980.[36]

According to Harvey A. Levine, the AAR's chief economist, improved operating results in the railroad industry were representative of "the strong traffic gains that railroads have experienced over the past two years as well as the industry's commitment to equal or exceed customer demands."[37] To meet those goals, rail companies flooded manufacturers with new orders. Railroads filed requisitions for 58,925 new cars in 1994, and the backlog of orders reached 38,970 cars, the highest since 1981.

While railroads invested heavily in car fleets, they also invested in technological improvements. Just as technological advances of the past permitted carriers to haul more tonnage, reduce employment, and achieve better fuel economy, new innovations offered modern systems the hope of more efficient service in the future.

According to Gus Welty, senior editor of *Railway Age*, not until the early 1990s were railroads capable of embarking on the full exploitation of new high-tech innovations. In the wake of the enactment of the Staggers Act, carriers became busy downsizing operations and streamlining corporate structures. By the early 1990s, however, financial improvement and reduced restructurings afforded railroads the opportunity to embrace new technology.[38]

Railroad companies utilized technological innovations to improve the manufacture and repair of locomotives and freight cars, the maintenance of right-of-way, and the quality of information systems. Locomotives were emerging with electronic fuel injection and increased fuel efficiency. Manufacturers like GE Transportation Systems, Morris Knudsen, and General Motors' Electro-Motive

Division began delivering locomotives that were powered by the high pressure injection of liquefied natural gas. These advanced units achieved greater fuel efficiency with significantly lower hazardous emissions.[39] CSX Transportation expected to spend $600–$650 million on such units over the next few years, while Southern Pacific estimated spending on these new locomotives to be in the $800–$900 million range in 1995.[40]

Two improvements in the manufacture of freight cars resulted in more efficient units during the early 1990s. First, electronic air-braking systems permitted carriers to achieve better braking performance, cut brake-related breakdowns, and more readily detect defects. Second, with the limitation of cars to a 286,000 pound weight-on-rail limit, carbuilders began using lightweight aluminum composites in car construction. Such cars permitted increased capacities.[41]

While technological improvements produced greater car capacities, other innovations facilitated quicker track repair with fewer interruptions in service than in the past. New machines like continuous-action tampers, high–speed undercutters, and wood tie replacement machines were designed with such efficiency in mind.[42]

Technological advancements also made rail operation safer. Train control systems were expected to help eliminate the problems which led to the one-hundred sixteen train wrecks involving thirty fatalities between 1988 and 1994. These would tie computers aboard locomotives to a central computer system. By means of wireless data links, the central computer system would monitor the entire industry's traffic, work crews, slowings, and stoppages.[43]

Advances in information systems were expected to enhance customer service and railway performance. Among these were Interline Service Management and Automatic Equipment Identification, both of which were designed to identify and track equipment in transit.[44] In addition, advances with simulators, such as the IIT Research Institute models used by Burlington Northern, offered more realistic training to conductors in the hope of improving safety.

While rail executives attempted to achieve greater financial and service benefits through technological innovation, they also hoped to generate gains through management reorganization. Railroad chiefs like Conrail's James Hagen and BN's Gerald Grinstein searched for ways to decentralize corporate decision making. They believed that adopting a matrix hierarchy was necessary to allow those in the field and therefore most familiar with daily operations to decide how best to improve the company. A decentralization policy would allow divisional services to run independantly, relying less on interdivisional guarantees and more on interdivisional cooperation. By reducing the responsibility of each division, executives hoped to generate greater efficiency and identify weaknesses within the transportation system as a whole.[45]

As railroads sought to achieve greater revenue and traffic gains through managerial restructuring and technological improvements, they were becoming total transportation companies. As explained by both Alvin Carpenter and Dick Davidson, CEOs of CSX Transportation and Union Pacific, respectively, the purpose of innovation and rationalization in the modern age is to create seamless interline quality transportation.[46] Shippers wanted timely and quality service in a single transaction, a desire that would only be fullfilled if rail carriers continued to modernize and coordinate their individual operations. By the 1990s, the nation's Class I rail carriers were moving in that direction.

FURTHER CONSOLIDATION

Early in the 1990s, the nation's Class I systems sought to achieve seamless interline quality service without the coordinating problems interline operating agreements generated. Shippers preferred single-line service as opposed to interline arrangements, and railroads represented the only modal link in which cooperation with other systems of the same mode was necessary to its market reach. In order to eliminate dependence on other systems, railroads again considered mergers with their rail partners. Executives attempted to provide the best rail access for shippers by owning all the rail access points. The only way to achieve such extended access and virtual control over the large rail transportation markets was through merger.

Nearly all of the holding companies of the nation's Class I systems engaged in merger discussions with other Class I conglomerates. Canadian Pacific was one of the earliest to consider combination. Its interest stemmed from Canada's proposal to sell the eastern lines of the ailing Canadian National. Shortly thereafter, the Norfolk Southern and Conrail started investigating a huge merger in the East. In the West, the Union Pacific was the busiest, acquiring control of the Chicago & North Western and attempting to block a Burlington Northern-Santa Fe combination. When the latter failed, UP opened merger discussions with Southern Pacific. Meanwhile, the Kansas City Southern and Illinois Central opened discussions looking toward a combination that would create the nation's largest midwestern carrier.

The two Canadian railroad holding companies with railroad properties in the United States discussed a merger. Through the early 1990s, the Canadian government considered privatizing the Canadian National, a rail system operated in much the same fashion as the U.S. government ran Conrail. By September 1994, Canadian Pacific, Canada's other main rail system, believed that it might benefit from the potential privatization. CP Rail System offered CN (through CN North America) C$1.4 billion ($1.1 billion U.S.) for the system's unprofitable eastern lines.[47] CP wanted the Grand Trunk Western lines east of Chicago to the Ontario border and its lines east of Winnipeg through Ontario, Quebec, New Brunswick, and Nova Scotia. In addition, Canadian Pacific desired a proportional number of locomotives, freight cars, and intermodal containers.

The agreement offered a number of advantages to Canadian Pacific. The GTW lines through the soon-to-be-completed Sarnia, Ontario, tunnel, and haulage rights over CSX lines through the Windsor-Detroit tunnel would allow CP to move freight between Ontario and Chicago. The CP could also sell the CN line north of the Great Lakes in Ontario and divert all the east-west traffic to its network linking Thunder Bay, Sudbury, and Toronto. CP Rail chairman Barry Scott noted that the transaction would cover about 25 percent of all rail traffic in eastern Canada.[48]

Despite the positive projections that the deal offered CP, CN officials had a number of concerns. First, the transaction was expected to result in the elimination over five years of from 2,500 to 16,000 workers. Also, CN management pointed out that its eastern rail assets were worth closer to C$3 billion than the C$1.4 billion that CP offered. More importantly, however, such a sale would leave the CP without competition in eastern Canada.

Canadian shippers had concerns about CP's assuming control of intermodal operations. CN maintained about 95 percent of the container business and had a proven track record, while CP was a relative unknown in that market. Shippers were not aware of the capabilities or quality of CP intermodal operations.[49]

Finally, the arrangement would draw some criticism from the ICC and Class I railroads in the United States. CP access to the new tunnel between Port Huron, Michigan, and Sarnia gave it the potential to divert water-carrier traffic from U.S. ports to Halifax, Nova Scotia. Transatlantic containerships serving U.S.-European markets could reduce sailing time a full day by docking in Halifax as opposed to Boston, New York, or Philadelphia.[50]

Despite arguments by Canadian Pacific defending its acquisition of the targeted lines, the plan fell apart. In December, Canada's Transport Minister, Doug Young, assuaged general concern over the issue with his announcement that the Canadian government was not ready to entertain unsolicited proposals for the acquisition of CN lines in eastern Canada. Although the announcement disappointed CP officials, rumors persisted that CP would spend between C$500 million and C$1 billion to acquire a major U.S. railroad if the CN proposal failed.[51]

While the Canadian Pacific was attempting to work out a combination in eastern Canada, a corporate battle between Norfolk Southern and CSX for unification with Conrail was taking shape in the eastern United States. Reportedly, NS and Conrail first started discussing the possibility of a merger in March 1994.[52] The proposal opened an old NS wound, festering since the mid-1980s when the federal government denied NS's first offer to purchase the northeastern giant. At that time, legislators found that a public offering of securities would be more lucrative than the NS bid. By the mid-1990s, however, Conrail was no longer a federally operated system, and the NS hoped that negotiations with a privatized Conrail would prove more favorable than the earlier ones with a government-operated Conrail.

The combination of the NS and Conrail would create the nation's third largest rail network with 26,700 miles of line.[53] The system would give NS direct access to the ports of New York, Boston, Philadelphia, and Baltimore. Moreover, the new carrier would offer single-line intermodal service throughout the eastern United States, with connection to New Orleans, Jacksonville, Boston, and Kansas City.

While such a deal would generate enormous benefits, both carriers were already highly profitable and extremely interactive. In 1993, Conrail's total revenues were $3.45 billion, while those of NS totaled $4.46 billion.[54] Moreover, since April 1993 the two systems were equal partners in Triple Crown Services, a nationwide intermodal trucking operation and the largest user of RoadRailer intermodal trailers.

However, NS found that the privatized Conrail was no more willing to agree to an inadequate bid for its assets than the government-controlled Conrail had been. Consequently nothing materialized from those discussions. Directors from both systems opted to remain independent. This situation remained until the summer of

1996.

Then on the fifteenth of October, Conrail announced that it had come to terms on a merger agreement with Norfolk Southern's competitor, CSX Transportation. CSX offered an astounding $8.4 billion in stock and cash, and the Conrail board of directors had accepted.

A combination between Conrail and CSX would have created a railroad leviathan with combined revenues of $14 billion. The system would span more than 29,000 miles through 22 states, stretching from Miami to Chicago to Boston. A unified company would offer seamless routes that run parallel to busy truck corridors such as I-81, I-85, and I-95; and the goods running up from the Southeast along CSX lines would gain access to New York, where Conrail dominated operations. CSX claimed that the combination would bump annual operating earnings $550 million.[55]

A week after the announcement of the CSX-Conrail agreement, NS made a hostile all-cash bid for Conrail of $9.1 billion, thus starting a corporate battle that continued into 1997. That battle included NS dragging CSX and Conrail into Court to fight a "poison pill" arrangement among Conrail stockholders, a Pennsylvania statute designed to prevent hostile takeovers, and a $300 million breach-of-promise clause in the CSX-Conrail agreement (either party backing out of the agreement pays the penalty to the other).[56] By 1997 the CSX bid was up to $9.4 billion in stock and cash and the NS bid reached $10.3 billion.

By March of that year, after months of fencing, the rivals announced a change in plans. Instead of continuing the battle, NS and CSX would begin working out a plan to divide Conrail between them. The purchase price for 70 percent of the Conrail shares not already owned by CSX or NS was set at $115 per share in cash, the very amount of NS's hostile tender offer.[57]

While rumors about a NS-Conrail combination were still spreading in 1994, the Union Pacific was already working on its own rail expansion. In February 1993, the UP filed an application with the Commission for permission to acquire control of the Chicago & North Western Transportation Company.[58] The latter operated 2,500 miles of main and 3,100 miles of branch line in the Upper Midwest. Merged with the Union Pacific Railroad and the Missouri Pacific Railroad, the new system would own 16,500 miles of main and 8,100 miles of branch line.

The Union Pacific had a very important reason for wanting to acquire the Chicago & North Western. The end-to-end combination would create a system that could effectively compete in the West and in midwestern corridors against the Burlington Northern, the Sante Fe, and the Southern Pacific. A unification would facilitate single-line service from the upper Midwest to the Gulf states, Mexico, and the West Coast. Revenue gains resulting from the union would be in excess of $183 million.[59]

By July of 1993, the Union Pacific and several western carriers asked that the Commission simply recognize UP's existing control of C&NW. UP pointed out that in addition to its 29.5 percent nonvoting common stock interest in C&NW Holdings, it was about to acquire another 34 percent after the C&NW's parents, Blackstone Capital Partners and DLJ Capital Corporation, completed a secondary stock offering of the shares they owned.[60] That would make UP the largest holder of C&NW stock. The only problem was that UP could not vote its shares without Commission approval.

UP argued that the Commission should allow UP to vote its shares, recognizing its significant interests in C&NW. In the past, the ICC had found that less stock ownership and board dominance than UP held of C&NW could amount to control of one system by another.[61] Considering that UP-C&NW marketing and operating coordinations were growing ever closer, UP argued that the Commission would have to recognize a level of control at some point.

This request attracted numerous objections from executives of competing carriers, some of whom also demanded trackage or haulage rights as a condition to the approval of the Union Pacific Corporation's acquisition.[62] Included among those requesting such rights were officials from the Kansas City Southern Railway, Southern Pacific Rail System, and the Chicago, Central & Pacific.

On September 26, 1993, the Commission ruled that UP would be allowed to vote shares it already owned and acquire 100 percent control of C&NW. The transaction was expected to help the two systems reduce rates and expand service. The Commission also mandated trackage and haulage rights for competitors threatened by the union.

By March 10, 1995, UP and C&NW decided to capitalize on their freedom to merge operations. UP began that process by purchasing 100 percent of the common stock of C&NW at $35 per share.[63] Among the expected benefits were net traffic increases of more than $105 million and $78.5 million in net revenue resulting from the consolidation of facilities and the coordination of traffic and equipment.[64]

In addition to the financial benefits, the combination also expected to generate service improvements. For example, shippers at C&NW locations in Minnesota, Iowa, northern Illinois, and Wisconsin would gain additional single-line access to the lower Mississippi Valley, the intermountain region, and the West Coast. Specifically, C&NW lines to the markets of the Twin Cities, Duluth, and other Lake Superior points would join with connections to Houston and Galveston, Dallas and Fort Worth, Oklahoma City, Tulsa, Wichita, and Memphis, all of which were served by the Burlington Northern.[65]

The UP-C&NW unification would also expand marketing opportunities. Increases in automobile traffic would emerge in the Omaha/Council Bluffs region and between the West Coast and the Twin Cities. In addition, the combination would augment intermodal movements between the Twin Cities, California, and the lower Mississippi Valley.[66] Furthermore, a union would permit UP and C&NW to compete more effectively with the BN in the shipment of corn products from Iowa to the Pacific Northwest and for coal movements from the Powder River Basin in Wyoming to midwestern power plants. Finally, producers in Iowa and Minnesota could expect greater flow of grain to processors there and in Nebraska and Illinois, while soybean products would reach destinations in California, Arkansas, Missouri, Oklahoma, and Texas, as well as in Mexico.[67]

Union Pacific Corporation waited only about a year after the Commission sanctioned its purchase of the C&NW before attempting another acquisition. This time, however, UP used a hostile takeover strategy. On October 5, 1994, the company offered a $3.4 billion stock bid for the Santa Fe Pacific Corporation. The move was an attempt by UP to thwart a Burlington Northern offer of $2.76 billion made in

June.[68] A BN-SF combination threatened the decade-long UP hegemony over the West, and UP's corporate chief, Drew Lewis, did not intend to let that come about without a fight.[69] Considering that a Burlington-Santa Fe union would create a 33,000-mile system through twenty-seven states, twice the length of CSXT or UP, and generate approximately $8 billion in revenue annually, Lewis believed he had little choice.[70]

The fight over the Santa Fe lasted four months. BN countered UP's offer with a $3.2 billion bid on October 27 in what it called its final offer.[71] Three days later, the UP countered BN's bid with an offer of $3.8 billion. However, Santa Fe did not want to merge with UP for anything less than an outrageous price, and the company limited its discussions with UP over lesser bids. Santa Fe increased its isolation from UP when it adopted a "shareholders rights plan" in late November. The plan permitted Santa Fe shareholders to buy shares in Santa Fe or an acquiring company at half price if anyone other than the Burlington Northern acquired more than 10 percent of the company's stock.

UP challenged this "poison pill" in court, claiming that the provision forced Santa Fe shareholders to favor a BN deal over anything UP had to offer. UP was worried about a stockholders meeting scheduled for February 1995 when Santa Fe shareholders would vote on whether or not to combine with the BN.[72] On January 26, UP asked for an expedited injunction blocking the "poison pill" provision before the meeting when Santa Fe would likely vote to unify with the BN. Unfortunately for the Union Pacific, however, Delaware's Court of Chancery refused to grant the request, made only eleven days before the vote. The judge pointed out that UP only became interested in such an injunction when it learned that Santa Fe had convinced Alleghany Corporation, a 7.2 percent stockholder of Santa Fe, to favor a combination with BN at the meeting. As it was unwilling to participate in an unlimited bidding war with BN, UP decided to end its attack.

By the time UP discontinued its attempts at stock control in January, it had created turmoil for its competitors. BN was being forced to pay about 50 percent more for the Santa Fe than in its original offer. In addition, UP saddled Santa Fe Pacific with an additional $1.1 billion in debt incurred in the effort to prevent UP from accomplishing a stock buyout.

Aside from the difficulties that the struggle with UP generated, supporters of the BN-Santa Fe combination expected the union to result in enormous financial and service benefits. The union of the BN and Santa Fe would divert $174.4 million worth of traffic from other rail carriers and $132.1 million from trucking companies. Most of these diversions would be the result of new single-line transportation to and within three different markets. The new system would provide new single-line transportation between the Southeast and the Southwest, connecting California, Arizona, and New Mexico markets to those in Oaklahoma, Texas, Arkansas, Missouri, Mississippi, Alabama, and Florida. Through intermodal connections single-line extensions would reach eastern Tennessee, the Carolinas, and Georgia.[73]

The combination would create new seamless service between the Northeast and the Southwest. For the first time, there would be a single-system operation between Minneapolis and Los Angeles; Des Moines and Phoenix; Minot, North Dakota, and

El Paso; Seattle and Albuquerque; Sioux Falls, South Dakota, and Beaumont, Texas.[74] Finally, the BN-Santa Fe venture would link northwestern states as well as central and western Canada to the Sunbelt states and to Mexico. Shippers of grain living in North Dakota would gain access to southwest markets served by Santa Fe. Farmers in Minnesota would be connected to feed, milling, and consumer markets in the Southwest and Mexico, and the movement of copper concentrates would be facilitated from mines in Butte, Montana, to El Paso and other destinations. Furthermore, BN and Santa Fe officials expected that BN Northern Corridor access to the Canadian provinces of British Columbia, Alberta, and Saskatchewan would attract minerals, chemicals, metals, and forest products via El Paso to burgeoning industrial and population centers in Mexico.[75]

As a single system the BN and Santa Fe would supersede the UP as the largest in the West, a situation the UP sought to change as quickly as possible. In order to regain its title and preserve its traffic, UP opened merger discussions with the Southern Pacific in August 1995. As early as August 4th, terms for an agreement called for UP to pay about $25 per share for SP in a transaction that would total $3.8 billion.

A union of the two systems would once more make UP the largest carrier financially in the West. A UP-SP union would be 25 percent larger than the BN-Santa Fe financially (with $9.5 billion in annual rail revenue), and the new system would have about 53,000 employees, exceeding the BN-Santa Fe employment level by 20 percent. The new carrier would operate 31,800 route miles and maintain 5,500 locomotives and 126,500 freight cars. Finally the combination, in addition to those of the BN-SF and UP-CN&W, would reduce from five to two the number of western railroads with operating revenues in excess of $1 billion.[76]

UP and SP officials expected numerous benefits from a combination. Southern Pacific chairman Philip Anschutz had just purchased SP in 1988 for $1 billion. By selling to UP for $1.1 billion, he stood to earn $100 million in profit for the 45 million shares he owned.[77] UP, on the other hand, would gain SP's route between Los Angeles and New Orleans via El Paso. The union would help tighten UP control of border crossings between the United States and Mexico, and UP would acquire the only route running along the Pacific Coast. Finally, the merger would combine the interests of both UP and SP in Mexico's forthcoming auction of the state-owned system, Ferrocarriles Nacionales de Mexico.[78] On August 12, 1996, more than a year after talks began, the Surface Transportation Board of the Department of Transportation approved the combination.[79] UP once again dominated the West.

Shortly after the Burlington Northern and the Santa Fe announced their plan to merge in June 1994 and before the Union Pacific and Southern Pacific were considering a merger, the Illinois Central Corporation announced its own plan to purchase the Kansas City Southern Railway for $1.6 billion.[80] The IC and KCS each operated approximately 2,500 miles of line, and together they were still dwarfed by several other Class I systems.[81] The $565 million in revenue of the IC and $465 million of the KCS in 1993 could not compare to the $2.4 billion and $4.7 billion in revenue of the SF and BN, respectively.

Nevertheless, the IC and KCS represented two very efficient railroads. The IC and KCS were among those systems with the lowest operating ratios in the industry. They were the two primary Mississippi Valley north-south rail links, and corporate managers expected their union to make operations more efficient than they already were.

The terms of the agreement were straightforward. Illinois Central would issue 21.26 million shares of its stock, inherit a $929 million debt from Kansas City Southern Industries, the railroad's parent, and purchase KCSI's $6 million in outstanding stock. Expected debt-to-capitalization ratio of about 51 percent and few job displacements would have likely generated Commission approval.[82]

By October, however, IC and KCSI called off merger talks. Neither side could work out the details, most of which neither would disclose entirely. What was known, however, was that investors in the stock market did not seem to like the idea. IC's stock declined in July after news of a tentative merger was released. By October 17th, the stock had declined $5 per share and cut the value of the arrangement by $100 million.[83]

By the mid-1990s, the U.S. railroad industry was again consolidating operations. As carriers became part of multimodal transportation networks, they were encouraged to adapt themselves to the single-system service desires of shippers. From the early 1980s, railroads enhanced their capabilities for providing seamless interline service, investing in ocean-going container operations, motor-carrier businesses, and intermodal facilities and equipment. For the Class I carriers, however, the rail leg of the intermodal journey still required the reduction of transfers from carrier to carrier. The Class I systems operating in the early 1990s recognized that need and scrambled to expand their market reach. They did it in the most rapid and efficient way, through the age-old tool of merger.

NOTES

1. U.S. General Accounting Office, Resources, Community, and Economic Development Division, *Railroad Regulation: Economic and Financial Impacts of the Staggers Rail Act of 1980* (GAO/RCED-90-80, May 16, 1990), 24. For more information on rate contracts, see Ronald R. Braeutigam, "Consequences of Regulatory Reform in the American Railroad Industry," *Southern Economic Journal* 59 (January 1993), 468–481; Tenpao Lee, Tae-kyun Kim and C. Phillip Baumel, "Impact of Deregulation on the Financial Performance of the Class I Railroads: Heuristic Models of Pooled Time-Series and Cross Sectional Data," *The Logistics and Transportation Review* 24 (September 1988), 281–297.

2. GAO, *Railroad Regulation*, 24.

3. Ibid., 52–53.

4. Ibid., 23.

5. Ibid., 59; for the study itself, see Ex Parte No. 387 (Sub-No.959), *Contract Rate Competitive Impact Report-Grain Shippers, Report to Congress*.

6. GAO, *Railroad Regulation*, 26.

7. Ibid. For more information on this issue, see U.S. General Accounting Office, Resources, Community, and Economic Development Division, *Railroad Retirement: Future Rail Employment and Trust Fund Solvency* (GAO/HRD-89-30, April 5, 1989).

8. GAO, *Railroad Regulation*, 27.

9. Ibid.

10. Ibid., 25.

11. Ibid., 28.

12. Ibid., 29. The Department of Defense was quoted by the General Accounting Office.

13. Ibid., 34.

14. Ibid., 38.

15. For details on how the cost of capital is determined, see *Railway Age* 192 (December 1991), DB39-DB40. Over the years the methodology for determining cost of capital has been challenged.

16. GAO, *Railroad Regulation*, 42. See also *Traffic Management* 31 (September 1992), 18–19.

17. U.S. GAO, *Railroad Regulation*, 30–31.

18. U.S. Congress, House, Committee on Energy and Commerce, *Staggers Rail Act Oversight: Hearings before the Subcommittee on Transportation, Tourism, and Hazardous Materials*, 100th Cong., 1st sess., May 20 and 28 and June 3, 1987, 547.

19. Ibid., 550.

20. Ibid., 552–553. For an in depth analysis of shortline relationships with clients, see Frederick J. Beier and James Cross, "Shortline-Client Relationships: Can Local Carriers Be More Than Small Railroads," *Transportation Journal* 33 (Winter 1993), 5–15.

21. Regionals differed from shortlines in size. Shortlines operated less than 250 miles of track, while regional systems operated more miles but did not attain Class I status. For details on the post-1984 experience with small and regional railroads, see John F. Due and Suzanne D. Leever, "The Post-1984 Experience with New Small and Regional Railroads," *Transportation Journal* 33 (Fall 1993), 40–53; *Railway Age* 190 (February 1989), 39–43.

22. U.S. Congress, Senate, *Short Line and Regional Railroads: Hearing before the Subcommittee on Surface Transportation*, 99th Cong., 2nd sess., July 25, 1986, 25.

23. A Supreme Court case in 1987, *Pittsburgh and Lake Erie Railroad v. Railroad Labor Executives*, upheld the Commission determination that labor protective provisions would not be required in shortline acquisitions. However, while this case was being tried, shortline sales dropped off drastically. Businesses were apparently worried about the potential loss of exemption privileges. It seemed as if they were interested in acquiring shortlines only if exemption from labor protection was assured.

24. U.S. Congress, *Short Line and Regional Railroads*, 26.

25. Ibid., 26.

26. Ibid.

27. Michael Babcock, Marvin Prater, and John Morrill, "A Profile of Short Line Railroad Success," *Transportation Journal* 34 (Fall 1994), 23.

28. ICC, *Annual Report, 1993*, 19. For more information on the factors affecting shortline performance, see Curtis M. Grimm and Harry J. Sapienza, "Determinants of Shortline Railroad Performance," *Transportation Journal* 32 (Spring 1993), 5–14.

29. *Traffic World* 242 (June19, 1995), 25–29.

30. Ibid.

31. U.S. Interstate Commerce Commission, Office of Economic and Environmental Analysis, *Class I Freight Railroads—Selected Earnings Data* (Washington, D.C.: Interstate Commerce Commission, 1994).

32. ICC, *Annual Report, 1989–1994*.

33. Ibid.

34. Association of American Railroads, *Trends: Railroads Record-Breaking Year Ends Strongly*, Pamphelet (Washington, D.C.: Association of American Railroads, January 5, 1995), 1.

35. Ibid., 2; *Journal of Commerce* 402 (November 21, 1994), 83; 403 (January 12, 1995), 3B; 403 (January 9, 1995), 563.

36. Association of American Railroads, *Trends: Rail Freight Car Fleet Increases*, Pamphlet (Washington, D.C.: Association of American Railroads, February 21, 1995), 1–2.

37. Ibid.

38. *Railway Age* 195 (September 1994), 55. See also 196 (January 1995), 33.

39. *Railway Age* 195 (September 1994), 56. The Union Pacific achieved similar success after it found that two 6,000-hp a.c. locomotives (a recent innovation) could provide enormous fuel savings and more rapid service than the traditional three 4,000-hp d.c. units. See *Railway Age* 196 (April 1995), 20; *Journal of Commerce* 398 (November 15, 1993), 6C.

40. *Railway Age* 195 (November 1994), 25–27; 195 (May 1994), 41–44.

41. *Railway Age* 195 (May 1994), 41–44.

42. Ibid.

43. *Computerworld* 28 (July 25, 1994), 24.

44. Ibid.; *Distribution* 94 (April 1995), 70; *Traffic Management* 33 (August 1994), 39–41. Conrail had a similar tracking system known as ACCESS. *Distribution* 93 (November 1994), 46–50.

45. *Railway Age* 195 (September 1994), 36–37; *Financial World* 161(March 1992), 52–55.

46. *Railway Age* 195 (May 1994), 41–44; 195 (March 1994), 38–39.

47. Canada's eastern lines cost CN and CP more than $2 billion in losses in 1993. *Traffic World* 240 (October 3, 1994), 10–11; *Traffic World*, 240 (November 14, 1994), 76.

48. Traffic World 240 (November 14, 1994), 76.

49. Ibid.; see also *Journal of Commerce* 401 (September 22, 1994), 33.

50. Journal of Commerce 401 (September 22, 1994), 33.

51. *Traffic World* 240 (December 19, 1994), 36.

52. *Traffic World* 239 (August 8, 1994), 9.

53. Ibid.

54. Ibid.

55. *Fortune* (November 11, 1996), 151–152.

56. *Railway Age* (November 1996), 23–26.

57. *Journal of Commerce* 411(March 4, 1997), 1A, 3B; 411(March 5, 1997), 1A, 3B.

58. Finance Docket No. 32133, *Union Pacific Corporation, Union Pacific Railroad Company and Missouri Pacific Railroad Company-Control-Chicago and North Western Holdings Corporation and the Chicago and North Western Transportation Company*, application, January 29, 1993, 1; *Distribution* 93 (April 1994), 20; *Railway Age* 194 (March 1993), 6.

59. Finance Docket No. 32133, application, 10–11.

60. *Traffic World* 235 (July 12, 1993), 28. For breakdown of stock ownership of C&NW, see Finance Docket No. 32133, application, 6.

61. Finance Docket No. 32133, application, 6.

62. *Traffic World* 237 (January 10, 1994), 38.

63. *Journal of Commerce* 404 (April 5, 1995), 1A; *Railway Age* 196 (April 1995), 6.

64. Finance Docket No. 32133, application, 19–20.

65. Ibid., 377.

66. Together UP and C&NW would gain control of 27 percent of railroad intermodal traffic, cover all West Coast ports, and operate terminals in 40 cities and subsidiary locations. *Journal of Commerce* 400 (July 13, 1994), 1A. See also *Financial Times* 7 (July 1994), 23.

67. Finance Docket No. 32133, application, 382–386.

68. *Wall Street Journal* 12 (July 1, 1994), 3.

69. *Business Week*, November 14, 1994, 100.

70. *Traffic World* 239 (July 11, 1994), 9.

71. *Wall Street Journal* 12 (October 28, 1994), 3.

72. *Traffic World* 241 (February 6, 1995), 10–11.

73. Finance Docket No. 32549 *Burlington Northern Inc. and Burnlington Northern Railroad Company-Control and Merger-Santa Fe Pacific Corporation and the Atchison, Topeka, and Santa Fe Railway Company*, application, 46–47.

74. Ibid., 220.

75. Ibid., 32–34.

76. *Journal of Commerce* 405 (August 4, 1995), 1A; *Wall Street Journal* 226 (August 4, 1995), A3–A4.

77. *Journal of Commerce* 405 (August 4, 1995), 8A.

78. Ibid.

79. Finance Docket No. 32760, *Union Pacific Corporation, Union Pacific Railroad Company, Missouri Pacific Railroad Company-Control-Southern Pacific Transportation Company, SPCL Corporation, and the Denver & Rio Grande Western*, 1.

80. *Traffic World* 235 (July 25, 1994), 9.

81. For example, the BN operated 24,500 miles of line by itself. *Traffic World* 239 (July 25, 1994), 9.

82. Ibid.

83. *Traffic World* 240 (October 31, 1994), 9.

11

Conclusion:
A Universal Language

The consolidation of the railroad industry between 1970 and 1995 was representative of a phenomenon sweeping corporate America. During the 1980s and 1990s, a wide array of businesses merged operations to a degree never before seen in the nation's history. By 1988, the aggregate value of merging enterprises reached an all-time high of $336 billion, a record that was broken in 1994 when the value of merging companies reached $342 billion.[1]

The combinations of the 1980s and 1990s came in the chemical, petroleum, drug, food, defense, banking, telecommunications, media, health care, and retail industries, among others. Companies used mergers for the same reasons that railroads found them attractive: to acquire new sources of capital, adjust to decreasing market bases, diversify investments, gain access to new markets, rationalize corporate structures, and eliminate internecine competition.

Economic ills provided the stimulus for large-scale combinations that began in the 1980s in the same manner that financial pressures prompted railroad unifications. The stagflation that plagued the nation in the late 1970s peaked with a recession in early 1980 and was highlighted by President Jimmy Carter's $1.5 billion in loan guarantees to an ailing Chrysler Corporation. The following year the malaise continued as automobile production was at its lowest point in twenty years, the cost of medical care soared to its highest level in history, and the nation's ten major airlines doubled operating losses recorded in 1980. In addition, inflation climbed to 14 percent in 1981, while unemployment levels increased from 7.4 percent to 10.8 percent by December 1982.[2]

Amidst these economic pressures, Congress offered to assist other industries by the same method it had sought to aid a struggling railroad system—deregualtion. Between 1978 and 1980, Congress began reducing federal regulation of numerous industries, including transportation, banking, and telecommunications. In 1981, the Reagan administration continued the process by lifting controls on oil prices and limiting the financing of regulatory agencies subject to the Office of Management and Budget.

Reacting to financial strains and taking advantage of deregulatory measures, corporations engaged in combinations that awed Americans in both their frequency and value. As early as 1981, for example, Du Pont Corportation, the chemical conglomerate, consummated the largest acquisition in history with its purchase of Conoco, Incorporated, for $7.6 billion.[3] Further consolidation in the chemical industry came in 1982 when the Allied Corporation acquired the Bendix Corporation for $1.9

billion.[4] In 1985, the chemical giant GAF launched a hostile $4.3 billion bid for Union Carbide, and two years later, Cain Chemical was formed from seven petrochemical plants in a leveraged buyout (LBO) worth $1 billion.[5]

Meanwhile, in other industries, corporate leaders took advantage of securities deregulation and provisions of the 1981 tax act which permitted faster write-offs for capital investment. In 1984, for example, two of the nation's mammoth oil companies expanded. In February, Texaco acquired Getty Oil for $10 billion; and in June, Chevron purchased Gulf for $13.2 billion.[6] Drug companies followed suit, as exemplified by Eastman Kodak, which captured national attention in 1988 with the acquisition of Sterling Drug for $5.1 billion.[7] The following year, two other pharmaceutical giants, Squibb Company and Bristol-Myers, merged in a transaction worth $12.6 billion.[8]

In the food industry, Kraft Company agreed to a $2.5 billion merger with Dart Industries in 1980, and Beatrice Company, Incorporated, purchased Esmark, Incorporated, for $2.7 billion in 1984. The Beatrice Company itself was swallowed two years later in a LBO by the investment firm, Kohlberg, Kravis & Roberts for $6.2 billion. In 1988, tobacco czar, Phillip Morris, which had agreed to pay $5.8 billion for General Foods three years earlier, acquired Kraft in an agreement valued at $13 billion.[9]

In the world of investment banking, Kohlberg, Kravis & Roberts (KKR) set the pace. In 1980, the company led a $420 million buyout of retailer Fred Mayer, a stepping stone to its first billion dollar deal that transpired in 1983 when the investment firm acquired Wometco Enterprises, the entertainment conglomerate. After leading a takeover of Motel 6 in 1984, KKR completed an LBO of the Beatrice Company and then of Safeway Stores in 1986, the latter appraised at $4.2 billion. After closing a $3.6 billion LBO of Owens-Illinois, a producer of glass containers, and a $1.8 billion LBO of the Duracell battery company, KKR made history in October 1988, when it consummated the largest deal in the nation's history in an LBO of RJR Nabisco, a diversified conglomerate with heavy investments in tobacco and food products, for $25 billion.[10]

The merger mania continued into the early 1990s, expanded to other industries, and involved companies of equally high value. For example, cutbacks in the defense industry stimulated a 1993 combination between the Northrop Corporation and Grumman Corporation valued at $2.2 billion and a merger of Lockheed Corporation and Martin Marietta to create a $23 billion defense titan.[11]

In the banking industry, mergers consolidated 80 percent of all business in the twenty-five largest banks by 1995. Some of the largest combinations included NBD Bancorp's $5.3 billion transaction with First Chicago Corporation, First Union Corporation's $5.1 billion acquisition of First Fidelity Bank Corporation, and Chemical Bank's $10 billion alliance with Chase Manhattan. The latter created the nation's largest bank, with assets worth a staggering $297 billion, displacing the long-time leader, Citicorp.[12]

In telecommunications, companies engaged in acquisitions as they expanded into global markets. Some of the more notable combinations included Bell Atlantic Corporation's union with Tele-Communications, Incorporated, in 1993, assessed at

$12 billion, and the purchase by British Telecommunications of a $4.3 billion stake in MCI Communications.[13] The following year Viacom, Incorporated, which had recently purchased Blockbuster Entertainment, acquired Paramount Communications for $9.7 billion; and LDDS Communications acquired WilTel, Incorporated, in a union worth $2.5 billion. The Sprint Corporation made headlines in 1995 when news that France Telecom and the Deutsche Bundespost Telekom were considering major investments in the U.S. firm.[14]

Acquisitions of media, health care, and retail corporations were equally brisk. Media companies battled to be the biggest in transactions that included Disney Company's purchase of Capital Cities/ABC for $19 billion and Time-Warner's combination with Turner Broadcasting for $7.5 billion.[15] In health care, Columbia Hospital became the nation's largest hospital conglomerate after its 1993 merger with Galen Health Care for $3.2 billion and HCA Healthcare Corporation for $5.7 billion.[16] Meanwhile, retail companies were not to be left behind as Federated Department Stores, Incorporated, and R. H. Macy & Company merged in late 1994 in a transaction worth $4.1 billion. The new $14.5 billion leviathan united eleven department store chains comprised of 357 stores.[17]

These developments demonstrated that a common thread running through the fabric of industrial America in the late twentieth century was the corporate merger. Railroad companies were among the first to revitalize its use. In part, this was the result of a financial crisis that brought the railroad industry to the brink of collapse as early as 1970, and it stemmed from the fact that railroad leaders had never really forgotten the power that corporate combinations afforded.

In 1970, the downfall of Penn Central and the northeastern railroad network forced the hand of Congress. Officials in Washington realized that drastic measures were necessary in order to revive a depressed industry. Legislators responded in two ways: they provided federal financial infusions and they reduced regulations governing railroad operations. The former stayed the impending collapse of the industry, and the latter provided the operating freedom railroads required to ensure long-term revitalization.

The liberation that railroads gained came in four major pieces of legislation. The Rail Passenger Service Act of 1970 permitted carriers to withdraw from the unprofitable passenger business, while a newly formed National Rail Passenger Service Corporation consolidated that service under one operation. The Railroad Regulatory Reform Act of 1973 created a semi-public company, Consolidated Rail Corporation, to combine the failing freight lines of the Northeast into a single system. Finally, the Railroad Revitalization and Regulatory Reform Act of 1976 and the Staggers Rail Act of 1980 permitted railroads the operational flexibility to eliminate the wasteful aspects of their individual operations and preserve the profitable facets of their particular systems.

Most railroad executives, like the Congressional legislators of the 1970s, believed that the corporate merger could help rail companies achieve both efficiency and profitability. This notion, however, was not anything new for railroad leaders. They had exploited the advantages of unifications in the nineteenth century, and they strived to maintain that right in the decades after 1887 when the federal regulatory structure first emerged and began to grow.

Railroad leaders learned quickly what Erastus Corning discovered in 1853 when he engineered the unification of fourteen short lines into the great New York Central. Corporate mergers could integrate the operations of different railroads under one managerial structure, provide market penetration, and eliminate internecine competition. Indirect benefits of combinations included a better utilization of rolling stock, a decline in fuel expenditures, and a reduction in employment costs per unit of output.

Unfortunately, the federal government interfered with the ability of railroads to combine operations with other systems for the first half of the twentieth century. In the decade before World War I, progressives inundated rail systems with so many regulations that meaningful industry growth was stifled, and financial problems and coordinating difficulties ensued. The imbroglio that followed absorbed the attention of the federal government which nationalized the railroad industry during the war—an experience in which federal regulators first discovered the difficulties encountered in operating a railroad profitably.

As a result of its experiences during nationalization, Congress passed the Transportation Act of 1920, and federal regulators spent the next twenty years trying to impose a federal plan of consolidation on the industry. Bureaucrats in Washington finally realized why rail executives were so keen on mergers, but they failed to understand that executives of individual rail systems would not agree to merge unless it was on their terms.

In 1940, Congress passed another Transportation Act. Under the stipulations of this law, railroad officials could decide for themselves when and with what other system their companies would merge. Regulators within the Interstate Commerce Commission would simply make sure that transactions were in the public interest. This approach appeared to be a breakthrough, and rail executives were eager to test the new policy.

By the early 1950s, after the nation readjusted itself after World War II, railroads experimented with the new regulatory environment. They spent the next two decades combining with each other in the hope of financial stability and market growth.

These corporate mergers, however, did not seem to solve the railroads' problems. Federal regulations were still too restrictive and did not allow rail carriers to achieve the full benefits that mergers could afford. As a result, the combination of small ailing systems frequently created larger struggling railroads.

To make matters worse, railroads had to deal with a growing threat to their markets from alternative modes of transportation. While automobile and airline transportation had relieved the railroad industry of its unprofitable passenger base by the mid-1960s, trucking companies and water carriers threatened to strip the industry of its profitable freight traffic.

With the regulatory revisions of the 1970s, however, railroads began to reap more of the benefits that combinations offered. Not only did regulators permit rail executives greater freedom to abandon unprofitable segments and acquire new lines, they also allowed rail leaders to circumvent regulations that restricted rail ownership of other modes of transportation. As a result, railroad officials gained access to markets that only motor and water carriers could exploit. The markets that railroads served suddenly increased.

Rail carriers took quick advantage of this new opportunity. Large rail systems grew even larger in a unification mania that reduced the number of Class I systems from seventy-three in 1970 to ten by 1997. Among the largest combinations was the Burlington Northern-Santa Fe union in 1994, creating a system spanning more than 30,000 miles and generating more than $8 billion annually.

Meanwhile, railroads expanded intermodally with equal enthusiasm. By the mid-1990s, nearly all of the Class I railroads owned or were affiliated with motor and water carriers. It was not uncommon to see rail systems constructing high-tech intermodal truck, barge, and port facilities to maximize intermodal operating efficiency. In addition, rail companies rebuilt bridges, tunnels, and overpasses to facilitate the movement of double-stacked container traffic and trailers on flatcars.

Expansion into intermodal markets provided railroads an important nitch in the modern transportation system. No longer were railroads in danger of financial collapse. As members of intermodal networks, rail carriers became an integral element in the door-to-door movement of freight in the United States and in the shipment of cargo to and from markets around the world. Railroads became part of global transportation enterprises, and in doing so, they developed into prosperous corporations.

This shift to globalism was extraordinarily timely for Class I railroads. A greater number of the nation's companies examined international markets when contemplating expansion in the 1980s and 1990s. Moreover, during the presidencies of Ronald Reagan, George Bush, and Bill Clinton the federal government continued to involve itself in international economic arrangements. During those administrations the United States participated in the eighth round of international trade negotiations under the General Agreement on Tariffs and Trade (GATT) and established one of the world's largest free-trade zones with Canada and Mexico by the North American Free Trade Agreement (NAFTA). The inclusion of railroads in an international transportation network was so opportune that it is difficult to determine whether the nation's rail carriers were part of generating the recent explosion in international business or were simply benefactors of that increased activity.

Despite such conjecture, one thing is certain: the corporate combination was the ingredient that made multimodal systems possible. It brought together disparate enterprises, transforming competing modes of transportation into compatible systems of hauling freight. It also linked railroads with businesses outside of transportation in ways that consolidated the role of producer and shipper. The merger was the communication link between railroads and other corporations whether inside or outside of transportation.

Considering the history of unifications among railroads and in corporate America in general, it may be said that the merger was the common language of growing enterprises. A unification could draw two or more businesses in the same industry together on a quest toward a common goal of efficiency and growth. A merger could generate cooperation between companies in different businesses in an effort to achieve increased profitability, and it could join the energy of diverse nations similar only in their concern for corporate expansion. By means of merger, as exemplified by its use in the railroad industry, corporations could accomplish that which hitherto had been impossible.

NOTES

1. *Business Week*, September 12, 1994, 30; *Institutional Investor* 29 (June 1995), 165–168.

2. Gorton Carruth, *What Happened When: A Chronology of Life and Events in America* (New York: Haper and Row, 1989), 1141.

3. *Business Week*, May 30, 1983, 73–74. See also *Business Week*, December 8, 1986, 60–64.

4. *Financial World* 151 (December 1–15 1982), 17–18.

5. *Fortune* 113 (February 3, 1986), 32–34; 124 (August 26, 1991), 65; *Business Week*, January 20, 1986, 26–27.

6. *Economist* 302 (February 21, 1987), 67.

7. *Business Week*, December 4, 1989, 72; *Fortune* 124 (August 26, 1991), 68.

8. Fortune 124 (August 26, 1991), 70.

9. Ibid., 58, 62, 64, 68; *Business Week*, June 3, 1985, 91–92; *Barron's* 65 (May 27, 1985), 16.

10. *Fortune* 124 (August 26, 1991), 61–69. For specifics on the RJR Nabisco deal, *Business Week*, August 30, 1993, 58–59; *Fortune* 127 (February 8, 1993), 118–125.

11. *Institutional Investor* 29 (January 1995), 70–71; *Aviation Week and Space Technology* 140 (April 11, 1994), 62–63; *Business Week*, September 12, 1994, 32.

12. *Barron's* 75 (September 18, 1995), 20; 75 (September 4, 1995), MW9; *Business Week*, September 11, 1995, 36; *Wall Street Journal*, July 13, 1995, A3; June 20, 1995, B1; September 1, 1995, B4; August 28, 1995, A1.

13. *Economist* 329 (October 16, 1993), 15–16; *Business Week*, November 1, 1993, 36–37; September 20, 1993, 96; *Wall Street Journal*, November 1, 1994, B8; July 29, 1994, A7C.

14. Business Week, October 4, 1993, 26–28; March 27, 1995, 180; *Wall Street Journal*, August 23, 1994, A3; October 17, 1995, A16.

15. *Barron's* 75 (August 7, 1995), 3–4; *Business Week*, October 9, 1995, 38.

16. *Wall Street Journal*, June 11, 1993, A3; June 26, 1995, B6C; *Business Week*, June 28, 1993, 33–34; October 9, 1995, 38–39.

17. *Business Week*, November 28, 1994, 116; *Wall Street Journal*, August 22, 1994, B5.

Appendix A:
Maps of Railroad Lines

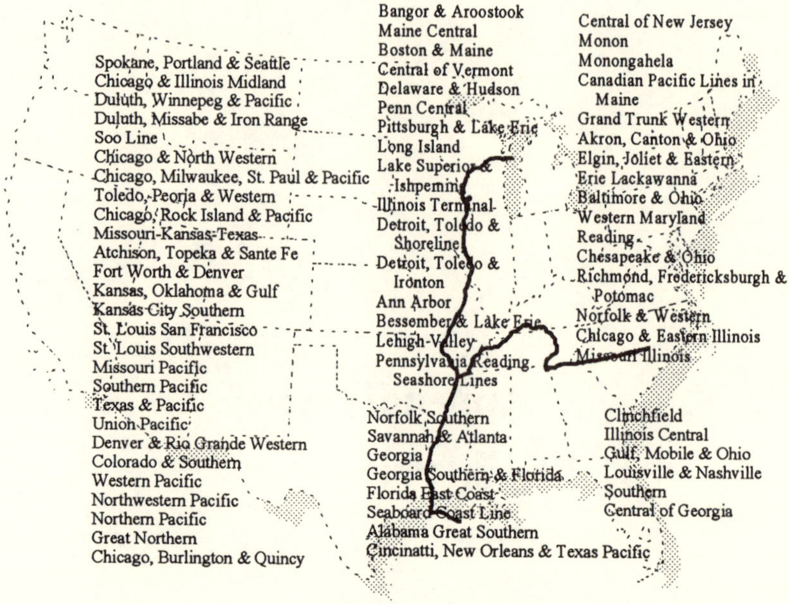

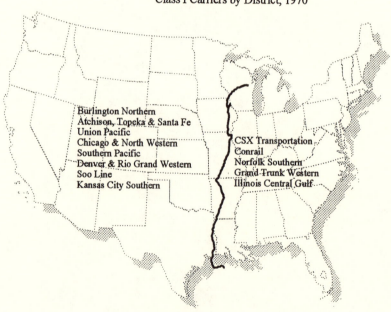

Spokane, Portland & Seattle
Chicago & Illinois Midland
Duluth, Winnepeg & Pacific
Duluth, Missabe & Iron Range
Soo Line
Chicago & North Western
Chicago, Milwaukee, St. Paul & Pacific
Toledo, Peoria & Western
Chicago, Rock Island & Pacific
Missouri-Kansas-Texas
Atchison, Topeka & Sante Fe
Fort Worth & Denver
Kansas, Oklahoma & Gulf
Kansas City Southern
St. Louis San Francisco
St. Louis Southwestern
Missouri Pacific
Southern Pacific
Texas & Pacific
Union Pacific
Denver & Rio Grande Western
Colorado & Southern
Western Pacific
Northwestern Pacific
Northern Pacific
Great Northern
Chicago, Burlington & Quincy

Bangor & Aroostook
Maine Central
Boston & Maine
Central of Vermont
Delaware & Hudson
Penn Central
Pittsburgh & Lake Erie
Long Island
Lake Superior &
   Ishpemin
Illinois Terminal
Detroit, Toledo &
   Shoreline
Detroit, Toledo &
   Ironton
Ann Arbor
Bessember & Lake Erie
Lehigh Valley
Pennsylvania Reading
Seashore Lines

Norfolk Southern
Savannah & Atlanta
Georgia
Georgia Southern & Florida
Florida East Coast
Seaboard Coast Line
Alabama Great Southern
Cincinatti, New Orleans & Texas Pacific

Central of New Jersey
Monon
Monongahela
Canadian Pacific Lines in
   Maine
Grand Trunk Western
Akron, Canton & Ohio
Elgin, Joliet & Eastern
Erie Lackawanna
Baltimore & Ohio
Western Maryland
Reading
Chesapeake & Ohio
Richmond, Fredericksburgh &
   Potomac
Norfolk & Western
Chicago & Eastern Illinois
Missouri Illinois

Clinchfield
Illinois Central
Gulf, Mobile & Ohio
Louisville & Nashville
Southern
Central of Georgia

Figure A.1
Class I Carriers by District, 1970

Burlington Northern
Atchison, Topeka & Santa Fe
Union Pacific
Chicago & North Western
Southern Pacific
Denver & Rio Grand Western
Soo Line
Kansas City Southern

CSX Transportation
Conrail
Norfolk Southern
Grand Trunk Western
Illinois Central Gulf

Figure A.2
Class I Carriers by District, 1995

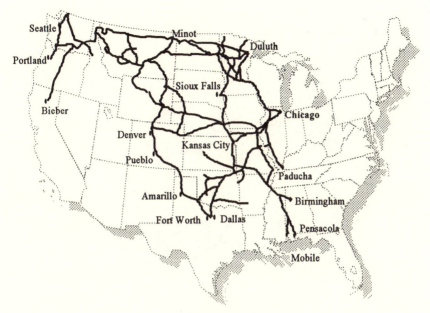

Figure A.3
Burlington Northern

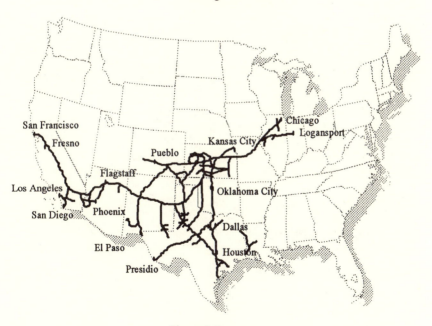

Figure A.4
Atchison, Topeka & Santa Fe

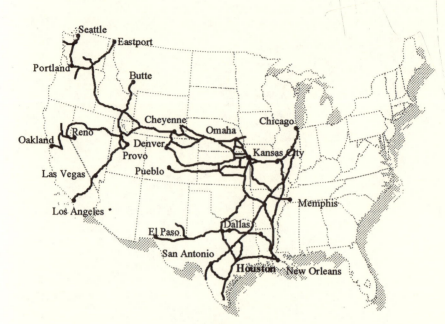

Figure A.5
Union Pacific

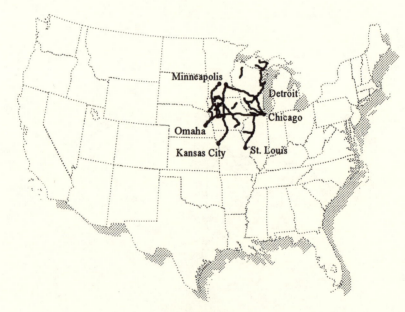

Figure A.6
Chicago & North Western

Figure A.7
Denver & Rio Grande Western

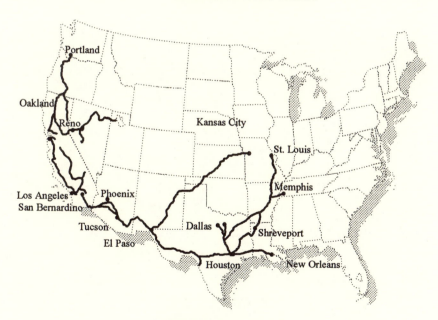

Figure A.8
Southern Pacific Transportation

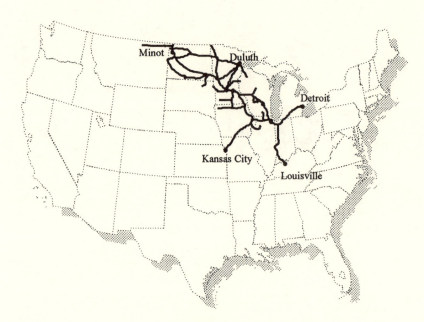

Figure A.9
Soo Line

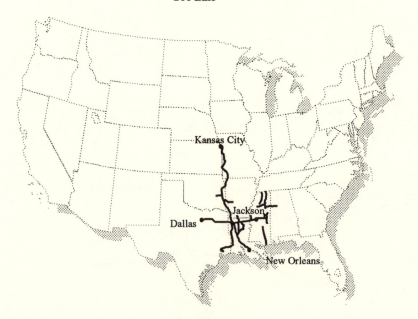

Figure A.10
Kansas City Southern

Figure A.11
CSX Transportation

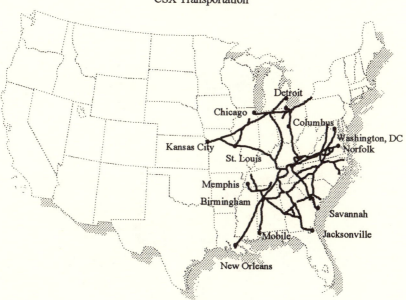

Figure A.12
Norfolk Southern

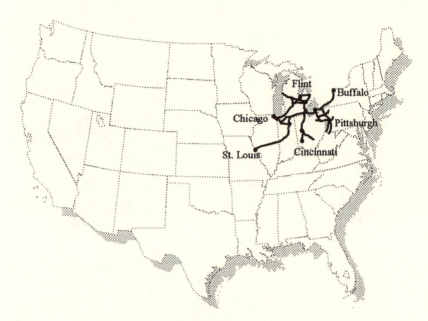

Figure A.13
Grand Trunk Western

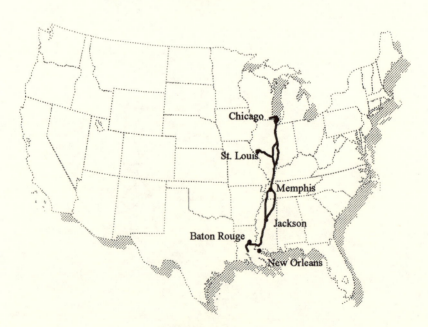

Figure A.14
Illinois Central Gulf

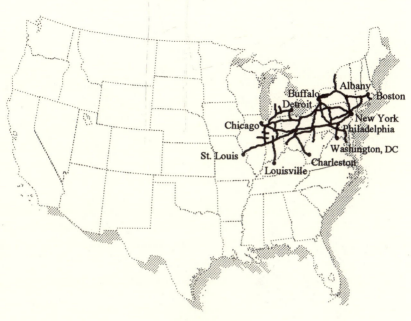

Figure A.15
Conrail

Appendix B:
Flow Charts of Railroad
Corporate Structures

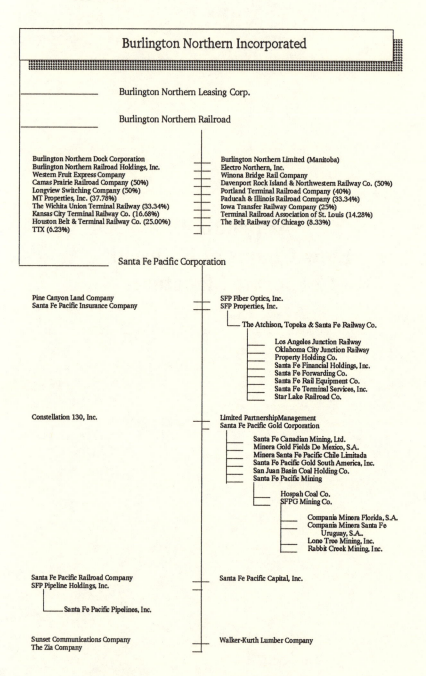

Figure B.1
Corporate Structure of Burlington Northern and Atchison,
Topeka & Santa Fe

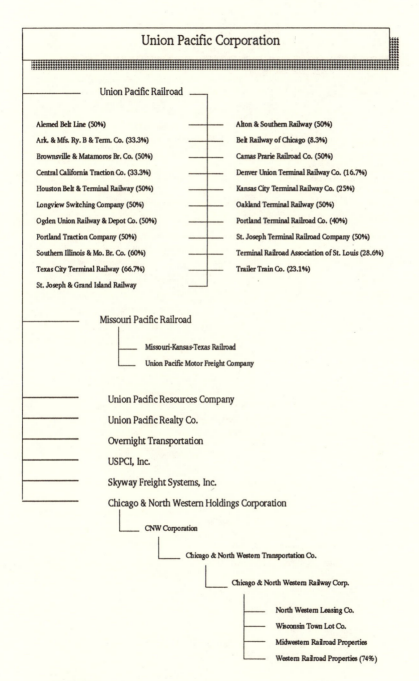

Figure B.2
Corporate Structure of Union Pacific and Chicago & North Western

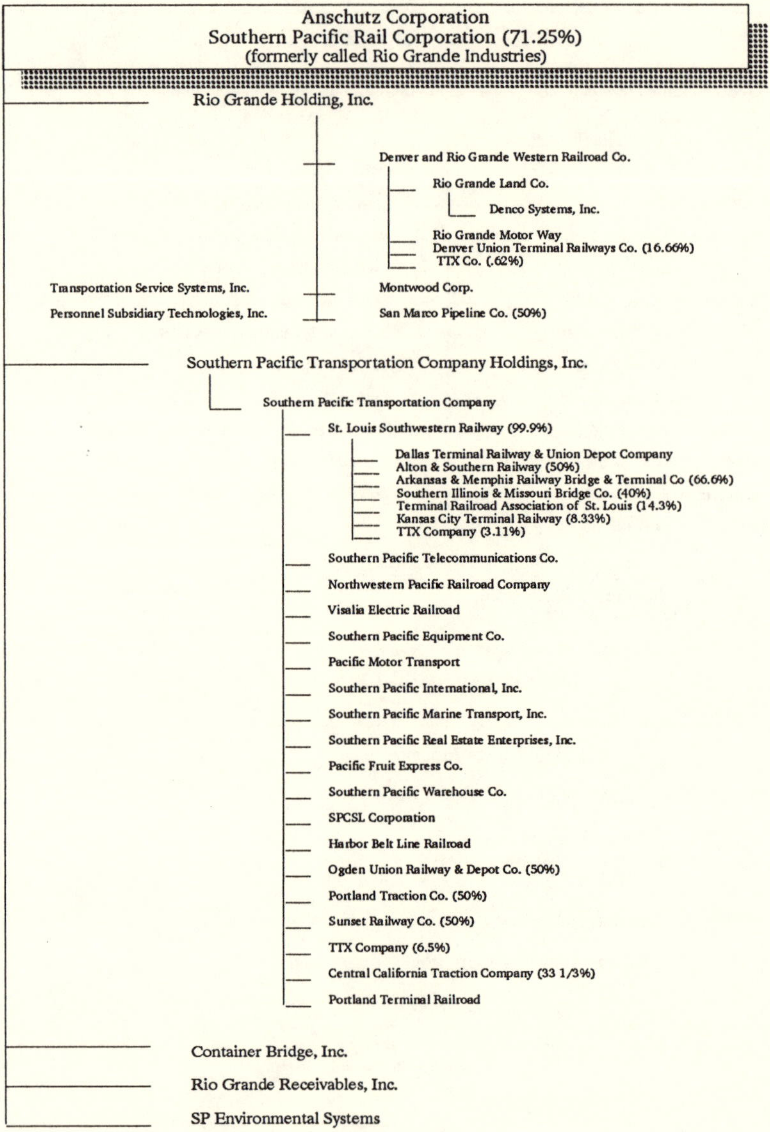

Anschutz Corporation Southern Pacific Rail Corporation (71.25%) (formerly called Rio Grande Industries)

Rio Grande Holding, Inc.

Denver and Rio Grande Western Railroad Co.

Rio Grande Land Co.

Denco Systems, Inc.

Rio Grande Motor Way
Denver Union Terminal Railways Co. (16.66%)
TTX Co. (.62%)

Transportation Service Systems, Inc.

Montwood Corp.

Personnel Subsidiary Technologies, Inc.

San Marco Pipeline Co. (50%)

Southern Pacific Transportation Company Holdings, Inc.

Southern Pacific Transportation Company

St. Louis Southwestern Railway (99.9%)

Dallas Terminal Railway & Union Depot Company
Alton & Southern Railway (50%)
Arkansas & Memphis Railway Bridge & Terminal Co (66.6%)
Southern Illinois & Missouri Bridge Co. (40%)
Terminal Railroad Association of St. Louis (14.3%)
Kansas City Terminal Railway (8.33%)
TTX Company (3.11%)

Southern Pacific Telecommunications Co.

Northwestern Pacific Railroad Company

Visalia Electric Railroad

Southern Pacific Equipment Co.

Pacific Motor Transport

Southern Pacific International, Inc.

Southern Pacific Marine Transport, Inc.

Southern Pacific Real Estate Enterprises, Inc.

Pacific Fruit Express Co.

Southern Pacific Warehouse Co.

SPCSL Corporation

Harbor Belt Line Railroad

Ogden Union Railway & Depot Co. (50%)

Portland Traction Co. (50%)

Sunset Railway Co. (50%)

TTX Company (6.5%)

Central California Traction Company (33 1/3%)

Portland Terminal Railroad

Container Bridge, Inc.

Rio Grande Receivables, Inc.

SP Environmental Systems

Figure B.3
Corporate Structure of Southern Pacific Transportation and
Denver & Rio Grande Western

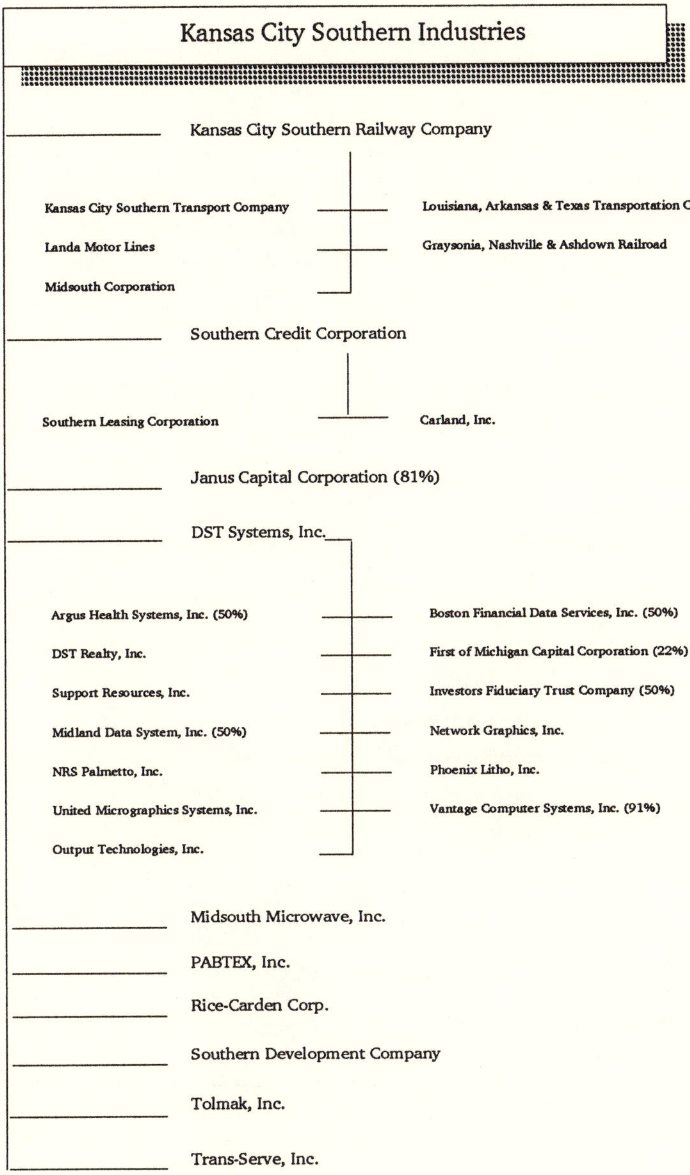

Kansas City Southern Industries

Kansas City Southern Railway Company

Kansas City Southern Transport Company	Louisiana, Arkansas & Texas Transportation Co.
Landa Motor Lines	Graysonia, Nashville & Ashdown Railroad
Midsouth Corporation	

Southern Credit Corporation

Southern Leasing Corporation	Carland, Inc.

Janus Capital Corporation (81%)

DST Systems, Inc.

Argus Health Systems, Inc. (50%)	Boston Financial Data Services, Inc. (50%)
DST Realty, Inc.	First of Michigan Capital Corporation (22%)
Support Resources, Inc.	Investors Fiduciary Trust Company (50%)
Midland Data System, Inc. (50%)	Network Graphics, Inc.
NRS Palmetto, Inc.	Phoenix Litho, Inc.
United Micrographics Systems, Inc.	Vantage Computer Systems, Inc. (91%)
Output Technologies, Inc.	

Midsouth Microwave, Inc.

PABTEX, Inc.

Rice-Carden Corp.

Southern Development Company

Tolmak, Inc.

Trans-Serve, Inc.

Figure B.4
Corporate Structure of Kansas City Southern

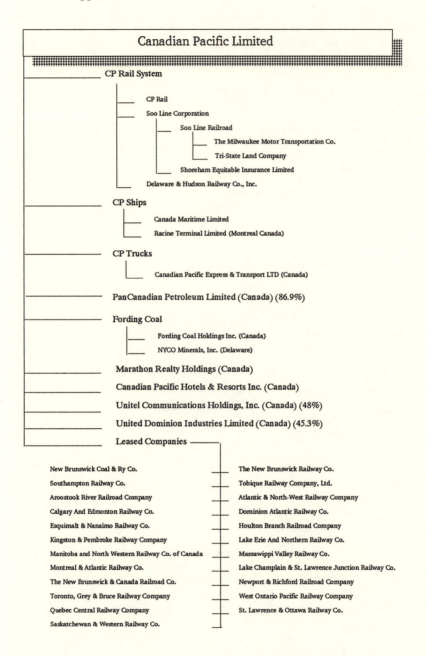

Figure B.5
Corporate Structure of Soo Line

Canadian National Railway Company

AMF Technotransport Inc.
Autoport Ltd.
CANAC International Inc.
CANAC International Ltd. (United States)
The Canada and Gulf Terminal Railway Company
Canadian National Express Company
Canadian National Railways Securities Trust
Canadian National Steamship Company, Limited
Canadian National Telegraph Company
Canadian National Transfer Company Limited
Canadian National Transportation, Limited
The Canadian Northern Quebec Railway Company (60%)
CANAT Limited (United States)
Central Vermont Railway, Inc. (United States)
Chapman Transport Limited
CN Exploration Inc.
C.N. (France) S.A. (France)
CNM Inc.
CN Tower Limited
CN Transactions Inc.
Domestic Three Leaasing Corp. (United States)
Domestic Four Leasing Corp. (United States)
EID Electronic Identification Systems Ltd.
Empire Freightways Limited
Grand Trunk Technologies
The Great North Western Telegraph Company of Canada (95%)
The Minnesota And Manitoba Railroad Company (United States)
The Minnesota and Ontario Bridge Company (United States)
Mount Royal Tunnel and Terminal Company, Limited
M.O.Q. Express Inc.
M.O.Q. Rail Inc.
The Northern Consolidated Holding Company Limited (73%)
17335 Canada Inc.
The Quebec and Lake St. John Railway Company (89%)
Royal Transportation Limited
St. Clair Tunnel Company (United States)
St. Clair Tunnel Construction Company (United States)
Grand Trunk Corporation (United States)

Duluth, Winnipeg And Pacific Railway Co.
GT Finance Company
Grand Trunk Western Railroad Incorporated

Jointly Operated and Other Companies In Which the System
Has Investments

The Belt Railway Company of Chicago	The Canada Southern Railway Company
CANAPREV Inc.	Campagnie De Gestion De Matane Inc.
La Corporation De Chauffage Urbain De Montreal	Detroit River Tunnel Company
Dome Consortium Investments Inc.	Domestic Two Leasing Corporation
Eurocanadian Shipholdings Limited	Halterm Limited
Intermodal Inc.	Lakespan Marine Inc.
Lakespan Marine Inc.	Railroad Association Insurance, Ltd.
Seabase Limited	Shawinigan Terminal Railway Company
Societe du port ferroviare de Baie Comeau-Hauterive	The Toronto Terminals Railway Company Limited
TTX Company	

Figure B.6
Corporate Structure of Grand Trunk Western

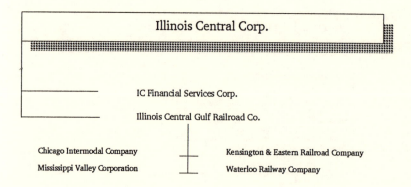

Figure B.7
Corporate Structure of Illinois Central Gulf

CSX Corporation

CSX Hotels, Inc.

DST Systems, Inc.

     CSX Realty Services, Inc.

CSX Technology, Inc.

CSX Intermodal, Inc.

American Commercial Lines, Inc.

Seal-Land Services, Inc.

Customized Transportation, Inc.

The Greenbrier Yudon Pacific Corp.

CSX Transportation

Adrian Realty Co.	Aeolus Transportation
Allegheny and Western Railway	The Atlantic Land And Improvement Company
The Baltimore & Cumberland Valley Railroad Co.	The Baltimore & Ohio Chicago Terminal Railroad Co.
CSX Associates, Inc.	CSX Capital Management, Inc.
CSX Logistics, Inc.	The Carrollton Railroad Company
Charlotte Docks Co.	Cincinnati Inter-Terminal Railroad Company
The Cleveland Terminal and Valley Railroad Company	Cybernetics And Systems, Inc.
Dayton And Michigan Railroad Company	Energy Resources And Logistics, Inc.
Fairfax Realty Co.	Fruitgrowers Express Co.
Gainsville Midland Railroad Co.	Holston Land Co., Inc.
The Home Avenue Railroad Company	L&N Development Co.
L&N Investment Corp.	The Lake Erie and Detroit River Railway Co.
The Mahoning State Line Railroad Co.	North Bank Development Co.
North Charleston Terminal Company	Raleland Car Corporation
Real Estate and Improvement Co. of Baltimore City	Richmond, Fredericksburg And Potomac Railway Co.
Seaboard Coast Line Railway Supplies, Inc.	Staten Island-Arlington, Inc.
Terminal Realty Baltimore Co.	The Toledo Ore Railroad Co.
Transkentucky Transportation Railroad	Transcontinental Terminals, Inc.
Washington and Western Maryland Railroad Company	Western Railway of Alabama
Staten Island Railroad Corporation	

Figure B.8
Corporate Structure of CSX Transportation

Norfolk Southern Corporation

Agency Media Services, Inc.

Atlantic Investment Company

Lamberts Point Barge Co., Inc.

Norfolk-Southern Properties, Inc.

Alexandria-Southern Properties, Inc.	Arrowood-Southern Properties, Inc.
Arrowood-Southern Company	Carlyle CA Corp.
Carlyle Development Corp.	Charlotte-Southern Corp.
Charlotte-Southern Hotel Corp.	Lambert's Point Docks
Nickelplate Improvement Company	Norfolk Southern Industrial Development Corp.
NS-Charlotte Tower Corp.	Sandusky Polk Corporation
Southern Region Industrial Realty, Inc.	Virginia Holding corp.

Norfolk Southern Railway Company

Airforce Pipeline, Inc.	Alabama Great Southern Railroad Co.
Atlanta & Charlotte Airline Railway Co.	Atlantic & East Carolina Railway Co.
Camp Lejeune Railroad Co.	Chesapeake Western Railway
Cincinnati, New Orleans & Texas Pacific Ry. Co.	Citico Realty Company
Elberton Southern Railway Co.	Georgia Midland Railway Co.
Georgia Southern & Florida Railway Co.	High Point, Randleman, Asheboro & Southern Railroad Co.
Interstate Railroad Co.	Lake Erie Dock Co.
Memphis and Charleston Railway Co.	Mobile and Birmingham Railroad Company
Norfolk and Portsmouth Belt Line Railroad	Norfolk and Western Railway Co.
North Carolina Midland Railroad Company	North Carolina Rail Investment Company
Richmond-Washington Company	Shenandoah-Virginia Corporation
South Western Railroad Co.	Southern Rail Terminals, Inc
Southern Rail Terminals of North Carolina	Southern Railway-Carolina Division
Southern Region Coal Transport, Inc.	Southern Region Materials Supply, Inc.
Southern Region Motor Transport, Inc.	State University Railroad Company
Tennessee, Alabama & Georgia Railway Co.	Tennessee Railway Company
Toledo Belt Railway Company	Virginia and Southwestern Railway
Yadkin Railroad Company	

North American Van Lines, Inc.

Alaska USA Van Lines, Inc.	Americas Quality Van Lines, Inc.
A Five Star Forwarding, Inc.	A Three Rivers Forwarding, Inc.
City Storage & Transfer, Inc.	Fleet Insurance Management, Inc.
Frontrunner Worldwide, Inc.	Great Falls North American, Inc.
Nacal, Inc.	Nalog, Inc.
Navtrans Container Lines, Inc.	Navtrans International Freight Forwarding, Inc.
Noram Forwarding, Inc.	North American Distribution Systems, Inc.
North American Forwarding, Inc.	North American Logistics, Ltd
North American Moving & Storage, Inc.	North American Transport Insurance Company
North American Van Lines of Texas	Relocation Management Systems
153843 Canada Inc. (Canada)	Cavalier Moving & Storage Company Ltd (Canada)
Colo Lake Moving & Storage Ltd (Alberta)	Curry Moving & Storage Ltd (Ontario)
Mid-Data Speditions GmbH (Germany)	NAVPAN (Panama)
NAVTRANS Intenat'l Speditions GmbH (Germany)	North American Van Lines Ltd. (United Kingdom)
North Americn Van Lines Canada Ltd (Canada)	North American Van Lines Alberta Ltd (Alberta)
North American Van Lines Atlantic Ltd (Novia Scotia)	Star Storage Ltd (Manitoba)
Tru-Flite Transporttion Systems, Inc. (Canada)	Westlake Moving & Storage, Ltd (Ontario)
Westmont Moving & Storage, Inc. (Quebec)	

NS Crown Services, Inc.

NS Fiber Optics, Inc.

NS Transportation Brokerage Corp.

Pocahontas Development Corp

Pocahontas Land Corp.

TCS Leasing, Inc.

Figure B.9
Corporate Structure of Norfolk Southern

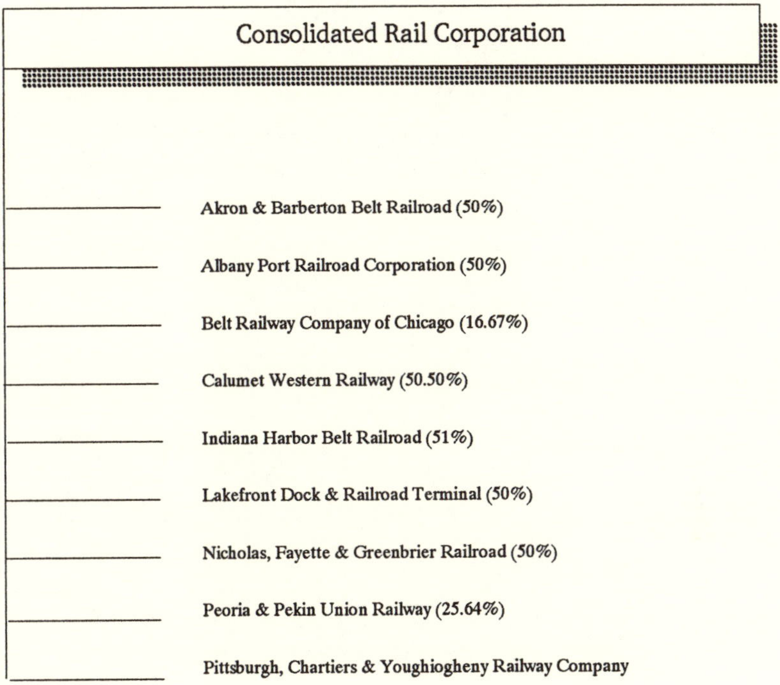

Consolidated Rail Corporation

Akron & Barberton Belt Railroad (50%)

Albany Port Railroad Corporation (50%)

Belt Railway Company of Chicago (16.67%)

Calumet Western Railway (50.50%)

Indiana Harbor Belt Railroad (51%)

Lakefront Dock & Railroad Terminal (50%)

Nicholas, Fayette & Greenbrier Railroad (50%)

Peoria & Pekin Union Railway (25.64%)

Pittsburgh, Chartiers & Youghiogheny Railway Company

Figure B.10
Corporate Structure of Consolidated Rail Corporation

Selected Bibliography

PRIMARY SOURCES

Interstate Commerce Commission Documents

Dockets (Modal Combinations)

Atchison, Topeka & Santa Fe-Control-Toledo, Peoria & Western 363 ICC 715.

Motor Carrier Finance Docket No. 17030 *Burlington Northern-Control Exempt-Stoops Express, Wingate Trucking, Taylor-Maid Transportation.*

Finance Docket No. 27770 *Burlington Northern Inc.-Control through Acquisition of Securities of-Green Bay & Western Railroad Company.*

Finance Docket No. 32549 *Burlington Northern Inc. And Burlington Northern Railroad Company-Control and Merger-Santa Fe Pacific Corporation and the Atchison, Topeka, and Santa Fe Railway Company.*

Finance Docket No. 28583 *Burlington Northern-Merger-St.Louis San Francisco.*

Finance Docket No. 31112 *Joint Application of Canadian Pacific Limited and Incan Ships Limited Under 49 U.S.C. 11321.*

Central of Georgia-Control-South Western 282 ICC 359.

Central of Georgia-Control-Savannah & Atlanta 282 ICC 39.

Central of Georgia, Georgia & Florida, Savannah & Atlanta-Consolidation-Central of Georgia 338 ICC 353.

Chesapeake & Ohio-Control-Baltimore & Ohio 317 ICC 261.

Chesapeake & Ohio and Baltimore & Ohio-Control-Western Maryland 328 ICC 684.

Chicago & Northwestern-Purchase-Minneapolis & St. Louis 312 ICC 285.

Chicago & Northwestern-Control-Chicago, Rock Island & Pacific 347 ICC 556.

Chicago, Milwaukee, St. Paul & Pacific Railroad Company-Reorganization-Acquisition-Grand Trunk Corporation 2 ICC 2d 161.

CSX Corporation-Control-Chessie System and Seaboard Coast Line Industries 363 ICC 521.

Finance Docket No. 31247 *CSX Corporation and American Commercial Lines Incorporated-Control-SCNO Barge Lines.*

CSX Corporation-Control-American Commercial Lines 2 ICC 2d 490.

Detroit, Toledo & Ironton Railroad Company et. al.-Control, Etc. 275 ICC 455.

Duluth, South Shore & Atlantic et al. Merger, etc. 312 ICC 341.

Finance Docket No. 28676 *Grande Trunk Western-Control-Detroit, Toledo & Ironton.*

Great Northern Pacific-Merger-Chicago, Burlington & Quincy-Merger-Great Northern 328 ICC 460; 331 ICC 228.

Gulf-Merger-Mobile & Ohio 236 ICC 61

Gulf, Mobile & Ohio-Purchase-Chicago & Alton 261 ICC 405.

Illinois Central Gulf-Acquisition-Gulf, Mobile & Ohio and Illinois Central, et. al. 338 ICC 805.

Finance Docket No. 28654 *Itel Corporation-Aquisition-Green Bay & Western.*

Joint Application of CSX Corporation and Sea-Land CorporationUnder 49 U.S.C. 11321. 3 ICC 2d 512.

Kansas City Southern Transport Company Incorporated, Common Carrier Application 10

MCC 221; 28 MCC 5.

Katy Industries, Incorporated-Control-Cenac Towing Company, Incorporated 342 ICC 666.

Louisville & Nashville Railroad Companyet al. Merger, Etc. 295 ICC 457.

Missouri Pacific-Merger-Texas & Pacific and Chicago & Eastern Illinois 348 ICC 414.

New York Railway-Control-Brooklyn Eastern District 360 ICC 60.

Nickle Plate-Control-Wheeling & Lake Erie 267 ICC 163.

Finance Docket No. 28499 *Norfolk & Western and Baltimore & OhIo-Control-Detroit, Toledo & Ironton.*

Norfolk & Western-Merger-St. Louis Railroad Company, Etc. 324 ICC 1.

Norfolk & Western-Merger-Virginian Railroad 307 ICC 401.

Norfolk & Western-Purchase-Illinois Terminal 363 ICC 882.

Norfolk & Western and New York, Chicago & St. Louis-Merger, Etc. 330 ICC 780.

Norfolk Southern Corporation-Control-North American Van Lines 1 ICC 2d842.

Norfolk Southern Corporation-Control-Norfolk & Western Railway and Southern Railway 366 ICC 173.

Northwestern Employeees Transportation-Purchase-Chicago & Northwestern 342 ICC 58.

Finance Docket No. 29430 (Sub-No. 1) *NWS Enterprises, Inc.-Control-Norfolk & Western Railway and Southern Railway,* December 4, 1980.

Pennsylvania-Control-Detroit, Toledo and Ironton 275 ICC 455.

Pennsylvania Railroad Company-Merger-New York Central Railroad Company 327 ICC 375; 328 ICC 304; 330 ICC 328; 331 ICC 754.

Pennsylvania Truck Lines Incorporated-Control-Barker Motor Freight 1 MCC 101; 5 MCC 9; 5 MCC 49.

Rio Grande Industries, Inc., SPTC Holding, Inc., and the Denver & Rio Grande Western Railroad Company-Control-Southern Pacific Transportation Company 4 ICC 2d 834.

Finance Docket No. 30400 *Santa Fe Southern Pacific Corporation-Control-Southern Pacific Transportation-Merger-Atchison, Topeka & Santa Fe and Southern Pacific Transportation.*

Seaboard Air Line-Merger-Atlantic Coast Line 320 ICC 122.

Soo Line and Chicago, Milwaukee, St. Paul & Pacific-Control-Green Bay & Western 354 ICC 451.

Southern Railway Company, Section 5(15) Application 342 ICC 416.

Southern-Control-Central of Georgia 317 ICC 557; 317 ICC 729; 331 ICC 151, 164.

Union Pacific Corporation and BTMC Corporation-Control-Overnite Transportation 4 ICC 2d 36.

Finance Docket No. 32011 *Union Pacific Corporation-Control-Skyway Freight Systems.*

Finance Docket No. 30000 *Union Pacific Corporation, Pacific Rail System, Inc., and Union Pacific Railroad Company-Control-Missouri Pacific Corporation and Missouri Pacific Railroad Company.*

Finance Docket No. 32133 *Union Pacific Corporation, Union Pacific Railroad and Missouri Pacific Railroad-Control-Chicago & North Western Holdings Corporation and the Chicago & North Western Transportation Company.*

Finance*Union Pacific Corporation, Union Pacific Railroad and Missouri Pacific Railroad-Control-Missouri-Kansas-Texas* 4 ICC 2d 409.

Finance Docket No. 32760 *Union Pacific Corporation, Union Pacific Railroad Company, Missouri Pacific Railroad Company-Control-Southern Pacific Transportation Company, SPCL Corporation, and the Denver and Rio Grande Western.*

Other ICC Dockets, Rulings, Reports

AAA Transfer, Incorporated, Ext-Cargo Containers 120 MCC 803.
Abandonment of Rail Lines and Discontinuances of Service 354 ICC 129.
Acquisition of Motor Carriers by Railroads 1 ICC 2d 716.
Chicago, Burlington & Quincy Railroad Company v. New York, Susquehana & Western Railroad Company 332 ICC 176.
Citrus Arizona and California to Eastern States 341 ICC 622.
Ex Parte 387 (Sub-No. 959) *Contract Rate Competitive Impact Report-Grain Shippers, Report to Congress.*
Demmurrage Rules and Charges, Nationwide 340 ICC 83.
Improvement of TOFC/COFC Regulation 364 ICC 391.
Improvement of TOFC/COFC Regulation 365 ICC 728.
Improvement of TOFC/COFC Regulations, Advance Notice of Proposed Rules 4 ICC 2d 28.
Ex Parte 230 (Sub-No. 6) *Improvement of TOFC/COFC Regulation (Railroad Affiliated Motor Carriers and other Motor Carriers).*
In the Matter of Consolidation of the Railway Properties of the Unites States into a Limited Number of Systems 159 ICC 522.
Incentive Per Diem Charges-1968 337 ICC 217.
Ex Parte 262 *Increased Freight Rates-1969.*
Increased Freight Rates-1970 and 1971 339 ICC 125.
Increased Freight Rates, 1972 341 ICC 290.
Increased Freight Rates and Charges-1972 340 ICC 358.
Ex Parte 318 *Increased Freight Rates and Charges- 1976.*
Ex Parte 313 *Increased Freight Rates and Charges- Labor Costs, 1975.*
Increased Freight Rates 341 ICC 288
Increased Freight Rates and Charges-Nationwide-1980 365 ICC 6.
Increased Freight Rates and Charges-Nationwide 359 ICC 740.
Ex Parte 374 *Increased Freight Rates and Charges-Western Railroads-2 Percent-1980.*
Ex Parte 303 *Increased Freight Rates-Nationwide.*
Inspection in Transit, Grain and Grain Products 339 ICC 364.
Interstate Commerce Commission. Office of Economic and Environmental Analysis. *Class I Freight Railroads- Selected Earnings Data, 1994.*
Investigation for the Transportation of Recyclable or Recycled Commodities 3 ICC 2d 650.
Investigation of Railroad Freight Rate Structure-Coal 345 ICC 493.
Investigation of Railroad Freight Rate Structure-Iron Ores 345 ICC 548.
Investigation of Railroad Freight Rate Structure-Paper and Paper Products 345 ICC 2092.
Investigation of Railroad Freight Rate Structure-Scrap Iron and Steel 345 ICC 867.
Joint Rates & Through Routes Freight Forwarder & NVO 365 ICC 136.
Market Dominance Determinations and Consideration of Product Competition 365 ICC 118.
Motor Carrier Operating Authority-Railroads 132 MCC 978.
Ex Parte 305 *Nationwide Increase of 10% in Freight Rates and Charges-1974.*
Ex Parte 343 *Nationwide Increase in Freight Rates and Charges-1977.*
Net Investment-Railroad Rate Base 344 ICC 55.
New Orleans Union Passenger Terminal Case 282 ICC 271.
Investigation & Suspension Docket 8701 *Notification of Unloaded Car, by Consignee to Railroad,* December 19, 1972.
Oaklahoma Railway Trustees Abandonment 257 ICC 177.
Procedures for Pending Rail Abandonment Cases, Notice decided March 24, 1976, served

March 31, 1976.

Protective Service Charges-1972 341 ICC 573.

Provisions on Vegetables and Melons, Transcontinental 340 ICC 807.

Rail General Exemption Authority-Fresh Fruits and Vegetables, March 21, 1979.

   Rail Market Dominance 365 ICC 116.

Directed Service Order No. 1237 *Regulation for the Return of Hopper Cars,* expired June 30, 1976.

Directed Service Order No. 1171 *Regulation for the Return of Open Top Hopper Cars,* issued April 30, 1975.

Directed Service Order No. 1182 *Substitution of Stock Cars for Hopper Cars,* issued January 15, 1975.

Special Procedures for Making Findings of Market Dominance as Required by the Railroad Revitalization and Regulatory Reform Act of 1976 353 ICC 874.

Substituted Service-Water-For Motor Service-Alaskan Trade 361 ICC 359.

U.S. Interstate Commerce Commission. *Annual Reports, 1970-1994.* Washington, DC: GPO, 1970-1994.

————————. Bureau of Transport Economics and Statistics. *Railroad Consolidation and the Public Interest: A Preliminary Examination* Washington, D.C.: U.S. Interstate Commerce Commission, 1962.

————————. Bureau of Transport Economics and Statistics. *Statistics of Railways in the United States* Washington, D.C.: U.S. Interstate Commerce Commission, 1940.

————————. Office of Economic and Environmental Analysis. *Class I Freight Railroads-- Selected Earnings Data* Washington, D.C.: U.S. Interstate Commerce Commission, 1994.

————————. Rail Services Planning Office. *Rail Merger Study: Alternatives to Merger* Washington, D.C.: Interstate Commerce Commission, August 18, 1977.

————————. Rail Services Planning Office. *Rail Merger Study: Final Report* [Washington, D.C.]: U.S. Interstate Commerce Commission, February 1, 1978.

————————. Rail Services Planning Office. *Rail Merger Study: Impacts on Other Carriers* Washington, D.C.: Interstate Commerce Commission, 12 August 1977.

————————. Rail Services Planning Office, *Rail Merger Study: Initial Paper* [Washington, DC]: U.S. Interstate Commerce Commission, 1977.

————————. Rail Services Planning Office. *Rail Merger Study: Labor* Washington, D.C.: Interstate Commerce Commission, 26 August 1977.

————————. Rail Services Planning Office. *Rail Merger Study: Service* Washington, D.C.: Interstate Commerce Commission, April 15, 1977.

————————. *Railroad Conglomerates and Other Corporate Structures: A Report to Congress as Directed by Section 903 of the Railroad Revitalization and Regulatory Reform Act of 1976* Washington, DC: GPO, 1977.

Wheat and Wheat Flour, Westbound 337 ICC 858.

Other Government Documents

Task Force on Railroad Productivity. *Improving Railroad Productivity: Final Report of the Task Force on Railroad Productivity.* Washington, D.C.: The National Commission on Productivity and the Council of Economic Advisers, November 1973.

U.S. Congress. House. *Amtrak Discontinuance Criteria.* Hearings before the Subcommittee on Transportation and Commerce of the Committee on Interstate and Foreign Commerce. 94th Cong., 2nd Sess., 1976.

————————. House. *Amtrak Reorganization Act of 1979: Conference Report to Accompany*

H.R. 39961. House Report 96-481. 96th Cong., 1st Sess., 1979.

——————. House. Committee on Energy and Commerce. *Staggers Rail Act Oversight: Hearings before the Subcommittee on Transportation, Tourism, and Hazardous Materials.* 100th Cong. 1st Sess., May 20, 28 and June 3, 1987.

——————. House. Committee on Interstate and Foreign Commerce. House Report 91-1580. *Passenger Train Service: Report to Accompany H.R. 17849.* 91st Cong., 2nd Sess., 1970.

——————. House. Committee on Interstate and Foreign Commerce. Subcommittee on Transportation and Commerce. Staff Report. *Materials Concerning the Effects of Government Regulation on Railroads and an Economic Profile of Railroads in the United States.* Washington, DC: GPO, 1975.

——————. House. *Passenger Train Service.* Supplemental Hearings before the Subcommittee on Transportation and Aeronautics of the Committee on Interstate and Foreign Commerce on H.R. 17849 and S. 3706. 91st Cong., 2nd Sess., 1970.

——————. House. *United States Railway Association Preliminary System Plan.* Hearings before the Subcommittee on Transportation and Commerce of the Committee on Interstate and Foreign Commerce on Oversight on the Implementation of the Rail Reorganization Act of 1973 and a Review of the Preliminary System Plan of the USRA. 94th Cong., 1st Sess., 1975.

——————. Senate. Committee on Commerce. Staff Report. *The American Railroad: Postures, Problems and Prospects.* A report prepared at the direction of Honorable Warren G. Magnuson, Chairman. 92nd Cong., 2nd Sess., August 28, 1972.

——————. Senate. Committee on Commerce, Science and Transportation. *Acquisition of Certain Railroads: Hearing Before the Subcommittee on Surface Transportation of the Committee on Science, Commerce and Transportation.* 101st Cong., 1st Sess., June 22, 1989.

——————. Senate. Committee on Commerce, Science and Transportation. Senate Report 97-96. *Amtrak Improvement Act of 1981: Report to Accompany S. 1199.* 97th Cong., 1st Sess., 1981.

——————. Senate. Committee on Science, Commerce and Transportation. *Sale of Conrail.* 99th Cong., 1st Sess., February 27 and 28 and April 4, 1985.

——————. Senate. *Department of Transportation and Related Agencies Appropriations for Fiscal Year 1977.* Hearings before a Subcommittee of the Committee of Appropriations on H.R. 14234. 94th Cong., 2nd Sess., 1976.

——————. Senate. *Short Line and Regional Railroads: Hearing before the Subcommittee on Surface Transportation.* 99th Cong., 2nd Sess., July 25, 1986.

U.S. Department of Commerce. Bureau of Census. *Historical Statistics of the United States, Colonial Times to 1957.* Washington, DC: GPO, 1960.

——————. Rationale of Federal Transportation Policy Washington, D.C.: U.S. Department of Commerce, 1960.

U.S. Department of Transportation. Federal Railroad Administration. *The Railroad Situation: Perspective on the Present, Past and Future of the Railroad Industry–Final Report.* Washington, DC: GPO, 1979.

——————. Federal Railroad Administration. *The Crew Size Dispute in the Railroad Industry.* Washington, D.C.: U.S. Department of Transportation, Federal Railroad Administration, 1979.

U.S. Economic Research Service. "Recent Railroad Merger Activity." *The Marketing and Transportation Situation.* Washington, D.C.: U.S. Department of Agriculture, 1961.

U.S. General Accounting Office. Resources, Community, and Economic Development Division. *Railroad Regulation: Economic and Financial Impacts of the Staggers Rail Act of 1980.*

GAO/RCED-90-80. Washington, D.C.: GAO, May 16, 1990.
————. Resources, Community, and Economic Development Division. *Railroad Retirement: Future Rail Employment and Trust Fund Solvency.* GAO/HRD-89-30. Washington, D.C.: GAO, April 5, 1989.

Statutes and Legislative Histories

Amtrak Authorization & Development Act. U.S. Code 106 STAT 3115.
Amtrak Authorization & Development Act. Legislative History. U.S. Code. Vol. 5, 3056–3077 (1992).
Amtrak Improvement Act of 1975. U.S. Code 89 STAT 92.
Amtrak Improvement Act of 1975. Legislative History. U.S. Code. Vol. 1, 165–177 (1975).
Amtrak Reauthorization and Improvement Act. U.S. Code 104 STAT 295.
Amtrak Reorganization Act of 1979. U.S. Code 93 STAT 537.
Emergency Transportation Act of 1933. Statutes at Large. Vol. 48, 214 (1933).
Intermodal Surface Transportation Efficiency Act of 1991. U.S. Code. 105 STAT 1914.
Interstate Commerce Act of 1887. Statutes at Large. Vol. 24, 379 (1887).
Omnibus Budget Reconciliation Act of 1981. U.S. Code 95 STAT 357.
Omnibus Budget Reconciliation Act of 1986. U.S. Code 100 STAT 1874.
Rail Passenger Service Act of 1970. U.S. Code. Vol. 1, 1557 (1970).
Rail Passenger Service Act of 1970. Legislative History. U.S. Code. Vol. 3, 4736–4754 (1970).
Railroad Revitalization and Regulatory Reform Act of 1976. U.S. Code 90 STAT 31.
Railroad Revitalization and Regulatory Reform Act of 1976. Legislative History. U.S. Code. Vol. 2, 14–246 (1976).
Regional Rail Reorganization Act of 1973. U.S. Code 87 STAT 1102.
Regional Rail Reorganization Act of 1973. Legislative History. U.S. Code. Vol. 1, 3242–3339 (1973).
Staggers Rail Act of 1980. U.S. Code 94 STAT 1895–1966.
Staggers Rail Act of 1980. Legislative History. U.S. Code. Vol. 10, 7378–7577 (1980).

Miscellaneous Documents

Abandonment of Railroad Lines, Commonwealth of Pennsylvania, et. al. v. United States Report 414 US 1017.
Association of American Railroads. *Analysis of Class I Railroads.* Series 17. Washington, D.C.: Association of American Railroads, 1995
————. *Consolidations and Mergers in the Transportation Industry.* Report to the Transportation Study Group under S. Res. 29 February 1960.
————. *Magna Carta for Transportation.* Washington, D.C.: Association of American Railroads, 1961.
————. *Mergers–Efficiency is the Target.* Background paper on mergers. Washington, D.C.: Association of American Railroads.
————. *Railroad Ten-Year Trends, 1985-1994.* Vol. 12. Washington, D.C.: Association of American Railroads, 1995.
————. *Railroad Transportation: A Statistical Record, 1921-1959.* Washington, D.C.: Association of American Railroads, 1960.
————. *Trends: Rail Freight Car Fleet Increases.* Pamphelet. Washington, D.C.: Association of American Railroads, February 21, 1995.

——————. *Trends: Railroads Record-Breaking Year Ends Strongly*. Pamphelet. Washington, D.C.: Association of American Railroads, January 5, 1995.

Regional Rail Reorganization Act Cases 419 U.S. 102.

Simat, Helliesen & Eichner, Inc. *Competition in the Railroad Industry*. Prepared for the United States Railway Association. Washington, D.C.: February 1975.

Transportation Association of America. *Transportation Facts and Trends*. 13th ed. Washington, D.C.: Transportation Association of America, 1977.

——————. *Transportation Facts and Trends*. 14th ed. Washington, D.C.:Transportation Association of America, 1978.

United States v. Florida East Coast Railway Company 410 U.S. 224.

Trade Journals/Periodicals

American Shipper

Aviation Week & Space Tech.

Barron's

Business Week

Computerworld

Distribution

Economist

Financial Times

Financial World

Forbes

Fortune

Industry Week

Institutional Investor

Journal of Commerce

Moody's Transport. Manual

Money

Nation

Newsweek

Oil and Gas Journal

Railway Age

Traffic Management

Traffic World

Transp. & Distribution

U.S. News & World Report

Wall Street Journal

SECONDARY MATERIALS

Aaron, Austin Godfrey. *Government Operation of the Railroads, 1918-1920*. Austin: Jenkins Publishing Company, 1974.

Allen, Benjamin J. "The Economic Effects of Rail Abandonment on Communities: A Case Study," *Transportation Journal* 15 (Fall 1975), 52–61.

Allen, Frederick Lewis. *Only Yesterday: An Informal History of the 1920s*. New York: Harper and Brothers, 1931.

Association of American Railroads. *Association of American Railroads: Born Out of Necessity*. Washington, D.C.: Association of American Railroads, 1988.

Athearn, Robert G. *Rebel of the Rockies: A History of the Denver & Rio Grande Western Railroad*. New Haven: Yale University Press, 1967.

Atterbury, W.W. "Railroad Consolidation." *Annals of the American Academy of Political and Social Science* 171 (January 1934), 166–171.

Ayre, Josephine. *History and Regulation of Trailer on Flatcar Movement*. Washington, D.C.: Department of Commerce, 1966.

Babcock, Michael, Marvin Prater, and John Morrill. "A Profile of Short Line Railroad Success." *Transportation Journal* 34 (Fall 1994), 22–31.

Beier, Frederick J. and James Cross. "Shortline-Client Relationships: Can Local Carriers Be More Than Small Railroads." *Transportation Journal* 33 (Winter 1993), 5–15.

Bernstein, Marver H. *Regulating Business by Independent Commission*. Princeton: Princeton

University Press, 1955.

Bok, Derek C. "Section 7 of the Clayton Act and the Merging of Law and Economics." *Harvard Law Review* 74 (December 1960): 226–255.

Boske, Leigh B. and Mark J. Wolfgram. "A Social Decision-Making Framework for Analyzing Rail Service Abandonment Impacts." *Transportation Journal* 16 (Summer 1977), 78–85.

Braeutigam, Ronald R. "Consequences of Regulatory Reform in the American Railroad Industry." *Southern Economic Journal* 59 (January 1993), 468–481.

Bryant Jr., Keith. Editor. *Encyclopedia of American Business History and Biography*. New York: Facts on File, 1988.

——————. *History of the Atchison, Topeka & Santa Fe Railway*. New York: Macmillan, 1974.

Buford, Curtis D. *Trailer Train Company: A Unique Force in the Railroad Industry*. New York: Newcomen Society in North America, 1982.

Burke, Davis. *The Southern Railway: Road of the Innovators*. Chapel Hill: University of North Carolina Press, 1985.

Carruth, Gorton. *What Happened When: A Chronology of Life and Events in America*. New York: Harper and Row Publishers, 1989.

Claytor, W. Graham Jr. "A Single Intermodal Transportation Company." *Transportation Journal* 11 (Spring 1972), 31–38.

Cottrell, W. Frederick. *The Railroaders*. Stanford: Stanford University Press, 1940.

Coyle, John J. and Edward Bardi. *The Management of Business Logistics*. 2nd ed. St. Paul, Minnesota: West Publishing Company, 1980.

Crane, Stanley. *Rise From the Wreckage: A Brief History of Conrail*. New York: Newcomen Society of U.S., 1988.

Cushman, Robert E. *The Independent Regulatory Commissions*. New York: Oxford University Press, 1941.

Dagget, Stuart. *Railroad Reorganization*. New York: August M. Kelly Publishers, 1967.

Daley, James M. "Holding Companies, Common Carriers, and Public Policy." *Transportation Journal* 19 (Winter 1979), 67–73.

Due, John F. and Suzanne D. Leever. "The Post-1984 Experience with New Small and Regional Railroads." *Transportation Journal* 33 (Fall 1993), 40–53.

Dunn, Paul C. *Selection and Training of Railroad Supervisors*. Cambridge, Massachusetts: Harvard University Press, 1942.

Fair, Marvin L. and Ernest N. Williams, Jr. *Transportation and Logistics*. 2nd ed. Dallas, Texas: Business Publications Incorporated, 1981.

Farris, Martin T. "The Multiple Meanings and Goals of Deregulation: A Commentary," *Transportation Journal* 21 (Winter 1981), 45–49.

Feinsand, Howard L. "The Diversifying Corporation: Section 7 Darwinism and the Elusive but Essential Test of the Marketplace." *St. John's Law Review* 44 (April 1970), 677–757.

Fellmeth, Robert C. *The Interstate Commerce Commission: The Public Interest and the ICC*. New York: Grossman, 1970.

Fuess, Claude Moore. *Joseph B. Eastman: Servant of the People*. New York: Columbia University Press, 1952.

Gallamore, Robert E. "Railroad Mergers: Costs, Competition and the Future Organization of the American Railroad Industry." Ph.D. diss., Harvard University, 1968.

Germaine, Gayton E., N. A. Glaskowsky, and J. L. Hoskett, *Highway Transportation Management*. New York: McGraw-Hill Book Company, 1963.

Gort, Michael and Thomas F. Hogarty. "New Evidence on Mergers." *Journal of Law and Economics* 13 (April 1970), 167–184.

Graham, Kenneth R. "Rail-Based Holding Companies: A View of Some Indicators of Strategy, Management Change and Financial Performance." *Transportation Journal* 19 (Summer 1980), 73–77.

Grant, Rogers H. *Erie Lackawanna: Death of an American Railroad, 1938-1992.* Stanford: Stanford University Press, 1994.

Grimm, Curtis M. and Harry J. Sapienza. "Determinants of Shortline Railroad Performance." *Transportation Journal* 32 (Spring 1993), 5–14.

Grodinsky, Julius. *Jay Gould: His Business Career, 1867-1892.* Philadelphia: University of Philadelphia Press, 1957.

Harper, Donald V. *Transportation in America: Users, Carriers, Government.* 2nd ed. Englewood Cliffs, New Jersey: Prentice-Hall, 1978.

Hartley, Scott. *Conrail.* Piscataway, N.J.: Railpace Company, 1990.

Healy, Kent T. *Performance of U.S. Railroads Since World War II.* New York: Vantage Press, 1985.

Heaver, Trevor D. "Multi-Modal Ownership–The Canadian Experience." *Transportation Journal* 11 (Fall 1971), 14–28.

Hicks, John D. *The Populist Revolt: History of the Farmer's Alliances and the People's Party.* Minneapolis: University of Minnesota Press, 1931.

Hidy, Ralph W., Muriel Hidy, and Roy V. Scott with Don Hofsommer. *The Great Northern Railway.* Boston: Harvard Business School Press, 1988.

Higgins, Robert C. *Analysis for Financial Management.* Homewood, Illinois: Dow Jones-Irwin, 1983.

Hilton, George W. *Amtrak: The National Railroad Passenger Corporation.* Washington, D.C.: American Enterprise Institute for Public Policy Research, 1975.

—————. *The Northeast Railroad Problem.* Washington: American Enterprise Institute for Public Policy Research, 1980.

Himmelberg, Robert F. (ed.) *Antitrust and Regulation During World War I and the Republican Era, 1917-1932.* New York: Garland Publishing, 1994.

Irwin, Manley R. and Kenneth B. Stanley. "Regulatory Circumvention and the Holding Company." *Journal of Economic Issues* 8 (June 1974), 395–411.

Jackson, Stanley. *J.P. Morgan, A Biography.* New York: Stein and Day, 1983.

Kerr, Austin K. *American Railroad Politics, 1914-1920: Wages, Rates and Efficiency.* Pittsburgh: University of Pittsburgh Press, 1968.

Kneafsey, James T. *Transportation Economic Analysis.* Lexington, Massachusetts: D.C. Heath and Company, 1975.

Kock, James. *Industrial Organization and Prices.* Englewood Cliffs: Prentice Hall, 1974.

Kolko, Gabriel. *Railroad Regulation, 1877-1916.* Princeton: Princeton University Press, 1965.

Lemly, James Hutton. *Gulf, Mobile & Ohio: A Railroad that Had to Expand or Expire.* Homewood, Illinois: R.D. Irwin, 1953.

Leonard, William M. *Railroad Consolidation under the Transportation Act of 1920.* New York: Columbia University Press, 1946.

Lev, Baruch and Gershon Mandelker. "The Microeconomic Consequences of Corporate Mergers." *Journal of Business* 45 (January 1972), 85–104.

Lieb, Robert C. *Labor in the Transportation Industries.* Washington, D.C.: U.S. Department of Transportation, 1973.

—————. *Transportation: The Domestic System.* Reston, Virginia: Reston Publishing Company, 1978.

—————. *Freight Transportation: A Study of Federal Intermodal Ownership Policy.* New York: Praeger Publishers, 1972.

Locklin, Phillip D. *Economics of Transportation*. 7th ed. Homewood, Illinois: Irwin, 1972.

Love, Jean, Wendell Cox, and Stephen Moore, "Amtrak at Twenty-Five: End of the Line for Taxpayer Subsidies," *Policy Analysis*, December 19, 1996.

Lovett, Robert A. *Forty Years After: An Appreciation of the Genius of Edward H. Harriman, 1848-1909*. New York: Newcomen Society in North America, 1949.

MacAvoy, Paul W. and John Snow. Editors. *Railroad Revitalization and Regulatory Reform: Ford Administration Papers on Regulatory Reform*. Washington, D.C.: American Enterprise Institute for Public Policy Research, 1977.

Mahoney, John H. *Intermodal Freight Transportation*. Westport, Connecticut: ENO Foundation for Transportation, 1985.

Martin, Albro. *Enterprise Denied: Origins of the Decline of the American Railroads, 1897-1917*. New York: Columbia University Press, 1971.

——————. *James J. Hill and the Opening of the Northwest*. New York: Oxford University Press, 1976.

——————. *Railroads Triumphant: The Growth Rejection, and Rebirth of a Vital American Force*. New York: Oxford University Press, 1992.

Meyer, Balthasar Henry. *A History of the Northern Securities Case*. New York: De Capo Press, 1972.

Morris, Stuart. "Stalled Professionalism: The Recruitment of Railway Officials in the United States, 1855-1940." *Business History Review* 47 (Autumn 1973), 317–334.

Mowry, George E. *The Era of Theordore Roosevelt, 1900-1912*. New York: Harper, 1958.

Muller, Gerhardt. *Intermodal Freight Transportation*. 2nd ed. Westport, Connecticut: ENO Foundation for Transportation, 1988.

Musolf, Lloyd. *Uncle Sam's Private, Profitseeking Corporations*. Lexington, Massachusetts: Lexington Books, 1983.

Narver, John. *Conglomerate Mergers and Market Competition*. Berkely and Los Angeles: University of California Press, 1967.

Nelson, James C. *Railroad Transportation and Public Policy*. Washington, D.C.: The Brookings Institution, 1959.

Newborn, Norton N. "Protection of Employees in Railroad Consolidations Under the Interstate Commerce Act." *Labor Law Journal* 23 (April 1972), 207–231.

Orenstein, Jeffrey. *United States Railroad Policy: Uncle Sam at the Throttle*. Chicago: Nelson-Hall, 1990.

Pegrum, Dudley F. *Transportation: Economics and Public Policy*. Homewood, Illinois: Richard D. Irwin, 1963.

Pfrommer, Frederick G. "Panel Discussion: The Effect of Diversification Into Other Modes of Transportation." *ICC Practitioner's Journal* 36 (September-October 1969), 1989–2011.

Reutter, Mark. "The Lost Promise of the American Railroad." *Wilson Quarterly* 18 (Winter 1994), 10–35.

Ripley, William. *Railway Problems*. Boston: Ginn and Company, 1913.

Saloutos, Theodore, and John D. Hicks. *Twentieth Century Populism: Agricultural Discontent and the Middle West, 1900-1939*. Lincoln: University of Nebraska Press, 1951.

Salsbury, Stephen. *No Way To Run A Railroad: the Untold Story of the Penn Central Crisis*. New York: McGraw-Hill, 1982.

Sattler, Edward L. "Diversified Holding Companies and their Impact on the Railroad Industry." *Transportation Journal* 20 (Fall 1980), 65–74.

Saunders, Richard. *Railroad Mergers and the Coming of Conrail*. Westport, Connecticut: Greenwood Press, 1978.

Scott, Roy V. *Railroad Development Programs in the Twentieth Century*. Iowa: Iowa State

University Press, 1985.

—————. "American Railroads and Agricultural Extension, 1900-1914: A Study in Railway Developmental Techniques," *Business History Review* 39 (Spring 1965), 74–98.

—————. "Railroads and Farmers: Educational Trains in Missouri, 1902-1914," *Agricultural History* 36 (January 1962), 3–15.

Sharfman, I.L. *The Interstate Commerce Commission: A Study in Administrative Law and Procedure*. New York: The Commonwealth Fund, 1931-1937.

Shils, Edward. "Industrial Unrest in the Nation's Rail Industry." *Labor Law Journal* 15 (February 1964), 81–110.

Sloss, James, Thomas J. Humphrey, and Forrest N. Krutter. "An Analysis and Evaluation of Past Experiences in Rationalizing Railroad Networks," *Studies In Railroad Operations and Economics*. Cambridge, Massachusetts: Institute of Technology, 1975.

Stone, Richard. *The Interstate Commerce Commission and the Railroad Industry: A History of Regulatory Policy*. New York: Praeger, 1991.

Stover, John. *History of Baltimore & Ohio Railroad*. West Lafayette, Indiana: Purdue University Press, 1987.

—————. *History of Illinois Central Railroad*. New York: Macmillan, 1975.

Stuart, Morris. "Stalled Professionalism: The Recruitment of Railway Officials in the United States, 1885-1940," *Business History Review* 47 (Autum 1973),   .

Taff, Charles A. *Commercial Motor Transportation*. 6th ed. Centerville, Maryland: Cornell Maritime Press, 1980.

Tenpao, Lee, Tae-Kyun Kim and C. Phillip Baumel. "Impact of Deregulation on the Fiancial Performance of the Class I Railroads: Heuristic Models of Pooled Time-Series and Cross-Sectional Data." *The Logistics and Transportation Review* 24 (September 1988), 281–297.

Waters, L. L. (Moderator). "Panel Discussion: Pros and Cons of Conglomerates as they Affect Transportation." *ICC Practitioner's Journal* 37 (September-October 1970), 963–986.

Whittaker, J.R. *Containerization*. 2nd ed. New York: John Wiley & Sons, 1975.

Wilson, George W. "Economic Analysis of Transportation: Twenty-Five Year Survey," *Transportation Journal* 26 (Fall 1986), 33–44.

Wyckoff, D. Daryl. *Railroad Management*. Lexington, Massachusetts: Lexington Books, 1976.

Wyckoff, D. Daryl and David H. Maister. *The Motor Carrier Industry*. Lexington: Lexington Books, 1977.

Index

About the Author

JAMES B. BURNS is an independent scholar. In the past, he has taught in the History Departments of the University of Maryland, Mississippi State University, Catonsville Community College, and Essex Community College.

ISBN 1-56720-166-0

EAN

9 781567 201666

90000>

HARDCOVER BAR CODE